Cra

Hap[illegible]

april, 11.79

GOOD STORIES
FOR GREAT HOLIDAYS

GOOD STORIES
FOR GREAT HOLIDAYS

(page 4)

THE BOYS LOOKED IN WONDER

GOOD STORIES FOR GREAT HOLIDAYS

ARRANGED FOR
STORY-TELLING AND READING ALOUD
AND FOR
THE CHILDREN'S OWN READING

BY

FRANCES JENKINS OLCOTT

WITH ILLUSTRATIONS

HOUGHTON MIFFLIN COMPANY

ISBN: 0–395–06967–X

THIRTY-SECOND PRINTING C

TO THE STORY-TELLER

This volume, though intended also for the children's own reading and for reading aloud, is especially planned for story-telling. The latter is a delightful way of arousing a gladsome holiday spirit, and of showing the inner meanings of different holidays. As stories used for this purpose are scattered through many volumes, and as they are not always in the concrete form required for story-telling, I have endeavored to bring together myths, legends, tales, and historical stories suitable to holiday occasions.

There are here collected one hundred and twenty stories for seventeen holidays — stories grave, gay, humorous, or fanciful; also some that are spiritual in feeling, and others that give the delicious thrill of horror so craved by boys and girls at Halloween time. The range of selection is wide, and touches all sides of wholesome boy and girl nature, and the tales have the power to arouse an appropriate holiday spirit.

As far as possible the stories are presented in their original form. When, however, they are too long for inclusion, or too loose in structure for story-telling purposes, they are adapted.

Adapted stories are of two sorts. *Condensed:*

in which case a piece of literature is shortened, scarcely any changes being made in the original language. *Rewritten:* here the plot, imagery, language, and style of the original are retained as far as possible, while the whole is moulded into form suitable for story-telling. Some few stories are built up on a slight framework of original matter.

Thus it may be seen that the tales in this volume have not been reduced to the necessarily limited vocabulary and uniform style of one editor, but that they are varied in treatment and language, and are the products of many minds.

A glance at the table of contents will show that not only have selections been made from modern authors and from the folklore of different races, but that some quaint old literary sources have been drawn on. Among the men and books contributing to these pages are the *Gesta Romanorum, Il Libro d'Oro,* Xenophon, Ovid, Lucian, the Venerable Bede, William of Malmesbury. John of Hildesheim, William Caxton, and the more modern Washington Irving, Hugh Miller, Charles Dickens, and Henry Cabot Lodge; also those immortals, Hans Andersen, the Brothers Grimm, Horace E. Scudder, and others.

The stories are arranged to meet the needs of story-telling in the graded schools. Reading-lists, showing where to find additional material for story-telling and collateral reading, are added. Grades in which the recommended stories are useful are indicated.

The number of selections in the volume, as well as the references to other books, is limited by the amount and character of available material. For instance, there is little to be found for Saint Valentine's Day, while there is an overwhelming abundance of fine stories for the Christmas season. Stories like Dickens's "Christmas Carol," Ouida's "Dog of Flanders," and Hawthorne's tales, which are too long for inclusion and would lose their literary beauty if condensed, are referred to in the lists. Volumes containing these stories may be procured at the public library.

A subject index is appended. This indicates the ethical, historical, and other subject-matter of interest to the teacher, thus making the volume serviceable for other occasions besides holidays.

In learning her tale the story-teller is advised not to commit it to memory. Such a method is apt to produce a wooden or glib manner of presentation. It is better for her to read the story over and over again until its plot, imagery, style, and vocabulary become her own, and then to retell it, as Miss Bryant says, "simply, vitally, joyously."

ACKNOWLEDGMENTS

THE compiler's thanks are due to the following publishers and authors who have allowed the publication of their stories in this volume: —

To the American Book Company for permission to use "A Brave Girl," by James Johonnot; "A Gunpowder Story," by John Esten Cooke; "Columbus and the Egg," and "Cornelia's Jewels," by James Baldwin; "Shippeitaro," by Mary F. Nixon-Roulet; "Signing of the Declaration of Independence," by H. A. Guerber; "The Proud Oak Tree," and "The Three Little Butterfly Brothers," from *Deutsches Drittes Lesebuch.*

To the Century Company for permission to use "Bill Brown's Test," by Cleveland Moffett.

To the *Cosmopolitan Magazine* for permission to use "A Prisoner's Valentine," by Millicent Olmsted.

To the Courier-Journal Job Printing Company for permission to use "Two Hero-Stories of the Civil War," by Ben La Bree.

To J. M. Dent and Sons, Ltd., for permission to use "The King of the Cats," by Ernest Rhys.

To E. P. Dutton and Company, for permission to use "Saint Christopher," by William Caxton; "The Lark and its Young Ones," and "The Smithy," by P. V. Ramaswami Raju.

To Ginn and Company for permission to use "Washington the Athlete," by Albert F. Blaisdell and Francis K. Ball.

To Henry Holt and Company for permission to use "A Flag Incident," by M. M. Thomas; and "Baucis and Philemon," by H. P. Maskell.

To J. B. Lippincott Company for permission to use "The Revenge of Coriolanus," by Charles Morris; "The Three Kings of Cologne," by H. S. Morris.

To Little, Brown and Company for permission to use "The Greedy Geese," from *Il Libro d'Oro*, translated by Mrs. Francis Alexander.

To Lothrop, Lee and Shepard Company for permission to use "Training for the Presidency," by Orison Swett Marden.

To the Macmillan Company for permission to use "Queen Margaret and the Robbers," by Albert F. Blaisdell; "The Boston Tea-Party," by John Andrews; "The Little Drummer-Boy," by Albert Bushnell Hart; "Burg Hill's on Fire," by Elizabeth W. Grierson.

To Milton Bradley Company for permission to use "The Fairy's New Year Gift," by Emilie Poulsson; "The Snowdrop," adapted by Bailey and Lewis.

To the New York State Museum for permission to use "The Elves," and "The Spirit of the Corn," by Harriet Maxwell Converse.

To the Presbyterian Board of Publication for permission to use "Betsy Ross and the Flag," by Harry Pringle Ford, published in *Forward Magazine*.

To G. P. Putnam's Sons for permission to use "He rescues the Birds," "The Colonel of the Zouaves," "Why Lincoln was called 'Honest Abe,'" by Noah Brooks; "The Magpie's Nest," and "The Strange Visitor," by Joseph Jacobs.

To Fleming H. Revell Company for permission to use "The Cañon Flowers," by Ralph Connor.

To Mr. William S. Walsh for permission to use "The Three Purses," and "The Thunder Oak."

To Houghton Mifflin Company for permission to use "Arachne," and "Cupid and Psyche," by Josephine Preston Peabody; "A Solomon come to Judgment," "George Pickett's Friend," "Lincoln and the Little Girl," by Charles W. Moores; "Hofus the Stone-Cutter," from the *Riverside Third Reader;* "Babes in the Woods," by John Burroughs; "Hansel and Grethel," by the Brothers Grimm; "The Busy Blue Jay," by Olive Thorne Miller; "The Dove who spoke Truth," by Abbie Farwell Brown; "The Dryad of the Old Oak," by James Russell Lowell; "The Elves and the Shoemaker," and "Young George and the Colt," by Horace E. Scudder; "The First Harvest Home in Plymouth," by W. De Loss Love, Jr.; "The Mother Murre," by Dallas Lore Sharp; "The Pine Tree," "The Little Match Girl," "The Loveliest Rose in the World," by Hans Christian Andersen; "Little Piccola," by Celia Thaxter; "The Nail," by the Brothers Grimm; "The Old Woman who became a Woodpecker," by Phœbe Cary; "The Pride of the Regiment," by Harry M. Kieffer; "The Quails," from the *Riverside Fourth Reader;* "The Stream that Ran Away," by Mary Austin; "The Star-Spangled Banner," by Eva March Tappan; "The Mutiny," by A. de Lamartine; "Washington at Yorktown," and "Washington's Modesty," by Henry Cabot Lodge; "Why the Evergreen Trees never lose their Leaves," by Florence Holbrook.

CONTENTS

[1] Confederate Memorial Day is celebrated in some States on April 26 and in others on May 10.

CONTENTS

BIRD DAY

ILLUSTRATIONS

From drawings by Clara M. Burd

GOOD STORIES
FOR GREAT HOLIDAYS

NEW YEAR'S DAY

GOOD STORIES FOR GREAT HOLIDAYS

THE FAIRY'S NEW YEAR GIFT

BY EMILIE POULSSON (ADAPTED)

Two little boys were at play one day when a Fairy suddenly appeared before them and said: "I have been sent to give you New Year presents."

She handed to each child a package, and in an instant was gone.

Carl and Philip opened the packages and found in them two beautiful books, with pages as pure and white as the snow when it first falls.

Many months passed and the Fairy came again to the boys. "I have brought you each another book," said she, "and will take the first ones back to Father Time who sent them to you."

"May I not keep mine a little longer?" asked Philip. "I have hardly thought about it lately. I 'd like to paint something on the last leaf that lies open."

"No," said the Fairy; "I must take it just as it is."

"I wish that I could look through mine just once," said Carl; "I have only seen one page at a time, for when the leaf turns over it sticks fast, and I can never open the book at more than one place each day."

"You shall look at your book," said the Fairy, "and Philip, at his." And she lit for them two little silver lamps, by the light of which they saw the pages as she turned them.

The boys looked in wonder. Could it be that these were the same fair books she had given them a year ago? Where were the clean, white pages, as pure and beautiful as the snow when it first falls? Here was a page with ugly, black spots and scratches upon it; while the very next page showed a lovely little picture. Some pages were decorated with gold and silver and gorgeous colors, others with beautiful flowers, and still others with a rainbow of softest, most delicate brightness. Yet even on the most beautiful of the pages there were ugly blots and scratches.

Carl and Philip looked up at the Fairy at last.

"Who did this?" they asked. "Every page was white and fair as we opened to it; yet now there is not a single blank place in the whole book!"

"Shall I explain some of the pictures to you?" said the Fairy, smiling at the two little boys. "See, Philip, the spray of roses blossomed on this page when you let the baby have your playthings; and this pretty bird, that looks as if it were singing with all its might, would never have been on this page if you had not tried to be kind and pleasant the other day, instead of quarreling."

"But what makes this blot?" asked Philip.

"That," said the Fairy sadly; "that came when you told an untruth one day, and this when you did not mind mamma. All these blots and scratches that look so ugly, both in your book and in Carl's, were made when you were naughty. Each pretty thing in your books came on its page when you were good."

"Oh, if we could only have the books again!" said Carl and Philip.

"That cannot be," said the Fairy. "See! they are dated for this year, and they must now go back into Father Time's bookcase, but I have brought you each a new one. Perhaps you can make these more beautiful than the others."

So saying, she vanished, and the boys were left alone, but each held in his hand a new book open at the first page.

And on the back of this book was written in letters of gold, "For the New Year."

THE LITTLE MATCH GIRL

BY HANS CHRISTIAN ANDERSEN (TRANSLATED)

IT was very, very cold; it snowed and it grew dark; it was the last evening of the year, New Year's Eve. In the cold and dark a poor little girl, with bare head and bare feet, was walking through the streets. When she left her own house she certainly had had slippers on; but what could they do? They were very big slippers, and her mother had used them till then, so big were they. The little maid lost them as she slipped across the road, where two carriages were rattling by terribly fast. One slipper was not to be found again, and a boy ran away with the other. He said he could use it for a cradle when he had children of his own.

So now the little girl went with her little naked feet, which were quite red and blue with the cold. In an old apron she carried a number of matches, and a bundle of them in her hand. No one had bought anything of her all day; no one had given her a copper. Hungry and cold she went, and drew herself together, poor little thing! The snowflakes fell on her long yellow hair, which curled prettily over her neck; but she did not think of that now. In all the windows lights were shining, and there was a glorious smell of roast goose out there in the street; it was no doubt New Year's Eve. Yes, she thought of that!

In a corner formed by two houses, one of which was a little farther from the street than the other, she sat down and crept close. She had drawn up her little feet, but she was still colder, and she did not dare to go home, for she had sold no matches, and she had not a single cent; her father would

beat her; and besides, it was cold at home, for they had nothing over them but a roof through which the wind whistled, though straw and rags stopped the largest holes.

Her small hands were quite numb with the cold. Ah! a little match might do her good if she only dared draw one from the bundle, and strike it against the wall, and warm her fingers at it. She drew one out. R-r-atch! how it spluttered and burned! It was a warm bright flame, like a little candle, when she held her hands over it; it was a wonderful little light! It really seemed to the little girl as if she sat before a great polished stove, with bright brass feet and a brass cover. The fire burned so nicely; it warmed her so well, — the little girl was just putting out her feet to warm these, too, — when out went the flame; the stove was gone; — she sat with only the end of the burned match in her hand.

She struck another; it burned; it gave a light; and where it shone on the wall, the wall became thin like a veil, and she could see through it into the room where a table stood, spread with a white cloth, and with china on it; and the roast goose smoked gloriously, stuffed with apples and dried plums. And what was still more splendid to behold, the goose hopped down from the dish, and waddled along the floor, with a knife and fork in its breast; straight to the little girl he came. Then

the match went out, and only the thick, damp, cold wall was before her.

She lighted another. Then she was sitting under a beautiful Christmas tree; it was greater and finer than the one she had seen through the glass door at the rich merchant's. Thousands of candles burned upon the green branches, and colored pictures like those in the shop windows looked down upon them. The little girl stretched forth both hands toward them; then the match went out. The Christmas lights went higher and higher. She saw that now they were stars in the sky: one of them fell and made a long line of fire.

"Now some one is dying," said the little girl, for her old grandmother, the only person who had been good to her, but who was now dead, had said: "When a star falls a soul mounts up to God."

She rubbed another match against the wall; it became bright again, and in the light there stood the old grandmother clear and shining, mild and lovely.

"Grandmother!" cried the child. "Oh, take me with you! I know you will go when the match is burned out. You will go away like the warm stove, the nice roast goose, and the great glorious Christmas tree!"

And she hastily rubbed the whole bundle of matches, for she wished to hold her grandmother fast. And the matches burned with such a glow

that it became brighter than in the middle of the day; grandmother had never been so large or so beautiful. She took the little girl up in her arms, and both flew in the light and the joy so high, so high! and up there was no cold, nor hunger, nor care — they were with God.

But in the corner by the house sat the little girl, with red cheeks and smiling mouth, frozen to death on the last evening of the Old Year. The New Year's sun rose upon the little body, that sat there with the matches, of which one bundle was burned. She wanted to warm herself, the people said. No one knew what fine things she had seen, and in what glory she had gone in with her grandmother to the New Year's Day.

THE TWELVE MONTHS

A SLAV LEGEND

BY ALEXANDER CHODZKO (ADAPTED)

THERE was once a widow who had two daughters, Helen, her own child by her dead husband, and Marouckla, his daughter by his first wife. She loved Helen, but hated the poor orphan because she was far prettier than her own daughter.

Marouckla did not think about her good looks, and could not understand why her stepmother should be angry at the sight of her. The hardest work fell to her share. She cleaned out the rooms, cooked, washed, sewed, spun, wove, brought in the hay, milked the cow, and all this without any help.

Helen, meanwhile, did nothing but dress herself in her best clothes and go to one amusement after another.

But Marouckla never complained. She bore the scoldings and bad temper of mother and sister with a smile on her lips, and the patience of a lamb. But this angelic behavior did not soften them. They became even more tyrannical and grumpy, for Marouckla grew daily more beautiful, while Helen's ugliness increased. So the stepmother determined to get rid of Marouckla, for she knew that while she remained, her own daughter would have no suitors. Hunger, every kind of privation, abuse, every means was used to make the girl's life miserable. But in spite of it all Marouckla grew ever sweeter and more charming.

One day in the middle of winter Helen wanted some wood-violets.

"Listen," cried she to Marouckla, "you must go up the mountain and find me violets. I want some to put in my gown. They must be fresh and sweet-scented — do you hear?"

"But, my dear sister, whoever heard of violets blooming in the snow?" said the poor orphan.

"You wretched creature! Do you dare to disobey me?" said Helen. "Not another word. Off with you! If you do not bring me some violets from the mountain forest I will kill you."

The stepmother also added her threats to those of Helen, and with vigorous blows they pushed Marouckla outside and shut the door upon her. The weeping girl made her way to the mountain. The snow lay deep, and there was no trace of any human being. Long she wandered hither and thither, and lost herself in the wood. She was hungry, and shivered with cold, and prayed to die.

Suddenly she saw a light in the distance, and climbed toward it till she reached the top of the mountain. Upon the highest peak burned a large fire, surrounded by twelve blocks of stone on which sat twelve strange beings. Of these the first three had white hair, three were not quite so old, three were young and handsome, and the rest still younger.

There they all sat silently looking at the fire. They were the Twelve Months of the Year. The great January was placed higher than the others. His hair and mustache were white as snow, and in his hand he held a wand. At first Marouckla was afraid, but after a while her courage returned, and drawing near, she said: —

"Men of God, may I warm myself at your fire? I am chilled by the winter cold."

The great January raised his head and answered: "What brings thee here, my daughter? What dost thou seek?"

"I am looking for violets," replied the maiden.

"This is not the season for violets. Dost thou not see the snow everywhere?" said January.

"I know well, but my sister Helen and my stepmother have ordered me to bring them violets from your mountain. If I return without them they will kill me. I pray you, good shepherds, tell me where they may be found."

Here the great January arose and went over to the youngest of the Months, and, placing his wand in his hand, said: —

"Brother March, do thou take the highest place."

March obeyed, at the same time waving his wand over the fire. Immediately the flames rose toward the sky, the snow began to melt and the trees and shrubs to bud. The grass became green, and from between its blades peeped the pale primrose. It was spring, and the meadows were blue with violets.

"Gather them quickly, Marouckla," said March.

Joyfully she hastened to pick the flowers, and having soon a large bunch she thanked them and ran home. Helen and the stepmother were amazed at the sight of the flowers, the scent of which filled the house.

"Where did you find them?" asked Helen.

"Under the trees on the mountain-side," said Marouckla.

Helen kept the flowers for herself and her mother. She did not even thank her stepsister for the trouble she had taken. The next day she desired Marouckla to fetch her strawberries.

"Run," said she, "and fetch me strawberries from the mountain. They must be very sweet and ripe."

"But whoever heard of strawberries ripening in the snow?" exclaimed Marouckla.

"Hold your tongue, worm; don't answer me. If I don't have my strawberries I will kill you," said Helen.

Then the stepmother pushed Marouckla into the yard and bolted the door. The unhappy girl made her way toward the mountain and to the large fire round which sat the Twelve Months. The great January occupied the highest place.

"Men of God, may I warm myself at your fire? The winter cold chills me," said she, drawing near.

The great January raised his head and asked: "Why comest thou here? What dost thou seek?"

"I am looking for strawberries," said she.

"We are in the midst of winter," replied January; "strawberries do not grow in the snow."

"I know," said the girl sadly, "but my sister and stepmother have ordered me to bring them strawberries. If I do not they will kill me. Pray, good shepherds, tell me where to find them."

The great January arose, crossed over to the

Month opposite him, and putting the wand in his hand, said: "Brother June, do thou take the highest place."

June obeyed, and as he waved his wand over the fire the flames leaped toward the sky. Instantly the snow melted, the earth was covered with verdure, trees were clothed with leaves, birds began to sing, and various flowers blossomed in the forest. It was summer. Under the bushes masses of star-shaped flowers changed into ripening strawberries, and instantly they covered the glade, making it look like a sea of blood.

"Gather them quickly, Marouckla," said June.

Joyfully she thanked the Months, and having filled her apron ran happily home.

Helen and her mother wondered at seeing the strawberries, which filled the house with their delicious fragrance.

"Wherever did you find them?" asked Helen crossly.

"Right up among the mountains. Those from under the beech trees are not bad," answered Marouckla.

Helen gave a few to her mother and ate the rest herself. Not one did she offer to her stepsister. Being tired of strawberries, on the third day she took a fancy for some fresh, red apples.

"Run, Marouckla," said she, "and fetch me fresh, red apples from the mountain."

"Apples in winter, sister? Why, the trees have neither leaves nor fruit!"

"Idle thing, go this minute," said Helen; "unless you bring back apples we will kill you."

As before, the stepmother seized her roughly and turned her out of the house. The poor girl went weeping up the mountain, across the deep snow, and on toward the fire round which were the Twelve Months. Motionless they sat there, and on the highest stone was the great January.

"Men of God, may I warm myself at your fire? The winter cold chills me," said she, drawing near.

The great January raised his head. "Why comest thou here? What does thou seek?" asked he.

"I am come to look for red apples," replied Marouckla.

"But this is winter, and not the season for red apples," observed the great January.

"I know," answered the girl, "but my sister and stepmother sent me to fetch red apples from the mountain. If I return without them they will kill me."

Thereupon the great January arose and went over to one of the elderly Months, to whom he handed the wand saying: —

"Brother September, do thou take the highest place."

September moved to the highest stone, and

waved his wand over the fire. There was a flare of red flames, the snow disappeared, but the fading leaves which trembled on the trees were sent by a cold northeast wind in yellow masses to the glade. Only a few flowers of autumn were visible. At first Marouckla looked in vain for red apples. Then she espied a tree which grew at a great height, and from the branches of this hung the bright, red fruit. September ordered her to gather some quickly. The girl was delighted and shook the tree. First one apple fell, then another.

"That is enough," said September; "hurry home."

Thanking the Months she returned joyfully. Helen and the stepmother wondered at seeing the fruit.

"Where did you gather them?" asked the stepsister.

"There are more on the mountain-top," answered Marouckla.

"Then, why did you not bring more?" said Helen angrily. "You must have eaten them on your way back, you wicked girl."

"No, dear sister, I have not even tasted them," said Marouckla. "I shook the tree twice. One apple fell each time. Some shepherds would not allow me to shake it again, but told me to return home."

"Listen, mother," said Helen. "Give me my

cloak. I will fetch some more apples myself. I shall be able to find the mountain and the tree. The shepherds may cry 'Stop!' but I will not leave go till I have shaken down all the apples."

In spite of her mother's advice she wrapped herself in her pelisse, put on a warm hood, and took the road to the mountain. Snow covered everything. Helen lost herself and wandered hither and thither. After a while she saw a light above her, and, following in its direction, reached the mountain-top.

There was the flaming fire, the twelve blocks of stone, and the Twelve Months. At first she was frightened and hesitated; then she came nearer and warmed her hands. She did not ask permission, nor did she speak one polite word.

"What hath brought thee here? What dost thou seek?" said the great January severely.

"I am not obliged to tell you, old graybeard. What business is it of yours?" she replied disdainfully, turning her back on the fire and going toward the forest.

The great January frowned, and waved his wand over his head. Instantly the sky became covered with clouds, the fire went down, snow fell in large flakes, an icy wind howled round the mountain. Amid the fury of the storm Helen stumbled about. The pelisse failed to warm her benumbed limbs.

The mother kept on waiting for her. She looked from the window, she watched from the doorstep, but her daughter came not. The hours passed slowly, but Helen did not return.

"Can it be that the apples have charmed her from her home?" thought the mother. Then she clad herself in hood and pelisse, and went in search of her daughter. Snow fell in huge masses. It covered all things. For long she wandered hither and thither, the icy northeast wind whistled in the mountain, but no voice answered her cries.

Day after day Marouckla worked, and prayed, and waited, but neither stepmother nor sister returned. They had been frozen to death on the mountain.

The inheritance of a small house, a field, and a cow fell to Marouckla. In course of time an honest farmer came to share them with her, and their lives were happy and peaceful.

THE MAIL-COACH PASSENGERS

BY HANS CHRISTIAN ANDERSEN (ADAPTED)

IT was bitterly cold. The sky glittered with stars, and not a breeze stirred. "Bump," — an old pot was thrown at a neighbor's door; and, "Bang! Bang!" went the guns, for they were greeting the New Year.

It was New Year's Eve, and the church clock was striking twelve. "Tan-ta-ra-ra, tan-ta-ra-ra!" sounded the horn, and the mail-coach came lumbering up. The clumsy vehicle stopped at the gate of the town; all the places had been taken, for there were twelve passengers in the coach.

"Hurrah! Hurrah!" cried the people in the town; for in every house the New Year was being welcomed; and, as the clock struck, they stood up, the full glasses in their hands, to drink success to the newcomer. "A happy New Year," was the cry; "a pretty wife, plenty of money, and no sorrow or care!"

The wish passed round, and the glasses clashed together till they rang again; while before the town-gate the mail-coach stopped with the twelve strange passengers. And who were these strangers? Each of them had his passport and his luggage with him; they even brought presents for me, and for you, and for all the people in the town. Who were they? What did they want? And what did they bring with them?

"Good-morning!" they cried to the sentry at the town-gate.

"Good-morning," replied the sentry, for the clock had struck twelve.

"Your name and profession?" asked the sentry of the one who alighted first from the carriage.

"See for yourself in the passport," he replied.

"I am myself!" — and a famous fellow he looked, arrayed in bearskin and fur boots. "Come to me to-morrow, and I will give you a New Year's present. I throw shillings and pence among the people. I give balls every night, no less than thirty-one; indeed, that is the highest number I can spare for balls. My ships are often frozen in, but in my offices it is warm and comfortable. *My name is January.* I am a merchant, and I generally bring my accounts with me."

Then the second alighted. He seemed a merry fellow. He was a director of a theater, a manager of masked balls, and a leader of all the amusements we can imagine. His luggage consisted of a great cask.

"We'll dance the bung out of the cask at carnival-time," said he. "I'll prepare a merry tune for you and for myself, too. Unfortunately I have not long to live, — the shortest time, in fact, of my whole family, — only twenty-eight days. Sometimes they pop me in a day extra; but I trouble myself very little about that. Hurrah!"

"You must not shout so," said the sentry.

"Certainly I may shout," retorted the man. "I'm Prince Carnival, traveling under *the name of February.*"

The third now got out. He looked the personification of fasting; but he carried his nose very high, for he was a weather prophet. In his buttonhole he wore a little bunch of violets, but they were very small.

"*March, March!*" the fourth passenger called after him, slapping him on the shoulder, "don't you smell something good? Make haste into the guard-room, they are feasting in there. I can smell it already! *Forward, Master March!*'

But it was not true. The speaker only wanted to make an *April Fool* of him, for with that fun the fourth stranger generally began his career. He looked very jovial, and did little work.

"If the world were only more settled!" said he; "but sometimes I'm obliged to be in a good humor, and sometimes a bad one. I can laugh or cry according to circumstances. I have my summer wardrobe in this box here, but it would be very foolish to put it on now!"

After him a lady stepped out of the coach. *She called herself Miss May.* She wore a summer dress and overshoes. Her dress was light green, and there were anemones in her hair. She was so scented with wild thyme that it made the sentry sneeze.

"Your health, and God bless you!" was her greeting.

How pretty she was! and such a singer! Not a theater singer nor a ballad-singer; no, but a singer of the woods. For she wandered through the gay, green forest, and had a concert there for her own amusement.

"Now comes the young lady," said those in the coach; and out stepped a young dame, delicate, proud, and pretty. *It was Mistress June.* In her service people become lazy and fond of sleeping for hours. She gives a feast on the longest day of the year, that there may be time for her guests to partake of the numerous dishes at her table. Indeed, she keeps her own carriage, but still she travels by the mail-coach with the rest because she wishes to show that she is not proud.

But she was not without a protector; her younger brother, *July*, was with her. He was a plump, young fellow, clad in summer garments, and wearing a straw hat. He had very little luggage because it was so cumbersome in the great heat. He had, however, swimming-trousers with him, which are nothing to carry.

Then came the mother herself, *Madame August*, a wholesale dealer in fruit, proprietress of a large number of fish-ponds, and a land-cultivator. She was fat and warm, yet she could use her hands well, and would herself carry out food to the laborers in the field. After work, came the recreations, dancing and playing in the greenwood, and the "harvest home." She was a thorough housewife.

After her a man stepped out of the coach. He is a painter, a master of colors, and is *named September*. The forest on his arrival has to change its colors, and how beautiful are those he chooses! The woods glow with red, and gold, and brown. This great master painter can whistle like a blackbird. There he stood with his color-pot in his hand, and that was the whole of his luggage.

A landowner followed, who in the month for sowing seed attends to his ploughing and is fond of field sports. *Squire October* brought his dog and his gun with him, and had nuts in his game-bag. "Crack! Crack!" He had a great deal of luggage, even a plough. He spoke of farming, but what he said could scarcely be heard for the coughing and sneezing of his neighbor.

It was November, who coughed violently as he got out. He had a cold, but he said he thought it would leave him when he went out woodcutting, for he had to supply wood to the whole parish. He spent his evenings making skates, for he knew, he said, that in a few weeks they would be needed.

At length the last passenger made her appearance, — *Old Mother December!* The dame was very aged, but her eyes glistened like two stars. She carried on her arm a flower-pot, in which a little fir tree was growing. "This tree I shall guard and cherish," she said, "that it may grow large by Christmas Eve, and reach from the floor to the ceiling, to be adorned with lighted candles, golden apples, and toys. I shall sit by the fireplace, and bring a story-book out of my pocket, and read aloud to all the little children. Then the toys on the tree will become alive, and the little waxen Angel at the top will spread out his wings of gold leaf, and fly down from his green perch. He will kiss every child in the room, yes, and all the little children who stand out in the street singing a carol about the 'Star of Bethlehem.'"

"Well, now the coach may drive away," said the sentry; "we will keep all the twelve months here with us."

"First let the twelve come to me," said the Captain on duty, "one after another. The passports I will keep here, each of them for one month. When that has passed, I shall write the behavior of each stranger on his passport. *Mr. January*, have the goodness to come here."

And *Mr. January* stepped forward.

When a year has passed, I think I shall be able to tell you what the twelve passengers have brought to you, to me, and to all of us. Just now I do not know, and probably even they do not know themselves, for we live in strange times.

LINCOLN'S BIRTHDAY

(FEBRUARY 12)

HE RESCUES THE BIRDS

BY NOAH BROOKS (ADAPTED)

ONCE, while riding through the country with some other lawyers, Lincoln was missed from the party, and was seen loitering near a thicket of wild plum trees where the men had stopped a short time before to water their horses.

"Where is Lincoln?" asked one of the lawyers.

"When I saw him last," answered another, "he had caught two young birds that the wind had blown out of their nest, and was hunting for the nest to put them back again."

As Lincoln joined them, the lawyers rallied him on his tender-heartedness, and he said: —

"I could not have slept unless I had restored those little birds to their mother."

LINCOLN AND THE LITTLE GIRL

BY CHARLES W. MOORES

IN the old days, when Lincoln was one of the leading lawyers of the State, he noticed a little girl of ten who stood beside a trunk in front of her home crying bitterly. He stopped to learn what was wrong, and was told that she was about to miss a long-promised visit to Decatur because the wagon had not come for her.

"You need n't let that trouble you," was his cheering reply. "Just come along with me and we shall make it all right."

Lifting the trunk upon his shoulder, and taking the little girl by the hand, he went through the streets of Springfield, a half-mile to the railway station, put her and her trunk on the train, and sent her away with a happiness in her heart that is still there.

TRAINING FOR THE PRESIDENCY

BY ORISON SWETT MARDEN

"I MEANT to take good care of your book, Mr. Crawford," said the boy, "but I've damaged it a good deal without intending to, and now I want to make it right with you. What shall I do to make it good?"

"Why, what happened to it, Abe?" asked the rich farmer, as he took the copy of Weems's "Life of Washington" which he had lent young Lincoln, and looked at the stained leaves and warped binding. "It looks as if it had been out through all last night's storm. How came you to forget, and leave it out to soak?"

"It was this way, Mr. Crawford," replied Abe.

"I sat up late to read it, and when I went to bed, I put it away carefully in my bookcase, as I call it, a little opening between two logs in the wall of our cabin. I dreamed about General Washington all night. When I woke up I took it out to read a page or two before I did the chores, and you can't imagine how I felt when I found it in this shape. It seems that the mud-daubing had got out of the weather side of that crack, and the rain must have dripped on it three or four hours before I took it out. I'm sorry, Mr. Crawford, and want to fix it up with you, if you can tell me how, for I have not got money to pay for it."

"Well," said Mr. Crawford, "come and shuck corn three days, and the book 's yours."

Had Mr. Crawford told young Abraham Lincoln that he had fallen heir to a fortune the boy could hardly have felt more elated. Shuck corn only three days, and earn the book that told all about his greatest hero!

"I don't intend to shuck corn, split rails, and the like always," he told Mrs. Crawford, after he had read the volume. "I'm going to fit myself for a profession."

"Why, what do you want to be, now?" asked Mrs. Crawford in surprise.

"Oh, I'll be President!" said Abe with a smile.

"You'd make a pretty President with all your

tricks and jokes, now, would n't you?" said the farmer's wife.

"Oh, I'll study and get ready," replied the boy, "and then maybe the chance will come."

WHY LINCOLN WAS CALLED "HONEST ABE"

BY NOAH BROOKS

In managing the country store, as in everything that he undertook for others, Lincoln did his very best. He was honest, civil, ready to do anything that should encourage customers to come to the place, full of pleasantries, patient, and alert.

On one occasion, finding late at night, when he counted over his cash, that he had taken a few cents from a customer more than was due, he closed the store, and walked a long distance to make good the deficiency.

At another time, discovering on the scales in the morning a weight with which he had weighed out a package of tea for a woman the night before, he saw that he had given her too little for her money. He weighed out what was due, and carried it to her, much to the surprise of the woman, who had not known that she was short in the amount of her purchase.

Innumerable incidents of this sort are related of Lincoln, and we should not have space to tell of the alertness with which he sprang to protect defenseless women from insult, or feeble children from tyranny; for in the rude community in which he lived, the rights of the defenseless were not always respected as they should have been. There were bullies then, as now.

A STRANGER AT FIVE-POINTS

(Adapted)

One afternoon in February, 1860, when the Sunday School of the Five-Point House of Industry in New York was assembled, the teacher saw a most remarkable man enter the room and take his place among the others. This stranger was tall, his frame was gaunt and sinewy, his head powerful, with determined features overcast by a gentle melancholy.

He listened with fixed attention to the exercises. His face expressed such genuine interest that the teacher, approaching him, suggested that he might have something to say to the children.

The stranger accepted the invitation with evident pleasure. Coming forward, he began to speak and at once fascinated every child in the room. His language was beautiful yet simple, his tones were musical, and he spoke with deep feeling.

The faces of the boys and girls drooped sadly

as he uttered warnings, and then brightened with joy as he spoke cheerful words of promise. Once or twice he tried to close his remarks, but the children shouted: "Go on! Oh! do go on!" and he was forced to continue.

At last he finished his talk and was leaving the room quietly when the teacher begged to know his name.

"Abra'm Lincoln, of Illinois," was the modest response.

A SOLOMON COME TO JUDGMENT

BY CHARLES W. MOORES

LINCOLN'S practical sense and his understanding of human nature enabled him to save the life of the son of his old Clary's Grove friend, Jack Armstrong, who was on trial for murder. Lincoln, learning of it, went to the old mother who had been kind to him in the days of his boyhood poverty, and promised her that he would get her boy free.

The witnesses were sure that Armstrong was guilty, and one of them declared that he had seen the fatal blow struck. It was late at night, he said, and the light of the full moon had made it possible for him to see the crime committed. Lincoln, on cross-examination, asked him only questions enough to make the jury see that it was the full moon that made it possible for the witness to see what occurred; got him to say two or three times that he was sure of it, and seemed to give up any further effort to save the boy.

But when the evidence was finished, and Lincoln's time came to make his argument, he called for an almanac, which the clerk of the court had ready for him, and handed it to the jury. They saw at once that on the night of the murder there was no moon at all. They were satisfied that the witness had told what was not true. Lincoln's case was won.

GEORGE PICKETT'S FRIEND

BY CHARLES W. MOORES

George Pickett, who had known Lincoln in Illinois, years before, joined the Southern army, and by his conspicuous bravery and ability had become one of the great generals of the Confederacy. Toward the close of the war, when a large part of Virginia had fallen into the possession of the Union army, the President called at General Pickett's Virginia home.

The general's wife, with her baby on her arm, met him at the door. She herself has told the story for us.

"'Is this George Pickett's home?' he asked.

"With all the courage and dignity I could

muster, I replied: 'Yes, and I am his wife, and this is his baby.'

"'I am Abraham Lincoln.'

"'The President!' I gasped. I had never seen him, but I knew the intense love and reverence with which my soldier always spoke of him.

"The stranger shook his head and replied: 'No; Abraham Lincoln, George's old friend.'

"The baby pushed away from me and reached out his hands to Mr. Lincoln, who took him in his arms. As he did so an expression of rapt, almost divine tenderness and love lighted up the sad face. It was a look that I have never seen on any other face. The baby opened his mouth wide and insisted upon giving his father's friend a dewy kiss.

"As Mr. Lincoln gave the little one back to me he said: 'Tell your father, the rascal, that I forgive him for the sake of your bright eyes.'"

LINCOLN THE LAWYER

BY Z. A. MUDGE (ADAPTED)

HE delighted to advocate the cases of those whom he knew to be wronged, but he would not defend the cause of the guilty. If he discovered in the course of a trial that he was on the wrong side, he lost all interest, and ceased to make any exertion.

Once, while engaged in a prosecution, he discovered that his client's cause was not a good one, and he refused to make the plea. His associate, who was less scrupulous, made the plea and obtained a decision in their favor. The fee was nine hundred dollars, half of which was tendered to Mr. Lincoln, but he refused to accept a single cent of it.

His honesty was strongly illustrated by the way he kept his accounts with his law-partner. When he had taken a fee in the latter's absence, he put one half of it into his own pocket, and laid the other half carefully away, labeling it "Billy," the name by which he familiarly addressed his partner. When asked why he did not make a record of the amount and, for the time being, use the whole, Mr. Lincoln answered: "Because I promised my mother never to use money belonging to another person."

THE COURAGE OF HIS CONVICTIONS

(Adapted)

Mr. Lincoln made the great speech of his famous senatorial campaign at Springfield, Illinois. The convention before which he spoke consisted of a thousand delegates together with the crowd that had gathered with them.

His speech was carefully prepared. Every

sentence was guarded and emphatic. It has since become famous as "The Divided House" speech. Before entering the hall where it was to be delivered, he stepped into the office of his law-partner, Mr. Herndon, and, locking the door, so that their interview might be private, took his manuscript from his pocket, and read one of the opening sentences: "I believe this government cannot endure permanently, half slave and half free."

Mr. Herndon remarked that the sentiment was true, but suggested that it might not be *good policy* to utter it at that time.

Mr. Lincoln replied with great firmness: "No matter about the *policy*. It is *true*, and the nation is entitled to it. The proposition has been true for six thousand years, and I will deliver it as it is written."

MR. LINCOLN AND THE BIBLE

BY Z. A. MUDGE (ADAPTED)

A VISITOR in Washington once had an appointment to see Mr. Lincoln at five o'clock in the morning. The gentleman made a hasty toilet and presented himself at a quarter of five in the waiting-room of the President. He asked the usher if he could see Mr. Lincoln.

"No," he replied.

"But I have an engagement to meet him this morning," answered the visitor.

"At what hour?" asked the usher.

"At five o'clock."

"Well, sir, he will see you at five."

The visitor waited patiently, walking to and fro for a few minutes, when he heard a voice as if in grave conversation.

"Who is talking in the next room?" he asked.

"It is the President, sir," said the usher, who then explained that it was Mr. Lincoln's custom to spend every morning from four to five reading the Scriptures, and praying.

HIS SPRINGFIELD FAREWELL ADDRESS

IT was on the morning of February 11, 1861, that the President-elect, together with his family and a small party of friends, bade adieu to the city of Springfield, which, alas! he was never to see again.

A large throng of Springfield citizens assembled at the railway station to see the departure, and before the train left Mr. Lincoln addressed them in the following words: —

"*My Friends:* No one, not in my position, can appreciate the sadness I feel at this parting. To this people I owe all that I am. Here I have lived more than a quarter of a century; here my children were born, and here one of them lies buried. I know not how soon I shall see you again. A duty devolves upon me which is, perhaps, greater than that which has devolved upon any other man since the days of Washington. He never would have succeeded except by the aid of Divine Providence, upon which he at all times relied. I feel that I cannot succeed without the same Divine aid which sustained him, and on the same Almighty Being I place my reliance for support; and I hope you, my friends, will all pray that I may receive that Divine assistance, without which I cannot succeed, but with which success is certain. Again I bid you an affectionate farewell."

SAINT VALENTINE'S DAY

(FEBRUARY 14)

SAINT VALENTINE

THE good Saint Valentine was a priest at Rome in the days of Claudius II. He and Saint Marius aided the Christian martyrs, and for this kind deed Saint Valentine was apprehended and dragged before the Prefect of Rome, who condemned him to be beaten to death with clubs and to have his head cut off. He suffered martyrdom on the 14th day of February, about the year 270.

At that time it was the custom in Rome, a very ancient custom, indeed, to celebrate in the month of February the Lupercalia, feasts in honor of a heathen god.

On these occasions, amidst a variety of pagan ceremonies, the names of young women were placed in a box, from which they were drawn by the men as chance directed.

The pastors of the early Christian Church in Rome endeavored to do away with the pagan element in these feasts by substituting the names of saints for those of maidens. And as the Lupercalia began about the middle of February, the pastors appear to have chosen Saint Valentine's Day for the celebration of this new feast.

So it seems that the custom of young men choosing maidens for valentines, or saints as patrons for the coming year, arose in this wise.

A PRISONER'S VALENTINE

BY MILLICENT OLMSTED (ADAPTED)

CHARLES, DUKE OF ORLÉANS, who was taken prisoner at the battle of Agincourt in 1415, and detained in England twenty-five years, was the author of the earliest known written valentines. He left about sixty of them. They were written during his confinement in the Tower of London, and are still to be seen among the royal papers in the British Museum.

One of his valentines reads as follows: —

"Wilt thou be mine? dear Love, reply —
Sweetly consent or else deny.
Whisper softly, none shall know,
Wilt thou be mine, Love? — aye or no?

"Spite of Fortune, we may be
Happy by one word from thee.
Life flies swiftly — ere it go
Wilt thou be mine, Love? — aye or no?"

A GIRL'S VALENTINE CHARM

AS TOLD BY HERSELF

(FROM THE CONNOISSEUR, 1775)

LAST Friday was Valentine's Day, and I'll tell you what I did the night before. I got five bay leaves, and pinned four of them to the four corners of my pillow, and the fifth to the middle; and then if I dreamt of my sweetheart, Betty said we would be married before the year was out.

But to make it more sure, I boiled an egg hard, and took out the yolk, and filled it with salt, and when I went to bed ate it, shell and all, without speaking or drinking after it.

We also wrote our lovers' names upon bits of paper, and rolled them up in clay and put them into water; and the first that rose up was to be our valentine. Would you think it? Mr. Blossom was my man, and I lay abed and shut my eyes all the morning, till he came to our house, for I would not have seen another man before him for all the world.

MR. PEPYS HIS VALENTINE

AS RELATED BY HIMSELF IN 1666

(ADAPTED)

THIS morning, came up to my wife's bedside, I being up dressing myself, little Will Mercer, to be her valentine; and brought her name writ upon blue paper in gold letters, done by himself, very pretty; and we were both well pleased with it.

But I am also this year my wife's valentine; and it will cost me five pounds; but that I must have laid out if we had not been valentines.

I find also that Mrs. Pierce's little girl is my valentine, she having drawn me; which I am not sorry for, it easing me of something more that I must have given to others.

But here I do first observe the fashion of drawing of mottoes as well as names; so that Pierce, who drew my wife, did draw also a motto, and this girl drew another for me. What mine was I have forgot, but my wife's was: "Most virtuous and most fair," which, as it may be used, or an anagram made upon each name, might be very pretty.

CUPID AND PSYCHE

BY JOSEPHINE PRESTON PEABODY

THE ENCHANTED PALACE

ONCE upon a time, through that Destiny that overrules the gods, Love himself gave up his immortal heart to a mortal maiden. And thus it came to pass: —

There was a certain king who had three beautiful daughters. The two elder married princes of great renown; but Psyche, the youngest, was so radiantly fair that no suitor seemed worthy of her. People thronged to see her pass through the city, and sang hymns in her praise, while strangers took her for the very goddess of beauty herself.

This angered Venus, and she resolved to cast down her earthly rival. One day, therefore, she called hither her son Love (Cupid, some name him), and bade him sharpen his weapons. He is an archer more to be dreaded than Apollo, for Apollo's arrows take life, but Love's bring joy or sorrow for a whole life long.

"Come, Love," said Venus. "There is a mortal maid who robs me of my honors in yonder city. Avenge your mother. Wound this precious Psyche, and let her fall in love with some churlish creature mean in the eyes of all men."

Cupid made ready his weapons, and flew down to earth invisibly. At that moment Psyche was asleep in her chamber; but he touched her heart with his golden arrow of love, and she opened her eyes so suddenly that he started (forgetting that he was invisible), and wounded himself with his own shaft. Heedless of the hurt, moved only by the loveliness of the maiden, he hastened to pour over her locks the healing joy that he ever kept by him, undoing all his work. Back to her dream the princess went, unshadowed by any thought of love. But Cupid, not so light of heart, returned to the heavens, saying not a word of what had passed.

Venus waited long; then, seeing that Psyche's heart had somehow escaped love, she sent a spell upon the maiden. From that time, lovely as she was, not a suitor came to woo; and her parents, who desired to see her a queen at least, made a journey to the Oracle, and asked counsel.

Said the voice: "The Princess Psyche shall never wed a mortal. She shall be given to one who waits for her on yonder mountain; he overcomes gods and men."

At this terrible sentence the poor parents were half-distraught, and the people gave themselves up to grief at the fate in store for their beloved princess. Psyche alone bowed to her destiny. "We have angered Venus unwittingly," she said, "and all for sake of me, heedless maiden that I am! Give me up, therefore, dear father and mother. If I atone, it may be that the city will prosper once more."

So she besought them, until, after many unavailing denials, the parents consented; and with a great company of people they led Psyche up the mountain, — as an offering to the monster of whom the Oracle had spoken, — and left her there alone.

Full of courage, yet in a secret agony of grief, she watched her kindred and her people wind down the mountain-path, too sad to look back, until they were lost to sight. Then, indeed, she wept, but a sudden breeze drew near, dried her tears, and caressed her hair, seeming to murmur comfort. In truth, it was Zephyr, the kindly West Wind, come to befriend her; and as she took heart, feeling some benignant presence, he lifted her in his arms, and carried her on wings as even as a sea-gull's, over the crest of the fateful mountain and into a valley below. There he left her, resting on a bank of hospitable grass, and there the princess fell asleep.

When she awoke, it was near sunset. She looked about her for some sign of the monster's approach; she wondered, then, if her grievous trial had been but a dream. Near by she saw a sheltering forest, whose young trees seemed to beckon as one maid beckons to another; and eager for the protection of the dryads, she went thither.

The call of running waters drew her farther and farther, till she came out upon an open place, where there was a wide pool. A fountain fluttered gladly in the midst of it, and beyond there stretched a white palace wonderful to see. Coaxed by the bright promise of the place, she drew near, and, seeing no one, entered softly. It was all kinglier than her father's home, and as she stood in wonder and awe, soft airs stirred about her. Little by little the silence grew murmurous like the woods, and one voice, sweeter than the rest, took words. "All that you see is yours, gentle high princess," it said. "Fear nothing; only command us, for we are here to serve you."

Full of amazement and delight, Psyche followed the voice from hall to hall, and through the lordly rooms, beautiful with everything that could delight a young princess. No pleasant thing was lacking. There was even a pool, brightly tiled and fed with running waters, where she bathed her weary limbs; and after she had put on the new and beautiful raiment that lay ready for her, she sat down to break her fast, waited upon and sung to by the unseen spirits.

Surely he whom the Oracle had called her husband was no monster, but some beneficent power, invisible like all the rest. When daylight waned he came, and his voice, the beautiful voice of a god, inspired her to trust her strange destiny and to look and long for his return. Often she begged him to stay with her through the day, that she might see his face; but this he would not grant.

"Never doubt me, dearest Psyche," said he. "Perhaps you would fear if you saw me, and love is all I ask. There is a necessity that keeps me hidden now. Only believe."

So for many days Psyche was content; but when she grew used to happiness, she thought once more of her parents mourning her as lost, and of her sisters who shared the lot of mortals while she lived as a goddess. One night she told her husband of these regrets, and begged that her sisters at least might come to see her. He sighed, but did not refuse.

"Zephyr shall bring them hither," said he.

And on the following morning, swift as a bird, the West Wind came over the crest of the high mountain and down into the enchanted valley, bearing her two sisters.

They greeted Psyche with joy and amazement, hardly knowing how they had come hither. But when this fairest of the sisters led them through her palace and showed them all the treasures that were hers, envy grew in their hearts and choked their old love. Even while they sat at feast with her, they grew more and more bitter; and hoping to find some little flaw in her good fortune, they asked a thousand questions.

"Where is your husband?" said they. "And why is he not here with you?"

"Ah," stammered Psyche. "All the day long — he is gone, hunting upon the mountains."

"But what does he look like?" they asked; and Psyche could find no answer.

When they learned that she had never seen him, they laughed her faith to scorn.

"Poor Psyche," they said. "You are walking in a dream. Wake, before it is too late. Have you forgotten what the Oracle decreed, — that you were destined for a dreadful creature, the fear of gods and men? And are you deceived by this show of kindliness? We have come to warn you. The people told us, as we came over the mountain, that your husband is a dragon, who feeds you well for the present, that he may feast the better, some day soon. What is it that you trust? Good words! But only take a dagger some night, and when the monster is asleep go, light a lamp, and look at him. You can put him to death easily, and all his riches will be yours — and ours."

Psyche heard this wicked plan with horror. Nevertheless, after her sisters were gone, she brooded over what they had said, not seeing their evil intent; and she came to find some wisdom in their words. Little by little, suspicion ate, like a moth, into her lovely mind; and at nightfall, in shame and fear, she hid a lamp and a dagger in her chamber. Towards midnight, when her husband was fast asleep, up she rose, hardly daring to breathe; and coming softly to his side, she uncovered the lamp to see some horror.

But there the youngest of the gods lay sleeping, — most beautiful, most irresistible of all immortals. His hair shone golden as the sun, his face was radiant as dear Springtime, and from his shoulders sprang two rainbow wings.

Poor Psyche was overcome with self-reproach. As she leaned towards him, filled with worship, her trembling hands held the lamp ill, and some burning oil fell upon Love's shoulder and awakened him.

He opened his eyes, to see at once his bride and the dark suspicion in her heart.

"O doubting Psyche!" he exclaimed with sudden grief, — and then he flew away, out of the window.

Wild with sorrow, Psyche tried to follow, but she fell to the ground instead. When she recovered her senses, she stared about her. She was alone, and the place was beautiful no longer. Garden and palace had vanished with Love.

THE TRIAL OF PSYCHE

Over mountains and valleys Psyche journeyed alone until she came to the city where her two envious sisters lived with the princes whom they had married. She stayed with them only long enough to tell the story of her unbelief and its penalty. Then she set out again to search for Love.

As she wandered one day, travel-worn but not hopeless, she saw a lofty palace on a hill near by, and she turned her steps thither. The place seemed deserted. Within the hall she saw no human being, — only heaps of grain, loose ears of corn half torn from the husk, wheat and barley, alike scattered in confusion on the floor. Without delay, she set to work binding the sheaves together and gathering the scattered ears of corn in seemly wise, as a princess would wish to see them. While she was in the midst of her task, a voice startled her, and she looked up to behold

Demeter herself, the goddess of the harvest, smiling upon her with good will.

"Dear Psyche," said Demeter, "you are worthy of happiness, and you may find it yet. But since you have displeased Venus, go to her and ask her favor. Perhaps your patience will win her pardon."

These motherly words gave Psyche heart, and she reverently took leave of the goddess and set out for the temple of Venus. Most humbly she offered up her prayer, but Venus could not look at her earthly beauty without anger.

"Vain girl," said she, "perhaps you have come to make amends for the wound you dealt your husband; you shall do so. Such clever people can always find work!"

Then she led Psyche into a great chamber heaped high with mingled grain, beans, and lentils (the food of her doves), and bade her separate them all and have them ready in seemly fashion by night. Heracles would have been helpless before such a vexatious task; and poor Psyche, left alone in this desert of grain, had not courage to begin. But even as she sat there, a moving thread of black crawled across the floor from a crevice in the wall; and bending nearer, she saw that a great army of ants in columns had come to her aid. The zealous little creatures worked in swarms, with such industry over the work they like best, that, when Venus came at night, she found the task completed.

"Deceitful girl," she cried, shaking the roses out of her hair with impatience, "this is my son's work, not yours. But he will soon forget you. Eat this black bread if you are hungry, and refresh your dull mind with sleep. To-morrow you will need more wit."

Psyche wondered what new misfortune could be in store for her. But when morning came, Venus led her to the brink of a river, and, pointing to the wood across the water, said: "Go now to yonder grove where the sheep with the golden fleece are wont to browse. Bring me a golden lock from every one of them, or you must go your ways and never come back again."

This seemed not difficult, and Psyche obediently bade the goddess farewell, and stepped into the water, ready to wade across. But as Venus disappeared, the reeds sang louder and the nymphs of the river, looking up sweetly, blew bubbles to the surface and murmured: "Nay, nay, have a care, Psyche. This flock has not the gentle ways of sheep. While the sun burns aloft, they are themselves as fierce as flame; but when the shadows are long, they go to rest and sleep, under the trees; and you may cross the river without fear and pick the golden fleece off the briers in the pasture."

Thanking the water-creatures, Psyche sat down to rest near them, and when the time came, she crossed in safety and followed their counsel. By twilight she returned to Venus with her arms full of shining fleece.

"No mortal wit did this," said Venus angrily. "But if you care to prove your readiness, go now, with this little box, down to Proserpina and ask her to enclose in it some of her beauty, for I have grown pale in caring for my wounded son."

It needed not the last taunt to sadden Psyche. She knew that it was not for mortals to go into Hades and return alive; and feeling that Love had forsaken her, she was minded to accept her doom as soon as might be.

But even as she hastened towards the descent, another friendly voice detained her. "Stay, Psyche, I know your grief. Only give ear and you shall learn a safe way through all these trials." And the voice went on to tell her how one might avoid all the dangers of Hades and come out unscathed. (But such a secret could not pass from mouth to mouth, with the rest of the story.)

"And be sure," added the voice, "when Proserpina has returned the box, not to open it, however much you may long to do so."

Psyche gave heed, and by this device, whatever it was, she found her way into Hades safely, and made her errand known to Proserpina, and was soon in the upper world again, wearied but hopeful.

"Surely Love has not forgotten me," she said. "But humbled as I am and worn with toil, how shall I ever please him? Venus can never need all the beauty in this casket; and since I use it for Love's sake, it must be right to take some." So saying, she opened the box, heedless as Pandora! The spells and potions of Hades are not for mortal maids, and no sooner had she inhaled the strange aroma than she fell down like one dead, quite overcome.

But it happened that Love himself was recovered from his wound, and he had secretly fled from his chamber to seek out and rescue Psyche. He found her lying by the wayside; he gathered into the casket what remained of the philter, and awoke his beloved.

"Take comfort," he said, smiling. "Return to our mother and do her bidding till I come again."

Away he flew; and while Psyche went cheerily homeward, he hastened up to Olympus, where all the gods sat feasting, and begged them to intercede for him with his angry mother.

They heard his story and their hearts were touched. Zeus himself coaxed Venus with kind words till at last she relented, and remembered that anger hurt her beauty, and smiled once more. All the younger gods were for welcoming

Psyche at once, and Hermes was sent to bring her hither. The maiden came, a shy newcomer among those bright creatures. She took the cup that Hebe held out to her, drank the divine ambrosia, and became immortal.

Light came to her face like moonrise, two radiant wings sprang from her shoulders; and even as a butterfly bursts from its dull cocoon, so the human Psyche blossomed into immortality.

Love took her by the hand, and they were never parted any more.

WASHINGTON'S BIRTHDAY

(FEBRUARY 22)

THREE OLD TALES

BY M. L. WEEMS (Adapted)

I. THE CHERRY TREE

When George was about six years old, he was made the wealthy master of a hatchet of which, like most little boys, he was extremely fond. He went about chopping everything that came his way.

One day, as he wandered about the garden amusing himself by hacking his mother's pea-sticks, he found a beautiful, young English cherry tree, of which his father was most proud. He tried the edge of his hatchet on the trunk of the tree and barked it so that it died.

Some time after this, his father discovered what had happened to his favorite tree. He came into the house in great anger, and demanded to know who the mischievous person was who had cut away the bark. Nobody could tell him anything about it.

Just then George, with his little hatchet, came into the room.

"George," said his father, "do you know who has killed my beautiful little cherry tree yonder in the garden? I would not have taken five guineas for it!"

This was a hard question to answer, and for a moment George was staggered by it, but quickly recovering himself he cried: —

"I cannot tell a lie, father, you know I cannot tell a lie! I did cut it with my little hatchet."

The anger died out of his father's face, and taking the boy tenderly in his arms, he said: —

"My son, that you should not be afraid to tell the truth is more to me than a thousand trees! yes, though they were blossomed with silver and had leaves of the purest gold!"

II. THE APPLE ORCHARD

One fine morning in the autumn Mr. Washington, taking little George by the hand, walked with him to the apple orchard, promising that he would show him a fine sight.

On arriving at the orchard they saw a fine sight, indeed! The green grass under the trees was strewn with red-cheeked apples, and yet the trees were bending under the weight of fruit that hung thick among the leaves.

"Now, George," said his father, "look, my son, see all this rich harvest of fruit! Do you remember when your good cousin brought you a fine, large apple last spring, how you refused to divide it with your brothers? And yet I told you then that, if you would be generous, God would give you plenty of apples this autumn."

Poor George could not answer, but hanging down his head looked quite confused, while with his little, naked, bare feet he scratched in the soft ground.

"Now, look up, my son," continued his father, "and see how the blessed God has richly provided us with these trees loaded with the finest fruit. See how abundant is the harvest. Some of the trees are bending beneath their burdens, while the ground is covered with mellow apples, more than you could eat, my son, in all your lifetime."

George looked in silence on the orchard, he marked the busy, humming bees, and heard the gay notes of the birds fluttering from tree to tree. His eyes filled with tears and he answered softly:—

"Truly, father, I never will be selfish any more."

III. THE GARDEN-BED

One day Mr. Washington went into the garden and dug a little bed of earth and prepared it for seed. He then took a stick and traced on the bed George's name in full. After this he strewed the tracing thickly with seeds, and smoothed all over nicely with his roller.

This garden-bed he purposely prepared close to a gooseberry-walk. The bushes were hung with the ripe fruit, and he knew that George would visit them every morning.

Not many days had passed away when one morning George came running into the house, breathless with excitement, and his eyes shining with happiness.

"Come here! father, come here!" he cried.

"What's the matter, my son?" asked his father.

"O come, father," answered George, "and I'll show you such a sight as you have never seen in all your lifetime."

Mr. Washington gave the boy his hand, which he seized with great eagerness. He led his father straight to the garden-bed, whereon in large letters, in lines of soft green, was written: —

GEORGE WASHINGTON

YOUNG GEORGE AND THE COLT

BY HORACE E. SCUDDER

There is a story told of George Washington's boyhood, — unfortunately there are not many stories, — which is to the point. His father had taken a great deal of pride in his blooded horses, and his mother afterward took pains to keep the stock pure. She had several young horses that had not yet been broken, and one of them in particular, a sorrel, was extremely spirited. No one had been able to do anything with it, and it was pronounced thoroughly vicious as people are apt to pronounce horses which they have not learned to master.

George was determined to ride this colt, and told his companions that if they would help him catch it, he would ride and tame it.

Early in the morning they set out for the pasture, where the boys managed to surround the sorrel, and then to put a bit into its mouth. Washington sprang upon its back, the boys dropped the bridle, and away flew the angry animal.

Its rider at once began to command. The horse resisted, backing about the field, rearing and plunging. The boys became thoroughly alarmed, but Washington kept his seat, never once losing his self-control or his mastery of the colt.

The struggle was a sharp one; when suddenly, as if determined to rid itself of its rider, the creature leaped into the air with a tremendous bound. It was its last. The violence burst a blood-vessel, and the noble horse fell dead.

Before the boys could sufficiently recover to consider how they should extricate themselves from the scrape, they were called to breakfast; and the mistress of the house, knowing that they had been in the fields, began to ask after her stock.

"Pray, young gentlemen," said she, "have you seen my blooded colts in your rambles? I hope they are well taken care of. My favorite, I am told, is as large as his sire."

The boys looked at one another, and no one liked to speak. Of course the mother repeated her question.

"The sorrel is dead, madam," said her son, "I killed him."

And then he told the whole story. They say that his mother flushed with anger, as her son often used to, and then, like him, controlled herself, and presently said, quietly: —

"It is well; but while I regret the loss of my favorite, I rejoice in my son who always speaks the truth."

WASHINGTON THE ATHLETE

BY ALBERT F. BLAISDELL AND FRANCIS K. BALL

Many stories are told of the mighty power of Washington's right arm. It is said that he once threw a stone from the bed of the stream to the top of the Natural Bridge, in Virginia.

Again, we are told that once upon a time he rounded a piece of slate to the size of a silver dollar, and threw it across the Rappahannock at Fredericksburg, the slate falling at least thirty feet on the other side. Many strong men have since tried the same feat, but have never cleared the water.

Peale, who was called the soldier-artist, was once visiting Washington at Mount Vernon. One day, he tells us, some athletic young men were pitching the iron bar in the presence of their host. Suddenly, without taking off his coat, Washington grasped the bar and hurled it, with little effort, much farther than any of them had done.

"We were, indeed, amazed," said one of the young men, "as we stood round, all stripped to the buff, and having thought ourselves very clever fellows, while the Colonel, on retiring, pleasantly said: —

" 'When you beat my pitch, young gentlemen, I'll try again.' "

At another time, Washington witnessed a wrestling-match. The champion of the day challenged him, in sport, to wrestle. Washington did not stop to take off his coat, but grasped the "strong man of Virginia." It was all over in a moment, for, said the wrestler, "In Washington's lionlike grasp I became powerless, and was hurled to the ground with a force that seemed to jar the very marrow in my bones."

In the days of the Revolution, some of the riflemen and the backwoodsmen were men of gigantic strength, but it was generally believed by good judges that their commander-in-chief was the strongest man in the army.

WASHINGTON'S MODESTY

BY HENRY CABOT LODGE (ADAPTED)

WASHINGTON as soon as Fort Duquesne had fallen hurried home, resigned his commission, and was married. The sunshine and glitter of the wedding day must have appeared to Washington deeply appropriate, for he certainly seemed to have all that heart of man could desire. Just twenty-seven, in the first flush of young manhood, keen of sense and yet wise in experience, life must have looked very fair and smiling. He had left the army with a well-earned fame, and had come home to take the wife of his choice, and enjoy the good will and respect of all men.

While away on his last campaign he had been elected a member of the House of Burgesses, and when he took his seat, on removing to Williamsburg, three months after his marriage, Mr. Robinson, the Speaker, thanked him publicly in eloquent words for his services to the country.

Washington rose to reply, but he was so utterly unable to talk about himself that he stood before the House stammering and blushing until the Speaker said: —

"Sit down, Mr. Washington, your modesty equals your valor, and that surpasses the power of any language I possess."

WASHINGTON AT YORKTOWN

BY HENRY CABOT LODGE

DURING the assault Washington stood in an embrasure of the grand battery, watching the advance of the men. He was always given to exposing himself recklessly when there was fighting to be done, but not when he was only an observer.

This night, however, he was much exposed to the enemy's fire. One of his aides, anxious and disturbed for his safety, told him that the place was perilous.

"If you think so," was the quiet answer, "you are at liberty to step back."

The moment was too exciting, too fraught with meaning, to think of peril. The old fighting spirit of Braddock's field was unchained for the last time. He would have liked to head the American assault, sword in hand, and as he could not do that, he stood as near his troops as he could, utterly regardless of the bullets whistling in the air about him. Who can wonder at his intense excitement at that moment?

Others saw a brilliant storming of two outworks, but to Washington the whole Revolution and all the labor and thought and conflict of six years were culminating in the smoke and din on those redoubts, while out of the dust and heat of the sharp, quick fight success was coming.

He had waited long, and worked hard, and his whole soul went out as he watched the troops cross the abatis and scale the works. He could have no thought of danger then, and when all was over, he turned to Knox and said: —

"The work is done, and well done. Bring me my horse."

RESURRECTION DAY (EASTER)

(MARCH OR APRIL)

A LESSON OF FAITH

BY MRS. ALFRED GATTY (ADAPTED)

"LET me hire you as a nurse for my poor children," said a butterfly to a quiet caterpillar, who was strolling along a cabbage-leaf in her odd, lumbering fashion.

"See these little eggs," continued the butterfly; "I do not know how long it will be before they come to life, and I feel very sick. If I should die, who will take care of my baby butterflies when I am gone? Will you, kind, mild, green caterpillar? They cannot, of course, live on your rough food. You must give them early dew, and honey from the flowers, and you must let them fly about only a little way at first. Dear me! it is a sad pity that you cannot fly yourself. Dear, dear! I cannot think what made me come and lay my eggs on a cabbage-leaf! What a place for young butterflies to be born upon! Here, take this gold-dust from my wings as a reward. Oh, how dizzy I am! Caterpillar! you will remember about the food —"

And with these words the butterfly drooped her wings and died. The green caterpillar, who had not had the opportunity of even saying "yes" or "no" to the request, was left standing alone by the side of the butterfly's eggs.

"A pretty nurse she has chosen, indeed, poor lady!" exclaimed she, "and a pretty business I have in hand. Why did she ever ask a poor crawling creature like me to bring up her dainty little ones! Much they'll mind me, truly, when they feel the gay wings on their backs, and can fly away."

However, the poor butterfly was dead, and there lay the eggs on the cabbage-leaf, and the green caterpillar had a kind heart, so she resolved to do her best.

"But two heads are better than one," said she; "I will consult some wise animal on the matter."

Then she thought and thought till at last she thought of the lark, and she fancied that because he went up so high, and nobody knew where he went to, he must be very clever and know a great deal.

Now in the neighboring cornfield there lived a lark, and the caterpillar sent a message to him, begging him to come and talk to her. When he came she told him all her difficulties, and asked him how she was to feed and rear the little butterfly creatures.

"Perhaps you will be able to inquire and learn something about it the next time you go up high," said the caterpillar timidly.

"Perhaps I can," answered the lark; and then he went singing upwards into the bright, blue sky, till the green caterpillar could not hear a sound, nor could she see him any more. So she began to walk round the butterfly's eggs, nibbling a bit of the cabbage-leaf now and then as she moved along.

"What a time the lark has been gone!" she cried at last. "I wonder where he is just now. He must have flown higher than usual this time. How I should like to know where he goes, and what he hears in that curious blue sky! He always sings going up and coming down, but he never lets any secret out."

And the green caterpillar took another turn round the butterfly's eggs.

At last the lark's voice began to be heard again. The caterpillar almost jumped for joy, and it was not long before she saw her friend descend with hushed note to the cabbage bed.

"News, news, glorious news, friend caterpillar!" sang the lark, "but the worst of it is, you won't believe me!"

"I believe anything I am told," said the caterpillar hastily.

"Well, then, first of all, I will tell you what those little creatures are to eat" — and the lark nodded his head toward the eggs. "What do you think it is to be? Guess!"

"Dew and honey out of the flowers, I am afraid!" sighed the caterpillar.

"No such thing, my good friend," cried the lark exultantly; "you are to feed them with cabbage-leaves!"

"Never!" said the caterpillar indignantly. "It was their mother's last request that I should feed them on dew and honey."

"Their mother knew nothing about the matter," answered the lark; "but why do you ask me, and then disbelieve what I say? You have neither faith nor trust."

"Oh, I believe everything I am told," said the caterpillar.

"Nay, but you do not," replied the lark. "Why, caterpillar, what do you think those little eggs will turn out to be?"

"Butterflies, to be sure," said the caterpillar.

"*Caterpillars!*" sang the lark; "and you'll find it out in time." And the lark flew away.

"I thought the lark was wise and kind," said the mild, green caterpillar to herself, once more beginning to walk round the eggs, "but I find that he is foolish and saucy instead. Perhaps he went up *too* high this time. How I wonder what he sees, and what he does up yonder!"

"I would tell you if you would believe me," sang the lark, descending once more.

"I believe everything I am told," answered the caterpillar.

"Then I'll tell you something else," cried the lark. "*You will one day be a butterfly yourself!*"

"Wretched bird," exclaimed the caterpillar, "you are making fun of me. You are now cruel as well as foolish! Go away! I will ask your advice no more."

"I told you you would not believe me," cried the lark.

"I believe everything I am told," persisted the caterpillar, — "everything that it is *reasonable* to believe. But to tell me that butterflies' eggs are caterpillars, and that caterpillars leave off crawling and get wings and become butterflies! — Lark! you do not believe such nonsense yourself! You know it is impossible!"

"I know no such thing," said the lark. "When I hover over the cornfields, or go up into the depths of the sky, I see so many wonderful things that I know there must be more. O caterpillar! it is because you *crawl*, and never get beyond your cabbage-leaf, that you call anything *impossible*."

"Nonsense," shouted the caterpillar, "I know what's possible and what's impossible. Look at my long, green body, and many legs, and then talk to me about having wings! Fool!"

"More foolish you!" cried the indignant lark.

"to attempt to reason about what you cannot understand. Do you not hear how my song swells with rejoicing as I soar upwards to the mysterious wonder-world above? Oh, caterpillar, what comes from thence, receive as I do, — on trust."

"What do you mean by that?" asked the caterpillar.

"*On faith*," answered the lark.

"How am I to learn faith?" asked the caterpillar.

At that moment she felt something at her side. She looked round, — eight or ten little green caterpillars were moving about, and had already made a hole in the cabbage-leaf. They had broken from the butterfly's eggs!

Shame and amazement filled the green caterpillar's heart, but joy soon followed. For as the first wonder was possible, the second might be so too.

"Teach me your lesson, lark," she cried.

And the lark sang to her of the wonders of the earth below and of the heaven above. And the caterpillar talked all the rest of her life of the time when she should become a butterfly.

But no one believed her. She nevertheless had learned the lark's lesson of faith, and when she was going into her chrysalis, she said: —

"I shall be a butterfly some day!"

But her relations thought her head was wandering, and they said, "Poor thing!"

And when she was a butterfly, and was going to die she said:—

"I have known many wonders, — *I have faith,* — I can trust even now for the wonder that shall come next."

A CHILD'S DREAM OF A STAR

BY CHARLES DICKENS

THERE was once a child, and he strolled about a good deal, and thought of a number of things. He had a sister, who was a child, too, and his constant companion. These two used to wonder all day long. They wondered at the beauty of the flowers; they wondered at the height and blueness of the sky; they wondered at the depth of the bright water; they wondered at the goodness and the power of God who made the lovely world.

They used to say to one another, sometimes: "Supposing all the children upon earth were to die, would the flowers, and the water, and the sky be sorry?" They believed they would be sorry. "For," said they, "the buds are the children of the flowers, and the little playful streams that gambol down the hillsides are the children of the water; and the smallest, bright specks playing at hide and seek in the sky all night, must surely be the children of the stars; and they would all be grieved to see their playmates, the children of men, no more."

There was one clear, shining star that used to come out in the sky before the rest, near the church spire, above the graves. It was larger and more beautiful, they thought, than all the others, and every night they watched for it, standing hand in hand at a window. Whoever saw it first cried out: "I see the star!" And often they cried out both together, knowing so well when it would rise, and where. So they grew to be such friends with it, that, before lying down in their beds, they always looked out once again, to bid it good-night; and when they were turning round to sleep, they used to say: "God bless the star!"

But while she was still very young, oh, very, very young, the sister drooped, and came to be so weak that she could no longer stand in the window at night; and then the child looked sadly out by himself, and when he saw the star turned round and said to the patient, pale face on the bed: "I see the star!" and then a smile would come upon the face, and a little weak voice used to say: "God bless my brother and the star!"

And so the time came all too soon, when the child looked out alone, and when there was no face on the bed; and when there was a little grave among the graves, not there before; and when the

GOD BLESS THE STAR

star made long rays down towards him, as he saw it through his tears.

Now, these rays were so bright, and they seemed to make such a shining way from earth to heaven, that when the child went to his solitary bed he dreamed about the star; and dreamed that, lying where he was, he saw a train of people taken up that sparkling road by angels. And the star, opening, showed him a great world of light, where many more such angels waited to receive them.

All these angels, who were waiting, turned their beaming eyes upon the people who were carried up into the star; and some came out from the long rows in which they stood, and fell upon the people's necks, and kissed them tenderly, and went away with them down avenues of light, and were so happy in their company, that lying in his bed he wept for joy.

But there were many angels who did not go with them, and among them one he knew. The patient face, that once had lain upon the bed, was glorified and radiant, but his heart found out his sister among all the host.

His sister's angel lingered near the entrance of the star, and said to the leader among those who had brought the people thither: —

"Is my brother come?"

And he said: "No."

She was turning hopefully away, when the child stretched out his arms, and cried: "O sister, I am here! Take me!" And then she turned her beaming eyes upon him, and it was night; and the star was shining into the room, making long rays down towards him, as he saw it through his tears.

From that hour forth, the child looked out upon the star as on the home he was to go to when his time should come; and he thought that he did not belong to the earth alone, but to the star, too, because of his sister's angel gone before.

There was a baby born to be a brother to the child; and while he was so little that he never yet had spoken word, he stretched his tiny form out on his bed, and died.

Again the child dreamed of the open star, and of the company of angels, and the train of people, and the rows of angels with their beaming eyes all turned upon those people's faces.

Said his sister's angel to the leader:—

"Is my brother come?"

And he said: "Not that one, but another."

As the child beheld his brother's angel in her arms, he cried: "O sister, I am here! Take me!" And she turned and smiled upon him, and the star was shining.

He grew to be a young man, and was busy at

his books, when an old servant came to him and said: —

"Thy mother is no more. I bring her blessing on her darling son."

Again at night he saw the star, and all that former company. Said his sister's angel to the leader: —

"Is my brother come?"

And he said: "Thy mother!"

A mighty cry of joy went forth through all the star, because the mother was reunited to her two children. And he stretched out his arms and cried: "O mother, sister, and brother, I am here! Take me!" And they answered him: "Not yet." And the star was shining.

He grew to be a man, whose hair was turning gray, and he was sitting in his chair by the fireside, heavy with grief, and with his face bedewed with tears, when the star opened once again.

Said his sister's angel to the leader: —

"Is my brother come?"

And he said: "Nay, but his maiden daughter."

And the man, who had been the child, saw his daughter, newly lost to him, a celestial creature among those three, and he said: "My daughter's head is on my sister's bosom, and her arm is around my mother's neck, and at her feet there is the baby of old time, and I can bear the parting from her, God be praised!"

And the star was shining.

Thus the child came to be an old man, and his once smooth face was wrinkled, and his steps were slow and feeble, and his back was bent. And one night as he lay upon his bed, his children standing round, he cried, as he had cried so long ago: —

"I see the star!"

They whispered one to another: "He is dying."

And he said: "I am. My age is falling from me like a garment, and I move towards the star as a child. And, O my Father, now I thank Thee that it has so often opened to receive those dear ones who await me!"

And the star was shining; and it shines upon his grave.

THE LOVELIEST ROSE IN THE WORLD

BY HANS CHRISTIAN ANDERSEN (ADAPTED)

ONCE there reigned a queen, in whose garden were found the most glorious flowers at all seasons and from all the lands of the world. But more than all others she loved the roses, and she had many kinds of this flower, from the wild dog-rose with its apple-scented green leaves to the most splendid, large, crimson roses. They grew against the garden walls, wound themselves around the pillars and wind-frames, and crept through the windows into the rooms, and all along the ceilings in the halls. And the roses were of many colors, and of every fragrance and form.

But care and sorrow dwelt in those halls. The queen lay upon a sick-bed, and the doctors said she must die.

"There is still one thing that can save her," said the wise man. "Bring her the loveliest rose in the world, the rose that is the symbol of the purest, the brightest love. If that is held before her eyes ere they close, she will not die."

Then old and young came from every side with roses, the loveliest that bloomed in each garden, but they were not of the right sort. The flower was to be plucked from the Garden of Love. But what rose in all that garden expressed the highest and purest love?

And the poets sang of the loveliest rose in the world, — of the love of maid and youth, and of the love of dying heroes.

"But they have not named the right flower," said the wise man. "They have not pointed out the place where it blooms in its splendor. It is not the rose that springs from the hearts of youthful lovers, though this rose will ever be fragrant in song. It is not the bloom that sprouts from the blood flowing from the breast of the hero who dies for his country, though few deaths are sweeter than his, and no rose is redder than the blood that flows then. Nor is it the wondrous flower to which man devotes many a sleepless night and much of his fresh life, — the magic flower of science."

"But I know where it blooms," said a happy mother, who came with her pretty child to the bedside of the dying queen. "I know where the loveliest rose of love may be found. It springs in the blooming cheeks of my sweet child, when, waking from sleep, it opens its eyes and smiles tenderly at me."

"Lovely is this rose, but there is a lovelier still," said the wise man.

"I have seen the loveliest, purest rose that blooms," said a woman. "I saw it on the cheeks of the queen. She had taken off her golden crown. And in the long, dreary night she carried her sick child in her arms. She wept, kissed it, and prayed for her child."

"Holy and wonderful is the white rose of a mother's grief," answered the wise man, "but it is not the one we seek."

"The loveliest rose in the world I saw at the altar of the Lord," said the good Bishop, "the young maidens went to the Lord's Table. Roses were blushing and pale roses shining on their fresh cheeks. A young girl stood there. She looked with all the love and purity of her spirit up to heaven. That was the expression of the highest and purest love."

"May she be blessed," said the wise man, "but not one of you has yet named the loveliest rose in the world."

Then there came into the room a child, the queen's little son.

"Mother," cried the boy, "only hear what I have read."

And the child sat by the bedside and read from the Book of Him who suffered death upon the cross to save men, and even those who were not yet born. "Greater love there is not."

And a rosy glow spread over the cheeks of the queen, and her eyes gleamed, for she saw that from the leaves of the Book there bloomed the loveliest rose, that sprang from the blood of Christ shed on the cross.

"I see it!" she said, "he who beholds this, the loveliest rose on earth, shall never die."

MAY DAY

(MAY 1)

THE SNOWDROP [1]

BY HANS CHRISTIAN ANDERSEN (ADAPTED)

THE snow lay deep, for it was winter-time. The winter winds blew cold, but there was one house where all was snug and warm. And in the house lay a little flower; in its bulb it lay, under the earth and the snow.

One day the rain fell and it trickled through the ice and snow down into the ground. And presently a sunbeam, pointed and slender, pierced down through the earth, and tapped on the bulb.

"Come in," said the flower.

"I can't do that," said the sunbeam; "I'm not strong enough to lift the latch. I shall be stronger when springtime comes."

"When will it be spring?" asked the flower of every little sunbeam that rapped on its door. But for a long time it was winter. The ground was still covered with snow, and every night there was ice in the water. The flower grew quite tired of waiting.

"How long it is!" it said. "I feel quite cramped. I must stretch myself and rise up a little. I must lift the latch, and look out, and say 'good-morning' to the spring."

[1] From *For the Children's Hour*, by Carolyn Sherwin Bailey and Clara M. Lewis. Copyright by the Milton Bradley Company.

So the flower pushed and pushed. The walls were softened by the rain and warmed by the little sunbeams, so the flower shot up from under the snow, with a pale green bud on its stalk and some long narrow leaves on either side. It was biting cold.

"You are a little too early," said the wind and the weather; but every sunbeam sang: "Welcome," and the flower raised its head from the snow and unfolded itself — pure and white, and decked with green stripes.

It was weather to freeze it to pieces, — such a delicate little flower, — but it was stronger than any one knew. It stood in its white dress in the white snow, bowing its head when the snowflakes fell, and raising it again to smile at the sunbeams, and every day it grew sweeter.

"Oh!" shouted the children, as they ran into the garden, "see the snowdrop! There it stands so pretty, so beautiful,—the first, the only one!"

THE THREE LITTLE BUTTERFLY BROTHERS

(From the German) [1]

There were once three little butterfly brothers, one white, one red, and one yellow. They played

[1] From *Deutsches Drittes Lesebuch,* by W. H. Weick and C. Grebner. Copyright, 1886, by Van Antwerp, Bragg & Co. American Book Company, publishers.

in the sunshine, and danced among the flowers in the garden, and they never grew tired because they were so happy.

One day there came a heavy rain, and it wet their wings. They flew away home, but when they got there they found the door locked and the key gone. So they had to stay out of doors in the rain, and they grew wetter and wetter.

By and by they flew to the red and yellow striped tulip, and said: "Friend Tulip, will you open your flower-cup and let us in till the storm is over?"

The tulip answered: "The red and yellow butterflies may enter, because they are like me, but the white one may not come in."

But the red and yellow butterflies said: "If our white brother may not find shelter in your flower-cup, why, then, we'll stay outside in the rain with him."

It rained harder and harder, and the poor little butterflies grew wetter and wetter, so they flew to the white lily and said: "Good Lily, will you open your bud a little so we may creep in out of the rain?"

The lily answered: "The white butterfly may come in, because he is like me, but the red and yellow ones must stay outside in the storm."

Then the little white butterfly said: "If you won't receive my red and yellow brothers, why, then, I'll stay out in the rain with them. We would rather be wet than be parted."

So the three little butterflies flew away.

But the sun, who was behind a cloud, heard it all, and he knew what good little brothers the butterflies were, and how they had held together in spite of the wet. So he pushed his face through the clouds, and chased away the rain, and shone brightly on the garden.

He dried the wings of the three little butterflies, and warmed their bodies. They ceased to sorrow, and danced among the flowers till evening, then they flew away home, and found the door wide open.

THE WATER-DROP

BY FRIEDRICH WILHELM CAROVÉ

(Adapted from the Translation by Sarah Austin)

There was once a child who lived in a little hut, and in the hut there was nothing but a little bed and a looking-glass; but as soon as the first sunbeam glided softly through the casement and kissed his sweet eyelids, and the finch and the linnet waked him merrily with their morning songs, he arose and went out into the green meadow.

And he begged flour of the primrose, and sugar of the violet, and butter of the buttercup. He shook dewdrops from the cowslip into the cup of the harebell, spread out a large lime-leaf, set his breakfast upon it, and feasted daintily. And he invited a humming-bee and a gay butterfly to partake of his feast, but his favorite guest was a blue dragon-fly.

The bee murmured a good deal about his riches, and the butterfly told his adventures. Such talk delighted the child, and his breakfast was the sweeter to him, and the sunshine on leaf and flower seemed more bright and cheering.

But when the bee had flown off to beg from flower to flower, and the butterfly had fluttered away to his play-fellows, the dragon-fly still remained, poised on a blade of grass. Her slender and burnished body, more brightly and deeply blue than the deep blue sky, glistened in the sunbeam. Her net-like wings laughed at the flowers because they could not fly, but must stand still and abide the wind and rain.

The dragon-fly sipped a little of the child's clear dewdrops and blue violet honey, and then whispered her winged words. Such stories as the dragon-fly did tell! And as the child sat motionless with his blue eyes shut, and his head rested on his hands, she thought he had fallen asleep; so she poised her double wings and flew into the rustling wood.

But the child had only sunk into a dream of

delight and was wishing he were a sunbeam or a moonbeam; and he would have been glad to hear more and more, and forever.

But at last as all was still, he opened his eyes and looked around for his dear guest, but she was flown far away. He could not bear to sit there any longer alone, and he rose and went to the gurgling brook. It gushed and rolled so merrily, and tumbled so wildly along as it hurried to throw itself head-over-heels into the river, just as if the great massy rock out of which it sprang were close behind it, and could only be escaped by a breakneck leap.

Then the child began to talk to the little waves and asked them whence they came. They would not stay to give him an answer, but danced away one over another; till at last, that the sweet child might not be grieved, a water-drop stopped behind a piece of rock.

"A long time ago," said the water-drop, "I lived with my countless sisters in the great Ocean, in peace and unity. We had all sorts of pastimes. Sometimes we mounted up high into the air, and peeped at the stars. Then we sank plump down deep below, and looked how the coral builders work till they are tired, that they may reach the light of day at last.

"But I was conceited, and thought myself much better than my sisters. And so, one day, when the sun rose out of the sea, I clung fast to one of his hot beams and thought how I should reach the stars and become one of them.

"But I had not ascended far when the sunbeam shook me off, and, in spite of all I could say or do, let me fall into a dark cloud. And soon a flash of fire darted through the cloud, and now I thought I must surely die; but the cloud laid itself down softly upon the top of a mountain, and so I escaped.

"Now I thought I should remain hidden, when, all on a sudden, I slipped over a round pebble, fell from one stone to another, down into the depths of the mountain. At last it was pitch dark and I could neither see nor hear anything.

"Then I found, indeed, that 'pride goeth before a fall,' for, though I had already laid aside all my unhappy pride in the cloud, my punishment was to remain for some time in the heart of the mountain. After undergoing many purifications from the hidden virtues of metals and minerals, I was at length permitted to come up once more into the free and cheerful air, and to gush from this rock and journey with this happy stream. Now will I run back to my sisters in the Ocean, and there wait patiently till I am called to something better."

So said the water-drop to the child, but scarcely had she finished her story, when the root of a

For-Get-Me-Not caught the drop and sucked her in, that she might become a floweret, and twinkle brightly as a blue star on the green firmament of earth.

THE SPRING BEAUTY

AN OJIBBEWAY LEGEND

BY HENRY R. SCHOOLCRAFT (ADAPTED)

AN old man was sitting in his lodge, by the side of a frozen stream. It was the end of winter, the air was not so cold, and his fire was nearly out. He was old and alone. His locks were white with age, and he trembled in every joint. Day after day passed, and he heard nothing but the sound of the storm sweeping before it the new-fallen snow.

One day while his fire was dying, a handsome young man approached and entered the lodge. His cheeks were red, his eyes sparkled. He walked with a quick, light step. His forehead was bound with a wreath of sweet-grass, and he carried a bunch of fragrant flowers in his hand.

"Ah, my son," said the old man, "I am happy to see you. Come in! Tell me your adventures, and what strange lands you have seen. I will tell you of my wonderful deeds, and what I can perform. You shall do the same, and we will amuse each other."

The old man then drew from a bag a curiously wrought pipe. He filled it with mild tobacco, and handed it to his guest. They each smoked from the pipe and then began their stories.

"I am Peboan, the Spirit of Winter," said the old man. "I blow my breath, and the streams stand still. The water becomes stiff and hard as clear stone."

"I am Seegwun, the Spirit of Spring," answered the youth. "I breathe, and flowers spring up in the meadows and woods."

"I shake my locks," said the old man, "and snow covers the land. The leaves fall from the trees, and my breath blows them away. The birds fly to a distant land, and the animals hide themselves from the cold."

"I shake my ringlets," said the young man, "and warm showers of soft rain fall upon the earth. The flowers lift their heads from the ground, the grass grows thick and green. My voice recalls the birds, and they come flying joyfully from the Southland. The warmth of my breath unbinds the streams, and they sing the songs of summer. Music fills the groves wherever I walk, and all nature rejoices."

And while they were talking thus a wonderful change took place. The sun began to rise. A gentle warmth stole over the place. Peboan, the Spirit of Winter, became silent. His head drooped, and the snow outside the lodge melted away. Seegwun, the Spirit of Spring, grew more radiant, and rose joyfully to his feet. The robin and the bluebird began to sing on the top of the lodge. The stream began to murmur at the door, and the fragrance of opening flowers came softly on the breeze.

The lodge faded away, and Peboan sank down and dissolved into tiny streams of water, that vanished under the brown leaves of the forest. Thus the Spirit of Winter departed, and where he had melted away, there the Indian children gathered the first blossoms, fragrant and delicately pink, — the modest Spring Beauty.

THE FAIRY TULIPS

ENGLISH FOLK-TALE

Once upon a time there was a good old woman who lived in a little house. She had in her garden a bed of beautiful striped tulips.

One night she was wakened by the sounds of sweet singing and of babies laughing. She looked out at the window. The sounds seemed to come from the tulip bed, but she could see nothing.

The next morning she walked among her flowers, but there were no signs of any one having been there the night before.

On the following night she was again wakened by sweet singing and babies laughing. She rose and stole softly through her garden. The moon was shining brightly on the tulip bed, and the flowers were swaying to and fro. The old woman looked closely and she saw, standing by each tulip, a little Fairy mother who was crooning and rocking the flower like a cradle, while in each tulip-cup lay a little Fairy baby laughing and playing.

The good old woman stole quietly back to her house, and from that time on she never picked a tulip, nor did she allow her neighbors to touch the flowers.

The tulips grew daily brighter in color and larger in size, and they gave out a delicious perfume like that of roses. They began, too, to bloom all the year round. And every night the little Fairy mothers caressed their babies and rocked them to sleep in the flower-cups.

The day came when the good old woman died, and the tulip-bed was torn up by folks who did not know about the Fairies, and parsley was planted there instead of the flowers. But the parsley withered, and so did all the other plants in the garden, and from that time nothing would grow there.

But the good old woman's grave grew beautiful, for the Fairies sang above it, and kept it green; while on the grave and all around it there sprang up tulips, daffodils, and violets, and other lovely flowers of spring.

THE STREAM THAT RAN AWAY

BY MARY AUSTIN (ADAPTED)

IN a short and shallow cañon running eastward toward the sun, one may find a clear, brown stream called the Creek of Piñon Pines; that is not because it is unusual to find piñon trees in that country, but because there are so few of them in the cañon of the stream. There are all sorts higher up on the slopes, — long-leaved yellow pines, thimble cones, tamarack, silver fir, and Douglas spruce; but in the cañon there is only a group of the low-headed, gray nut pines which the earliest inhabitants of that country called piñons.

The Cañon of Piñon Pines has a pleasant outlook and lies open to the sun. At the upper end there is no more room by the stream border than will serve for a cattle trail; willows grow in it, choking the path of the water; there are brown birches here and ropes of white clematis tangled over thickets of brier rose.

Low down, the ravine broadens out to inclose a meadow the width of a lark's flight, blossomy and wet and good. Here the stream ran once in a maze of soddy banks and watered all the ground, and afterward ran out at the cañon's mouth across the mesa in a wash of bone-white boulders as far as it could. That was not very far, for it was a slender stream. It had its source on the high crests and hollows of the near-by mountain, in the snow banks that melted and seeped downward through the rocks. But the stream did not know any more of that than you know of what happened to you before you were born, and could give no account of itself except that it crept out from under a great heap of rubble far up in the Cañon of the Piñon Pines.

And because it had no pools in it deep enough for trout, and no trees on its borders but gray nut pines; because, try as it might, it could never get across the mesa to the town, the stream had fully made up its mind to run away.

"Pray, what good will that do you?" said the pines. "If you get to the town, they will turn you into an irrigating ditch, and set you to watering crops."

"As to that," said the stream, "if I once get started I will not stop at the town."

Then it would fret between its banks until the spangled frills of the mimulus were all tattered with its spray. Often at the end of the summer it was worn quite thin and small with running, and not able to do more than reach the meadow.

"But some day," it whispered to the stones, "I shall run quite away."

If the stream had been inclined for it, there was no lack of good company on its own borders. Birds nested in the willows, rabbits came to drink; one summer a bobcat made its lair up the bank opposite the brown birches, and often the deer fed in the meadow.

In the spring of one year two old men came up into the Cañon of Piñon Pines. They had been miners and partners together for many years. They had grown rich and grown poor, and had seen many hard places and strange times. It was a day when the creek ran clear and the south wind smelled of the earth. Wild bees began to whine among the willows, and the meadow bloomed over with poppy-breasted larks.

Then said one of the old men: "Here is good meadow and water enough; let us build a house and grow trees. We are too old to dig in the mines."

"Let us set about it," said the other; for that is the way with two who have been a long time together, — what one thinks of, the other is for doing.

So they brought their possessions, and they built a house by the water border and planted trees. One of the men was all for an orchard but the other preferred vegetables. So they did each what he liked, and were never so happy as when walking in the garden in the cool of the day, touching the growing things as they walked, and praising each other's work.

They were very happy for three years. By this time the stream had become so interested it had almost forgotten about running away. But every year it noted that a larger bit of the meadow was turned under and planted, and more and more the men made dams and ditches by which to turn the water into their gardens.

"In fact," said the stream, "I am being made into an irrigating ditch before I have had my fling in the world. I really must make a start."

That very winter, by the help of a great storm, the stream went roaring down the meadow, over the mesa, and so clean away, with only a track of muddy sand to show the way it had gone.

All that winter the two men brought water for drinking from a spring, and looked for the stream to come back. In the spring they hoped still, for that was the season they looked for the orchard to bear. But no fruit grew on the trees, and the seeds they planted shriveled in the earth. So by the end of summer, when they understood that the water would not come back at all, they went sadly away.

Now the Creek of Piñon Pines did not have a happy time. It went out in the world on the wings of the storm, and was very much tossed about and mixed up with other waters, lost and bewildered.

Everywhere it saw water at work, turning mills, watering fields, carrying trade, falling as hail, rain, and snow; and at the last, after many journeys it found itself creeping out from under the rocks of the same old mountain, in the Cañon of Piñon Pines.

"After all, home is best," said the little stream to itself, and ran about in its choked channels looking for old friends.

The willows were there, but grown shabby and dying at the top; the birches were quite dead, and there was only rubbish where the white clematis had been. Even the rabbits had gone away.

The little stream ran whimpering in the meadow, fumbling at the ruined ditches to comfort the fruit trees which were not quite dead. It was very dull in those days living in the Cañon of Piñon Pines.

"But it is really my own fault," said the stream. So it went on repairing the borders as best it could.

About the time the white clematis had come back to hide the ruin of the brown birches, a young man came and camped with his wife and child in the meadow. They were looking for a place to make a home.

"What a charming place!" said the young wife; "just the right distance from town, and a stream all to ourselves. And look, there are fruit trees already planted. Do let us decide to stay!"

Then she took off the child's shoes and stockings to let it play in the stream. The water curled all about the bare feet and gurgled delightedly.

"Ah, do stay," begged the happy water. "I can be such a help to you, for I know how a garden should be irrigated in the best manner."

The child laughed, and stamped the water up to his bare knees. The young wife watched anxiously while her husband walked up and down the stream border and examined the fruit trees.

"It is a delightful place," he said, "and the soil is rich, but I am afraid the water cannot be depended upon. There are signs of a great drought within the last two or three years. Look, there is a clump of birches in the very path of the stream, but all dead; and the largest limbs of the fruit trees have died. In this country one must be able to make sure of the water-supply. I suppose the people who planted them must have abandoned the place when the stream went dry. We must go on farther."

So they took their goods and the child and went on farther.

"Ah, well," said the stream, "that is what is to be expected when one has a reputation for neglecting one's duty. But I wish they had stayed. That baby and I understood each other."

It had made up its mind not to run away again, though it could not be expected to be quite cheerful after all that had happened. If you go to the Cañon of Piñon Pines you will notice that the stream, where it goes brokenly about the meadow, has a mournful sound.

THE ELVES

AN IROQUOIS LEGEND

BY HARRIET MAXWELL CONVERSE (ADAPTED)

THE little Elves of Darkness, so says the old Iroquois grandmother, were wise and mysterious. They dwelt under the earth, where were deep forests and broad plains. There they kept captive all the evil things that wished to injure human beings, — the venomous reptiles, the wicked spiders, and the fearful monsters. Sometimes one of these evil creatures escaped and rushed upward to the bright, pure air, and spread its poisonous breath over the living things of the upper-world. But such happenings were rare, for the Elves of Darkness were faithful and strong, and did not willingly allow the wicked beasts and reptiles to harm human beings and the growing things.

When the night was lighted by the moon's soft rays, and the woods of the upper-world were sweet with the odor of the spring-flowers, then the Elves of Darkness left the under-world, and creeping from their holes, held a festival in the woods. And under many a tree, where the blades of grass had refused to grow, the Little People danced until rings of green sprang up beneath their feet. And to the festival came the Elves of Light, — among whom were Tree-Elves, Flower-Elves, and Fruit-Elves. They too danced and made merry.

But when the moonlight faded away, and day began to break, then the Elves of Darkness scampered back to their holes, and returned once more to the under-world; while the Elves of Light began their daily tasks.

For in the springtime these Little People of the Light hid in sheltered places. They listened to the complaints of the seeds that lay covered in the ground, and they whispered to the earth until the seeds burst their pods and sent their shoots upward to the light. Then the little Elves wandered over the fields and through the woods, bidding all growing things to look upon the sun.

The Tree-Elves tended the trees, unfolding their leaves, and feeding their roots with sap from the earth. The Flower-Elves unwrapped the baby buds, and tinted the petals of the opening flowers, and played with the bees and the butterflies.

But the busiest of all were the Fruit-Elves. Their greatest care in the spring was the strawberry plant. When the ground softened from the frost, the Fruit-Elves loosened the earth around each strawberry root, that its shoots might push through to the light. They shaped the plant's leaves, and turned its blossoms toward the warm rays of the sun. They trained its runners, and assisted the timid fruit to form. They painted the luscious berry, and bade it ripen. And when the first strawberries blushed on the vines, these guardian Elves protected them from the evil insects that had escaped from the world of darkness underground.

And the old Iroquois grandmother tells, how once, when the fruit first came to earth, the Evil Spirit, Hahgwehdaetgah, stole the strawberry plant, and carried it to his gloomy cave, where he hid it away. And there it lay until a tiny sunbeam pierced the damp mould, and finding the little vine carried it back to its sunny fields. And ever since then the strawberry plant has lived and thrived in the fields and woods. But the Fruit-Elves, fearing lest the Evil One should one day steal the vine again, watch day and night over their favorite. And when the strawberries ripen they give the juicy, fragrant fruit to the Iroquois children as they gather the spring flowers in the woods.

THE CAÑON FLOWERS

BY RALPH CONNOR (ADAPTED)

AT first there were no cañons, but only the broad, open prairie. One day the Master of the Prairie, walking out over his great lawns, where were only grasses, asked the Prairie: "Where are your flowers?"

And the Prairie said: "Master, I have no seeds."

Then he spoke to the birds, and they carried seeds of every kind of flower and strewed them far and wide, and soon the Prairie bloomed with crocuses and roses and buffalo beans and the yellow crowfoot and the wild sunflowers and the red lilies, all the summer long.

Then the Master came and was well pleased; but he missed the flowers he loved best of all, and he said to the Prairie: "Where are the clematis and the columbine, the sweet violets and wind-flowers, and all the ferns and flowering shrubs?"

And again the Prairie answered: "Master, I have no seeds."

And again he spoke to the birds and again they carried all the seeds and strewed them far and wide.

But when next the Master came, he could not find the flowers he loved best of all, and he said: "Where are those, my sweetest flowers?"

And the Prairie cried sorrowfully: "O Master, I cannot keep the flowers, for the winds sweep fiercely, and the sun beats upon my breast, and they wither up and fly away."

Then the Master spoke to the Lightning, and with one swift blow the Lightning cleft the Prairie to the heart. And the Prairie rocked and groaned in agony, and for many a day moaned bitterly over its black, jagged, gaping wound.

But a little river poured its waters through the cleft, and carried down deep, black mould, and once more the birds carried seeds and strewed them in the cañon. And after a long time the rough rocks were decked out with soft mosses and trailing vines, and all the nooks were hung with clematis and columbine, and great elms lifted their huge tops high up into the sunlight, and down about their feet clustered the low cedars and balsams, and everywhere the violets and wind-flowers and maiden-hair grew and bloomed till the cañon became the Master's place for rest and peace and joy.

CLYTIE, THE HELIOTROPE

BY OVID (ADAPTED)

THERE was once a Nymph named Clytie, who gazed ever at Apollo as he drove his sun-chariot through the heavens. She watched him as he rose in the east attended by the rosy-fingered Dawn and the dancing Hours. She gazed as he ascended the heavens, urging his steeds still higher in the fierce heat of the noonday. She looked with wonder as at evening he guided his steeds downward to their many-colored pastures under the western sky, where they fed all night on ambrosia.

Apollo saw not Clytie. He had no thought for her, but he shed his brightest beams upon her sister the white Nymph Leucothoë. And when Clytie perceived this she was filled with envy and grief.

Night and day she sat on the bare ground weeping. For nine days and nine nights she never raised herself from the earth, nor did she take food or drink; but ever she turned her weeping eyes toward the sun-god as he moved through the sky.

And her limbs became rooted to the ground. Green leaves enfolded her body. Her beautiful face was concealed by tiny flowers, violet-colored and sweet with perfume. Thus was she changed into a flower and her roots held her fast to the ground; but ever she turned her blossom-covered face toward the sun, following with eager gaze his daily flight. In vain were her sorrow and tears, for Apollo regarded her not.

And so through the ages has the Nymph turned

her dew-washed face toward the heavens, and men no longer call her Clytie, but the sun-flower, heliotrope.

HYACINTHUS

BY OVID (ADAPTED)

ONCE when the golden-beamed Apollo roamed the earth, he made a companion of Hyacinthus, the son of King Amyclas of Lacedæmon; and him he loved with an exceeding great love, for the lad was beautiful beyond compare.

The sun-god threw aside his lyre, and became the daily comrade of Hyacinthus. Often they played games, or climbed the rugged mountain ridges. Together they followed the chase or fished in the quiet and shadowy pools; and the sun-god, unmindful of his dignity, carried the lad's nets and held his dogs.

It happened on a day that the two friends stripped off their garments, rubbed the juice of the olive upon their bodies, and engaged in throwing the quoit. First Apollo poised it and tossed it far. It cleaved the air with its weight and fell heavily to earth. At that moment Hyacinthus ran forwards and hastened to take up the disc, but the hard earth sent it rebounding straight into his face, so that he fell wounded to the ground.

Ah! then, pale and fearful, the sun-god hastened to the side of his fallen friend. He bore up the lad's sinking limbs and strove to stanch his wound with healing herbs. All in vain! Alas! the wound would not close. And as violets and lilies, when their stems are crushed, hang their languid blossoms on their stalks and wither away, so did Hyacinthus droop his beautiful head and die.

Then the sun-god, full of grief, cried aloud in his anguish: "O Beloved! thou fallest in thy early youth, and I alone am the cause of thy destruction! Oh, that I could give my life for thee or with thee! but since Fate will not permit this, thou shalt ever be with me, and thy praise shall dwell on my lips. My lyre struck with my hand, my songs, too, shall celebrate thee! And thou, dear lad, shalt become a new flower, and on thy leaves will I write my lamentations."

And even as the sun-god spoke, behold! the blood that had flowed from Hyacinthus's wound stained the grass, and a flower, like a lily in shape, sprang up, more bright than Tyrian purple. On its leaves did Apollo inscribe the mournful characters: "ai, ai," which mean "alas! alas!"

And as oft as the spring drives away the winter, so oft does Hyacinthus blossom in the fresh, green grass.

ECHO AND NARCISSUS

BY OVID (ADAPTED)

LONG ago, in the ancient world, there was born to the blue-eyed Nymph Liriope, a beautiful boy, whom she called Narcissus. An oracle foretold at his birth that he should be happy and live to a good old age if he "never saw himself." As this prophecy seemed ridiculous his mother soon forgot all about it.

Narcissus grew to be a stately, handsome youth. His limbs were firm and straight. Curls clustered about his white brow, and his eyes shone like two stars. He loved to wander among the meadow flowers and in the pathless woodland. But he disdained his playmates, and would not listen to their entreaties to join in their games. His heart was cold, and in it was neither hate nor love. He lived indifferent to youth or maid, to friend or foe.

Now, in the forest near by dwelt a Nymph named Echo. She had been a handmaiden of the goddess Juno. But though the Nymph was beautiful of face, she was not loved. She had a noisy tongue. She told lies and whispered slanders, and encouraged the other Nymphs in many misdoings. So when Juno perceived all this, she ordered the troublesome Nymph away from her court, and banished her to the wildwood, bidding her never speak again except in imitation of other peoples' words. So Echo dwelt in the woods, and forever mocked the words of youths and maidens.

One day as Narcissus was wandering alone in the pathless forest, Echo, peeping from behind a tree, saw his beauty, and as she gazed her heart was filled with love. Stealthily she followed his footsteps, and often she tried to call to him with endearing words, but she could not speak, for she no longer had a voice of her own.

At last Narcissus heard the sound of breaking branches, and he cried out: "Is there any one here?"

And Echo answered softly: "Here!"

Narcissus, amazed, looking about on all sides and seeing no one, cried: "Come!"

And Echo answered: "Come!"

Narcissus cried again: "Who art thou? Whom seekest thou?"

And Echo answered: "Thou!"

Then rushing from among the trees she tried to throw her arms about his neck, but Narcissus fled through the forest, crying: "Away! away! I will die before I love thee!"

And Echo answered mournfully: "I love thee!"

And thus rejected, she hid among the trees, and

buried her blushing face in the green leaves. And she pined, and pined, until her body wasted quite away, and nothing but her voice was left. And some say that even to this day her voice lives in lonely caves and answers men's words from afar.

Now, when Narcissus fled from Echo, he came to a clear spring, like silver. Its waters were unsullied, for neither goats feeding upon the mountains nor any other cattle had drunk from it, nor had wild beasts or birds disturbed it, nor had branch or leaf fallen into its calm waters. The trees bent above and shaded it from the hot sun, and the soft, green grass grew on its margin.

Here Narcissus, fatigued and thirsty after his flight, laid himself down beside the spring to drink. He gazed into the mirror-like water, and saw himself reflected in its tide. He knew not that it was his own image, but thought that he saw a youth living in the spring.

He gazed on two eyes like stars, on graceful slender fingers, on clustering curls worthy of Apollo, on a mouth arched like Cupid's bow, on blushing cheeks and ivory neck. And as he gazed his cold heart grew warm, and love for this beautiful reflection rose up and filled his soul.

He rained kisses on the deceitful stream. He thrust his arms into the water, and strove to grasp the image by the neck, but it fled away. Again he kissed the stream, but the image mocked his love. And all day and all night, lying there without food or drink, he continued to gaze into the water. Then raising himself, he stretched out his arms to the trees about him, and cried: —

"Did ever, O ye woods, one love as much as I! Have ye ever seen a lover thus pine for the sake of unrequited affection?"

Then turning once more, Narcissus addressed his reflection in the limpid stream: —

"Why, dear youth, dost thou flee away from me? Neither a vast sea, nor a long way, nor a great mountain separates us! only a little water keeps us apart! Why, dear lad, dost thou deceive me, and whither dost thou go when I try to grasp thee? Thou encouragest me with friendly looks. When I extend my arms, thou extendest thine; when I smile, thou smilest in return; when I weep, thou weepest; but when I try to clasp thee beneath the stream, thou shunnest me and fleest away! Grief is taking my strength, and my life will soon be over! In my early days am I cut off, nor is Death grievous to me, now that he is about to remove my sorrows!"

Thus mourned Narcissus, lying beside the woodland spring. He disturbed the water with his tears, and made the woods to resound with his sighs. And as the yellow wax is melted by the fire, or the hoar frost is consumed by the heat of the sun, so did Narcissus pine away, his body wasting by degrees.

And often as he sighed: "Alas!" the grieving Echo from the wood answered: "Alas!"

With his last breath he looked into the water and sighed: "Ah, youth beloved, farewell!" and Echo sighed: "Farewell!"

And Narcissus, laying his weary head upon the grass, closed his eyes forever. The Water-Nymphs wept for him, and the Wood-Dryads lamented him, and Echo resounded their mourning. But when they sought his body it had vanished away, and in its stead had grown up by the brink of the stream a little flower, with silver leaves and golden heart, — and thus was born to earth the woodland flower, Narcissus.

MOTHERS' DAY

(SECOND SUNDAY IN MAY)

THE LARK AND ITS YOUNG ONES

A HINDU FABLE

BY P. V. RAMASWAMI RAJU (ADAPTED)

A CHILD went up to a lark and said: "Good lark, have you any young ones?"

"Yes, child, I have," said the mother lark, "and they are very pretty ones, indeed." Then she pointed to the little birds and said: "This is Fair Wing, that is Tiny Bill, and that other is Bright Eyes."

"At home, we are three," said the child, "myself and two sisters. Mother says that we are pretty children, and she loves us."

To this the little larks replied: "Oh, yes, *our* mother is fond of us, too."

"Good mother lark," said the child, "will you let Tiny Bill go home with me and play?"

Before the mother lark could reply, Bright Eyes said: "Yes, if you will send your little sister to play with us in our nest."

"Oh, she will be so sorry to leave home," said the child; "she could not come away from our mother."

"Tiny Bill will be so sorry to leave our nest,"

answered Bright Eyes, "and he will not go away from *our* mother."

Then the child ran away to her mother, saying: "Ah, every one is fond of home!"

CORNELIA'S JEWELS

BY JAMES BALDWIN [1]

It was a bright morning in the old city of Rome many hundred years ago. In a vine-covered summer-house in a beautiful garden, two boys were standing. They were looking at their mother and her friend, who were walking among the flowers and trees.

"Did you ever see so handsome a lady as our mother's friend?" asked the younger boy, holding his tall brother's hand. "She looks like a queen."

"Yet she is not so beautiful as our mother," said the elder boy. "She has a fine dress, it is true; but her face is not noble and kind. It is our mother who is like a queen."

"That is true," said the other. "There is no woman in Rome so much like a queen as our own dear mother."

Soon Cornelia, their mother, came down the walk to speak with them. She was simply dressed

[1] From *Fifty Famous Stories Retold.* Copyright, 1896, by American Book Company.

in a plain, white robe. Her arms and feet were bare, as was the custom in those days; and no rings or chains glittered about her hands and neck. For her only crown, long braids of soft brown hair were coiled about her head; and a tender smile lit up her noble face as she looked into her sons' proud eyes.

"Boys," she said, "I have something to tell you."

They bowed before her, as Roman lads were taught to do, and said: "What is it, mother?"

"You are to dine with us to-day, here in the garden; and then our friend is going to show us that wonderful casket of jewels of which you have heard so much."

The brothers looked shyly at their mother's friend. Was it possible that she had still other rings besides those on her fingers? Could she have other gems besides those which sparkled in the chains about her neck?

When the simple outdoor meal was over, a servant brought the casket from the house. The lady opened it. Ah, how those jewels dazzled the eyes of the wondering boys! There were ropes of pearls, white as milk, and smooth as satin; heaps of shining rubies, red as the glowing coals; sapphires as blue as the sky that summer day; and diamonds that flashed and sparkled like the sunlight.

The brothers looked long at the gems. "Ah!" whispered the younger; "if our mother could only have such beautiful things!"

At last, however, the casket was closed and carried carefully away.

"Is it true, Cornelia, that you have no jewels?" asked her friend. "Is it true, as I have heard it whispered, that you are poor?"

"No, I am not poor," answered Cornelia, and as she spoke she drew her two boys to her side; "for here are my jewels. They are worth more than all your gems."

The boys never forgot their mother's pride and love and care; and in after years, when they had become great men in Rome, they often thought of this scene in the garden. And the world still likes to hear the story of Cornelia's jewels.

QUEEN MARGARET AND THE ROBBERS

BY ALBERT F. BLAISDELL (ADAPTED)

ONE day when roses were in bloom, two noblemen came to angry words in the Temple Gardens, by the side of the river Thames. In the midst of their quarrel one of them plucked a white rose from a bush, and, turning to those who were near him, said: —

"He who will stand by me in this quarrel, let

him pluck a white rose with me, and wear it in his hat."

Then the other gentleman tore a red rose from another bush, and said: —

"Let him who will stand by me pluck a red rose, and wear it as his badge."

Now this quarrel led to a great civil war, which was called "The War of the Roses," for every soldier wore a white or red rose in his helmet to show to which side he belonged.

The leaders of the "Red Rose" sided with King Henry the Sixth and his wife, Queen Margaret, who were fighting for the English throne. Many great battles were fought, and wicked deeds were done in those dreadful times.

In a battle at a place called Hexham, the king's party was beaten, and Queen Margaret and her little son, the Prince of Wales, had to flee for their lives. They had not gone far before they met a band of robbers, who stopped the queen and stole all her rich jewels, and, holding a drawn sword over her head, threatened to take her life and that of her child.

The poor queen, overcome by terror, fell upon her knees and begged them to spare her only son, the little prince. But the robbers, turning from her, began to fight among themselves as to how they should divide the plunder, and, drawing their weapons, they attacked one another. When the queen saw what was happening she sprang to her feet, and, taking the prince by the hand, made haste to escape.

There was a thick wood close by, and the queen plunged into it, but she was sorely afraid and trembled in every limb, for she knew that this wood was the hiding-place of robbers and outlaws. Every tree seemed to her excited fancy to be an armed man waiting to kill her and her little son.

On and on she went through the dark wood, this way and that, seeking some place of shelter, but not knowing where she was going. At last she saw by the light of the moon a tall, fierce-looking man step out from behind a tree. He came directly toward her, and she knew by his dress that he was an outlaw. But thinking that he might have children of his own, she determined to throw herself and her son upon his mercy.

When he came near she addressed him in a calm voice and with a stately manner.

"Friend," said she, "I am the queen. Kill me if thou wilt, but spare my son, thy prince. Take him, I will trust him to thee. Keep him safe from those that seek his life, and God will have pity on thee for all thy sins."

The words of the queen moved the heart of the outlaw. He told her that he had once fought on her side, and was now hiding from the soldiers of the "White Rose." He then lifted the little prince in his arms, and, bidding the queen follow, led the way to a cave in the rocks. There he gave them food and shelter, and kept them safe for two days, when the queen's friends and attendants, discovering their hiding-place, came and took them far away.

If you ever go to Hexham Forest, you may see this robber's cave. It is on the bank of a little stream that flows at the foot of a hill, and to this day the people call it "Queen Margaret's Cave."

THE REVENGE OF CORIOLANUS

BY CHARLES MORRIS (ADAPTED)

CAIUS MARCIUS was a noble Roman youth, who fought valiantly, when but seventeen years of age, in the battle of Lake Regillus, and was there crowned with an oaken wreath, the Roman reward for saving the life of a fellow soldier. This he showed with joy to his mother, Volumnia, whom he loved exceedingly, it being his greatest pleasure to receive praise from her lips.

He afterward won many more crowns in battle, and became one of the most famous of Roman soldiers. One of his memorable exploits took place during a war with the Volscians, in which the Romans attacked the city of Corioli. Through

Caius's bravery the place was taken, and the Roman general said: "Henceforth, let him be called after the name of this city." So ever after he was known as Caius Marcius Coriolanus.

Courage was not the only marked quality of Coriolanus. His pride was equally great. He was a noble of the nobles, so haughty in demeanor and so disdainful of the commons that they grew to hate him bitterly.

At length came a time of great scarcity of food. The people were on the verge of famine, to relieve which shiploads of corn were sent from Sicily to Rome. The Senate resolved to distribute this corn among the suffering people, but Coriolanus opposed this, saying: "If they want corn, let them promise to obey the Patricians, as their fathers did. Let them give up their tribunes. If they do this we will let them have corn, and take care of them."

When the people heard of what the proud noble had said, they broke into a fury, and a mob gathered around the doors of the Senate house, prepared to seize and tear him in pieces when he came out. But the tribunes prevented this, and Coriolanus fled from Rome, exiled from his native land by his pride and disdain of the people.

The exile made his way to the land of the Volscians and became the friend of Rome's great enemy, whom he had formerly helped to conquer. He aroused the Volscians' ire against Rome, to a greater degree than before, and placing himself at the head of a Volscian army greater than the Roman forces, marched against his native city. The army swept victoriously onward, taking city after city, and finally encamping within five miles of Rome.

The approach of this powerful host threw the Romans into dismay. They had been assailed so suddenly that they had made no preparations for defense, and the city seemed to lie at the mercy of its foes. The women ran to the temples to pray for the favor of the gods. The people demanded that the Senate should send deputies to the invading army to treat for peace.

The Senate, no less frightened than the people, obeyed, sending five leading Patricians to the Volscian camp. These deputies were haughtily received by Coriolanus, who offered them such severe terms that they were unable to accept them. They returned and reported the matter, and the Senate was thrown into confusion. The deputies were sent again, instructed to ask for gentler terms, but now Coriolanus refused even to let them enter his camp. This harsh repulse plunged Rome into mortal terror.

All else having failed, the noble women of Rome, with Volumnia, the mother of Coriolanus, at their head, went in procession from the city to the Volscian camp to pray for mercy.

It was a sad and solemn spectacle, as this train of noble ladies, clad in their habiliments of woe, and with bent heads and sorrowful faces, wound through the hostile camp, from which they were not excluded as the deputies had been. Even the Volscian soldiers watched them with pitying eyes, and spoke no scornful word as they moved slowly past.

On reaching the midst of the camp, they saw Coriolanus on the general's seat, with the Volscian chiefs gathered around him. At first he wondered who these women could be; but when they came near, and he saw his mother at the head of the train, his deep love for her welled up so strongly in his heart that he could not restrain himself, but sprang up and ran to meet and kiss her.

The Roman matron stopped him with a dignified gesture. "Ere you kiss me," she said, "let me know whether I speak to an enemy or to my son; whether I stand here as your prisoner or your mother."

He stood before her in silence, with bent head, and unable to answer.

"Must it, then, be that if I had never borne a son, Rome would have never seen the camp of an enemy?" said Volumnia, in sorrowful tones. "But I am too old to endure much longer your shame and my misery. Think not of me, but of your wife and children, whom you would doom to death or to life in bondage."

Then Virgilia, his wife, and his children, came forward and kissed him, and all the noble ladies in the train burst into tears and bemoaned the peril of their country.

Coriolanus still stood silent, his face working with contending thoughts. At length he cried out in heart-rending accents: "O mother! What have you done to me?"

Then clasping her hand he wrung it vehemently, saying: "Mother, the victory is yours! A happy victory for you and Rome! but shame and ruin for your son."

Thereupon he embraced her with yearning heart, and afterward clasped his wife and children to his breast, bidding them return with their tale of conquest to Rome. As for himself, he said, only exile and shame remained.

Before the women reached home, the army of the Volscians was on its homeward march. Coriolanus never led it against Rome again. He lived and died in exile, far from his wife and children.

The Romans, to honor Volumnia, and those who had gone with her to the Volscian camp, built a temple to "Woman's Fortune," on the spot where Coriolanus had yielded to his mother's entreaties.

THE WIDOW AND HER THREE SONS

(Adapted)

One day a poor woman approached Mr. Lincoln for an interview. She was somewhat advanced in years and plainly clad, wearing a faded shawl and worn hood.

"Well, my good woman," said Mr. Lincoln, "what can I do for you this morning?"

"Mr. President," answered she, "my husband and three sons all went into the army. My husband was killed in the battle of ——. I get along very badly since then living all alone, and I thought that I would come and ask you to release to me my eldest son."

Mr. Lincoln looked in her face for a moment, and then replied kindly: —

"Certainly! Certainly! If you have given us *all*, and your prop has been taken away, you are justly entitled to one of your boys."

He then made out an order discharging the young man, which the woman took away, thanking him gratefully.

She went to the front herself with the President's order, and found that her son had been mortally wounded in a recent battle, and taken to the hospital.

She hastened to the hospital. But she was too

late, the boy died, and she saw him laid in a soldier's grave.

She then returned to the President with his order, on the back of which the attendant surgeon had stated the sad facts concerning the young man it was intended to discharge.

Mr. Lincoln was much moved by her story, and said: "I know what you wish me to do now, and I shall do it without your asking. I shall release to you your second son."

Taking up his pen he began to write the order, while the grief-stricken woman stood at his side and passed her hand softly over his head, and stroked his rough hair as she would have stroked her boy's.

When he had finished he handed her the paper, saying tenderly, his eyes full of tears: —

"Now you have one of the two left, and I have one, that is no more than right."

She took the order and reverently placing her hand upon his head, said: —

"The Lord bless you, Mr. President. May you live a thousand years, and may you always be the head of this great nation."

MEMORIAL DAY

(APRIL OR MAY)

FLAG DAY

(JUNE 14)

BETSY ROSS AND THE FLAG

BY HARRY PRINGLE FORD (ADAPTED)

ON the 14th day of June, 1777, the Continental Congress passed the following resolution: "*Resolved,* That the flag of the thirteen United States be thirteen stripes alternate red and white; that the Union be thirteen stars, white in a blue field, representing a new constellation."

We are told that previous to this, in 1776, a committee was appointed to look after the matter, and together with General Washington they called at the house of Betsy Ross, 239 Arch Street, Philadelphia.

Betsy Ross was a young widow of twenty-four heroically supporting herself by continuing the upholstery business of her late husband, young John Ross, a patriot who had died in the service of his country. Betsy was noted for her exquisite needlework, and was engaged in the flag-making business.

The committee asked her if she thought she could make a flag from a design, a rough drawing of which General Washington showed her. She replied, with diffidence, that she did not know whether she could or not, but would try. She noticed, however, that the star as drawn had six points, and informed the committee that the correct star had but five. They answered that as a great number of stars would be required, the more regular form with six points could be more easily made than one with five.

She responded in a practical way by deftly folding a scrap of paper; then with a single clip of her scissors she displayed a true, symmetrical, five-pointed star.

This decided the committee in her favor. A rough design was left for her use, but she was permitted to make a sample flag according to her own ideas of the arrangement of the stars and the proportions of the stripes and the general form of the whole.

Sometime after its completion it was presented to Congress, and the committee had the pleasure of informing Betsy Ross that her flag was accepted as the Nation's standard.

THE STAR-SPANGLED BANNER

BY EVA MARCH TAPPAN (ADAPTED)

IN 1814, while the War of 1812 was still going on, the people of Maryland were in great trouble, for a British fleet began to attack Baltimore. The enemy bombarded the forts, including Fort McHenry. For twenty-four hours the terrific bombardment went on.

"If Fort McHenry only stands, the city is safe," said Francis Scott Key to a friend, and they gazed anxiously through the smoke to see if the flag was still flying.

These two men were in the strangest place that could be imagined. They were in a little American vessel fast moored to the side of the British admiral's flagship. A Maryland doctor had been seized as a prisoner by the British, and the President had given permission for them to go out under a flag of truce, to ask for his release. The British commander finally decided that the prisoner might be set free; but he had no idea of allowing the two men to go back to the city and carry any information. "Until the attack on Baltimore is ended, you and your boat must remain here," he said.

The firing went on. As long as daylight lasted they could catch glimpses of the Stars and Stripes whenever the wind swayed the clouds of smoke. When night came they could still see the banner now and then by the blaze of the cannon. A little after midnight the firing stopped. The two men paced up and down the deck, straining their eyes to see if the flag was still flying. "Can the fort have surrendered?" they questioned. "Oh, if morning would only come!"

At last the faint gray of dawn appeared. They could see that some flag was flying, but it was too dark to tell which. More and more eagerly they gazed. It grew lighter, a sudden breath of wind caught the flag, and it floated out on the breeze. It was no English flag, it was their own Stars and Stripes. The fort had stood, the city was safe. Then it was that Key took from his pocket an old letter and on the back of it he wrote the poem, "The Star-Spangled Banner."

The British departed, and the little American boat went back to the city. Mr. Key gave a copy of the poem to his uncle, who had been helping to defend the fort. The uncle sent it to the printer, and had it struck off on some handbills. Before the ink was dry the printer caught up one and hurried away to a restaurant, where many patriots were assembled. Waving the paper, he cried, "Listen to this!" and he read: —

"O say, can you see, by the dawn's early light,
What so proudly we hailed at the twilight's last gleaming,
Whose broad stripes and bright stars, through the perilous fight,
O'er the ramparts we watch'd were so gallantly streaming?
And the rockets' red glare, the bombs bursting in air,
Gave proof through the night that our flag was still there.
O say, does the star-spangled banner yet wave
O'er the land of the free and the home of the brave?"

"Sing it! sing it!" cried the whole company. Charles Durang mounted a chair and then for the first time "The Star-Spangled Banner" was sung. The tune was "To Anacreon in Heaven," an air which had long been a favorite. Halls, theaters, and private houses rang with its strains.

The fleet was out of sight even before the poem was printed. In the middle of the night the admiral had sent to the British soldiers this message, "I can do nothing more," and they hurried on board the vessels. It was not long before they left Chesapeake Bay altogether, — perhaps with the new song ringing in their ears as they went.

THE LITTLE DRUMMER-BOY

BY ALBERT BUSHNELL HART (ADAPTED)

A FEW days before a certain regiment received orders to join General Lyon, on his march to Wilson's Creek, the drummer-boy of the regiment was taken sick, and carried to the hospital.

Shortly after this there appeared before the captain's quarters, during the beating of the réveille, a good-looking, middle-aged woman, dressed in deep mourning, leading by the hand a sharp, sprightly looking boy, apparently about twelve or thirteen years of age.

Her story was soon told. She was from East Tennessee, where her husband had been killed by the Confederates, and all her property destroyed. Being destitute, she thought that if she could procure a situation for her boy as drummer, she could find employment for herself.

While she told her story, the little fellow kept his eyes intently fixed upon the countenance of the captain. And just as the latter was about to say that he could not take so small a boy. the lad spoke out: —

"Don't be afraid, Captain," said he, "I can drum."

This was spoken with so much confidence that the captain smiled and said to the sergeant: —

"Well, well, bring the drum, and order our fifer to come here."

In a few moments a drum was produced and the fifer, a round-shouldered, good-natured fellow, who stood six feet tall, made his appearance. Upon being introduced to the lad, he stooped down, resting his hands on his knees, and, after peering into the little fellow's face for a moment, said: —

"My little man, can you drum?"

"Yes, sir," answered the boy promptly. "I drummed for Captain Hill in Tennessee."

The fifer immediately straightened himself, and, placing his fife to his lips, played the "Flowers of Edinburgh," one of the most difficult things to follow with the drum. And nobly did the little fellow follow him, showing himself to be master of the drum.

When the music ceased the captain turned to the mother and observed: —

"Madam, I will take the boy. What is his name?"

"Edward Lee," she replied. Then placing her hand upon the captain's arm, she continued in a choking voice, "If he is not killed! — Captain, — you will bring him back to me?"

"Yes, yes," he replied, "we shall be certain to bring him back to you. We shall be discharged in six weeks."

An hour after, the company led the regiment out of camp, the drum and fife playing "The Girl I left behind me."

Eddie, as the soldiers called him, soon became a great favorite with all the men of the company. When any of the boys returned from foraging, Eddie's share of the peaches, melons, and other good things was meted out first. During the heavy and fatiguing marches, the long-legged fifer often waded through the mud with the little drummer mounted on his back, and in the same fashion he carried Eddie when fording streams.

During the fight at Wilson's Creek, a part of the company was stationed on the right of Totten's battery, while the balance of the company was ordered down into a deep ravine, at the left, in which it was known a party of Confederates was concealed.

An engagement took place. The contest in the ravine continued some time. Totten suddenly wheeled his battery upon the enemy in that quarter, and they soon retreated to high ground behind their lines.

In less than twenty minutes after Totten had driven the Confederates from the ravine, the word passed from man to man throughout the army, "Lyon is killed!" And soon after, hostilities having ceased upon both sides, the order came for the main part of the Federal force to fall back upon Springfield, while the lesser part was to camp upon the ground, and cover the retreat.

That night a corporal was detailed for guard duty. His post was upon a high eminence that overlooked the deep ravine in which the men had engaged the enemy. It was a dreary, lonesome beat. The hours passed slowly away, and at length the morning light began to streak along the western sky, making surrounding objects visible.

Presently the corporal heard a drum beating up the morning call. At first he thought it came from the camp of the Confederates across the creek, but as he listened he found that it came from the deep ravine. For a few moments the sound stopped, then began again. The corporal listened closely. The notes of the drum were familiar to him, — and then he knew that it was the drummer-boy from Tennessee playing the morning call.

Just then the corporal was relieved from guard duty, and, asking permission, went at once to Eddie's assistance. He started down the hill, through the thick underbrush, and upon reaching the bottom of the ravine, he followed the sound of the drum, and soon found the lad seated upon the ground, his back leaning against a fallen tree, while his drum hung upon a bush in front of him.

As soon as the boy saw his rescuer he dropped his drumsticks, and exclaimed: —

"O Corporal! I am so glad to see you! Give me a drink."

The soldier took his empty canteen, and immediately turned to bring some water from the brook that he could hear rippling through the bushes near by, when, Eddie, thinking that he was about to leave him, cried out: —

"Don't leave me, Corporal, I can't walk."

The corporal was soon back with the water, when he discovered that both the lad's feet had been shot away by a cannon-ball.

After satisfying his thirst, Eddie looked up into the corporal's face and said: —

"You don't think I shall die, do you? This man said I should not, — he said the surgeon could cure my feet."

The corporal now looked about him and discovered a man lying in the grass near by. By his dress he knew him to belong to the Confederate army. It appeared that he had been shot and had fallen near Eddie. Knowing that he could not live, and seeing the condition of the drummer-boy, he had crawled to him, taken off his buck-skin suspenders, and had corded the little fellow's legs below the knees, and then he had laid himself down and died.

While Eddie was telling the corporal these particulars, they heard the tramp of cavalry coming down the ravine, and in a moment a scout of the enemy was upon them, and took them both prisoners.

The corporal requested the officer in charge to take Eddie up in front of him, and he did so, carrying the lad with great tenderness and care. When they reached the Confederate camp the little fellow was dead.

A FLAG INCIDENT

BY M. M. THOMAS (ADAPTED)

WHEN marching to Chattanooga the corps had reached a little wooded valley between the mountains. The colonel, with others, rode ahead, and, striking into a bypath, suddenly came upon a secluded little cabin surrounded by a patch of cultivated ground.

At the door an old woman, eighty years of age, was supporting herself on a crutch. As they rode up she asked if they were "Yankees," and upon their replying that they were, she said: "Have you got the Stars and Stripes with you? My father fought the Tories in the Revolution, and my old eyes ache for a sight of the true flag before I die."

To gratify her the colonel sent to have the colors brought that way. When they were unfurled and planted before her door, she passed her trembling hands over them and held them close to her eyes that she might view the stars once more. When the band gave her "Yankee Doodle," and the "'Star-Spangled Banner," she sobbed like a child, as did her daughter, a woman of fifty, while her three little grandchildren gazed in wonder.

They were Eastern people, who had gone to New Orleans to try to improve their condition. Not being successful, they had moved from place to place to better themselves, until finally they had settled on this spot, the husband having taken several acres of land here for a debt.

Then the war burst upon them. The man fled to the mountains to avoid the conscription, and they knew not whether he was alive or dead. They had managed to support life, but were so retired that they saw very few people.

Leaving them food and supplies, the colonel and the corps passed on.

TWO HERO-STORIES OF THE CIVIL WAR

BY BEN LA BREE (ADAPTED)

I. BRAVERY HONORED BY A FOE

IN a rifle-pit, on the brow of a hill near Fredericksburg, were a number of Confederate soldiers who had exhausted their ammunition in the vain attempt to check the advancing column of Hooker's finely equipped and disciplined army which was crossing the river. To the relief of these few came the brigade in double-quick time. But no sooner were the soldiers intrenched than the firing on the opposite side of the river became terrific.

A heavy mist obscured the scene. The Federal soldiers poured a merciless fire into the trenches. Soon many Confederates fell, and the agonized cries of the wounded who lay there calling for water, smote the hearts of their helpless comrades.

"Water! Water!" But there was none to give, the canteens were empty.

"Boys," exclaimed Nathan Cunningham, a lad of eighteen, the color-bearer for his regiment, "I can't stand this any more. They want water, and water they must have. So let me have a few canteens and I'll go for some."

Carefully laying the colors, which he had borne on many a field, in a trench, he seized some canteens, and, leaping into the mist, was soon out of sight.

Shortly after this the firing ceased for a while, and an order came for the men to fall back to the main line.

As the Confederates were retreating they met Nathan Cunningham, his canteens full of water, hurrying to relieve the thirst of the wounded men in the trenches. He glanced over the passing column and saw that the faded flag, which he had carried so long, was not there. The men in their haste to obey orders *had forgotten or overlooked the colors.*

Quickly the lad sped to the trenches, intent now not only on giving water to his comrades, but on rescuing the flag and so to save the honor of his regiment.

His mission of mercy was soon accomplished. The wounded men drank freely. The lad then found and seized his colors, and turned to rejoin his regiment. Scarcely had he gone three paces when a company of Federal soldiers appeared ascending the hill.

"Halt and surrender," came the stern command, and a hundred rifles were leveled at the boy's breast.

"*Never!* while I hold the colors," was his firm reply.

The morning sun, piercing with a lurid glare

the dense mist, showed the lad proudly standing with his head thrown back and his flag grasped in his hand, while his unprotected breast was exposed to the fire of his foe.

A moment's pause. Then the Federal officer gave his command: —

"Back with your pieces, men, don't shoot that brave boy."

And Nathan Cunningham, with colors flying over his head, passed on and joined his regiment.

His comrades in arms still tell with pride of his brave deed and of the generous act of a foe.

II. THE BRAVERY OF RICHARD KIRTLAND

Richard Kirtland was a sergeant in the Second Regiment of South Carolina Volunteers. The day after the great battle of Fredericksburg, Kershaw's brigade occupied the road at the foot of Marye's Hill.

One hundred and fifty yards in front of the road, on the other side of a stone wall, lay Sykes's division of the United States Army. Between these troops and Kershaw's command a skirmish fight was continued through the entire day. The ground between the lines was literally covered with dead and dying Federal soldiers.

All day long the wounded were calling, "Water! water! water!"

In the afternoon, Sergeant Kirtland, a Confederate soldier, went to the headquarters of General Kershaw, and said with deep emotion: "General, all through last night and to-day I have been hearing those poor wounded Federal soldiers out there cry for water. Let me go and give them some."

"Don't you know," replied the general, "that you would get a bullet through you the moment you stepped over the wall?"

"Yes, sir," said the sergeant; "but if you will let me go I am willing to try it."

The general reflected a minute, then answered: "Kirtland, I ought not to allow you to take this risk, but the spirit that moves you is so noble I cannot refuse. Go, and may God protect you!"

In the face of almost certain death the sergeant climbed the wall, watched with anxiety by the soldiers of his army. Under the curious gaze of his foes, and exposed to their fire, he dropped to the ground and hastened on his errand of mercy. Unharmed, untouched, he reached the nearest sufferer. He knelt beside him, tenderly raised his drooping head, rested it gently on his breast, and poured the cooling life-giving water down the parched throat. This done he laid him carefully down, placed the soldier's knapsack under his head, straightened his broken limbs, spread his coat over him, replaced the empty canteen with a full one, then turned to another sufferer.

By this time his conduct was understood by friend and foe alike and the firing ceased on both sides.

For an hour and a half did he pursue his noble mission, until he had relieved the wounded on all parts of the battlefield. Then he returned to his post uninjured.

Surely such a noble deed is worthy of the admiration of men and angels.

THE YOUNG SENTINEL

BY Z. A. MUDGE (ADAPTED)

IN the summer of 1862, a young man belonging to a Vermont regiment was found sleeping at his post. He was tried and sentenced to be shot. The day was fixed for the execution, and the young soldier calmly prepared to meet his fate.

Friends who knew of the case brought the matter to Mr. Lincoln's attention. It seemed that the boy had been on duty one night, and on the following night he had taken the place of a comrade too ill to stand guard. The third night he had been again called out, and, being utterly exhausted, had fallen asleep at his post.

As soon as Mr. Lincoln understood the case, he signed a pardon, and sent it to the camp. The morning before the execution arrived, and the President had not heard whether the pardon had reached the officers in charge of the matter. He began to feel uneasy. He ordered a telegram to be sent to the camp, but received no answer. State papers could not fix his mind, nor could he banish the condemned soldier boy from his thoughts.

At last, feeling that he *must know* that the lad was safe, he ordered the carriage and rode rapidly ten miles over a dusty road and beneath a scorching sun. When he reached the camp he found that the pardon had been received and the execution stayed.

The sentinel was released, and his heart was filled with lasting gratitude. When the campaign opened in the spring, the young man was with his regiment near Yorktown, Virginia. They were ordered to attack a fort, and he fell at the first volley of the enemy.

His comrades caught him up and carried him bleeding and dying from the field. "Bear witness," he said, "that I have proved myself not a coward, and I am not afraid to die." Then, making a last effort, with his dying breath he prayed for Abraham Lincoln.

THE COLONEL OF THE ZOUAVES

BY NOAH BROOKS (ADAPTED)

AMONG those who accompanied Mr. Lincoln, the President-elect, on his journey from Illinois to the national capital, was Elmer E. Ellsworth, a young man who had been employed in the law office of Lincoln and Herndon, Springfield.

He was a brave, handsome, and impetuous youth, and was among the first to offer his services to the President in defense of the Union, as soon as the mutterings of war were heard.

Before the war he had organized a company of Zouaves from the Chicago firemen, and had delighted and astonished many people by the exhibitions of their skill in the evolutions through which they were put while visiting some chief cities of the Republic.

Now, being commissioned a second lieutenant in the United States Army, he went to New York and organized from the firemen of that city a similar regiment, known as the Eleventh New York.

Colonel Ellsworth's Zouaves, on the evening of May 23, were sent with a considerable force to occupy the heights overlooking Washington and Alexandria, on the banks of the Potomac, opposite the national capital.

Next day, seeing a Confederate flag flying from the Marshall House, a tavern in Alexandria kept by a secessionist, he went up through the building to the roof and pulled it down. While on his way down the stairs, with the flag in his arms, he was met by the tavern-keeper, who shot and killed him instantly. Ellsworth fell, dyeing the

Confederate flag with the blood that gushed from his heart. The tavern-keeper was instantly killed by a shot from Private Brownell, of the Ellsworth Zouaves, who was at hand when his commander fell.

The death of Ellsworth, needless though it may have been, caused a profound sensation throughout the country, where he was well known. He was among the very first martyrs of the war, as he had been one of the first volunteers.

Lincoln was overwhelmed with sorrow. He had the body of the lamented young officer taken to the White House, where it lay in state until the burial took place, and, even in the midst of his increasing cares, he found time to sit alone and in grief-stricken meditation by the bier of the dead young soldier of whose career he had cherished so great hopes.

The life-blood from Ellsworth's heart had stained not only the Confederate flag, but a gold medal found under his uniform, bearing the legend: "*Non solum nobis, sed pro patria*"; "Not for ourselves alone, but for the country."

GENERAL SCOTT AND THE STARS AND STRIPES

BY E. D. TOWNSEND (ADAPTED)

ONE day, as the general was sitting at his table in the office, the messenger announced that a person desired to see him a moment in order to present a gift.

A German was introduced, who said that he was commissioned by a house in New York to present General Scott with a small silk banner. It was very handsome, of the size of a regimental flag, and was made of a single piece of silk stamped with the Stars and Stripes of the proper colors.

The German said that the manufacturers who had sent the banner, wished to express thus the great respect they felt for General Scott, and their sense of his importance to the country in that perilous time.

The general was highly pleased, and, in accepting the gift, assured the donors that the flag should hang in his room wherever he went, and enshroud him when he died.

As soon as the man was gone, the general desired that the stars might be counted to see if *all* the States were represented. They were *all* there.

The flag was then draped between the windows over the couch where the general frequently reclined for rest during the day. It went with him in his berth when he sailed for Europe, after his retirement, and enveloped his coffin when he was interred at West Point.

INDEPENDENCE DAY

(JULY 4)

THE DECLARATION OF INDEPENDENCE

BY WASHINGTON IRVING

WHILE danger was gathering round New York, and its inhabitants were in mute suspense and fearful anticipations, the General Congress at Philadelphia was discussing, with closed doors, what John Adams pronounced: "The greatest question ever debated in America, and as great as ever was or will be debated among men." The result was, a resolution passed unanimously on the 2d of July, "that these United Colonies are, and of right ought to be, free and independent States."

"The 2d of July," adds the same patriot statesman, "will be the most memorable epoch in the history of America. I am apt to believe that it will be celebrated by succeeding generations as the great anniversary festival. It ought to be commemorated as the day of deliverance, by solemn acts of devotion to Almighty God. It ought to be solemnized with pomp and parade, with shows, games, sports, guns, bells, bonfires, and illuminations, from one end of this continent to the other, from this time forth forevermore."

The glorious event has, indeed, given rise to an

annual jubilee; but not on the day designated by Adams. The *Fourth* of July is the day of national rejoicing, for on that day the "Declaration of Independence," that solemn and sublime document, was adopted.

Tradition gives a dramatic effect to its announcement. It was known to be under discussion, but the closed doors of Congress excluded the populace. They awaited, in throngs, an appointed signal. In the steeple of the State House was a bell, imported twenty-three years previously from London by the Provincial Assembly of Pennsylvania. It bore the portentous text from Scripture: "Proclaim Liberty throughout all the land, unto all the inhabitants thereof." A joyous peal from that bell gave notice that the bill had been passed. It was the knell of British domination.

THE SIGNING OF THE DECLARATION OF INDEPENDENCE

BY H. A. GUERBER [1]

John Hancock, President of Congress, was the first to sign the Declaration of Independence, writing his name in large, plain letters, and saying: —

[1] From *The Story of the Thirteen Colonies.* Copyright, 1898, by H. A. Guerber. American Book Company, publishers.

"There! John Bull can read my name without spectacles. Now let him double the price on my head, for this is my defiance."

Then he turned to the other members, and solemnly declared: —

"We must be unanimous. There must be no pulling different ways. We must all hang together."

"Yes," said Franklin, quaintly: "we must all hang together, or most assuredly we shall all hang separately."

We are told that Charles Carroll, thinking that his writing looked shaky, added the words, "of Carrollton," so that the king should not be able to make any mistake as to whose name stood there.

A BRAVE GIRL

BY JAMES JOHONNOT (ADAPTED) [1]

IN the year 1781 the war was chiefly carried on in the South, but the North was constantly troubled by bands of Tories and Indians, who would swoop down on small settlements and make off with whatever they could lay their hands on.

During this time General Schuyler was staying at his house, which stood just outside the stockade or walls of Albany. The British commander

[1] From *Stories of Heroic Deeds.* Copyright, 1887, by D. Appleton and Company. American Book Company, publishers.

sent out a party of Tories and Indians to capture the general.

When they reached the outskirts of the city they learned from a Dutch laborer that the general's house was guarded by six soldiers, three watching by night and three by day. They let the Dutchman go, and as soon as the band was out of sight he hastened to Albany and warned the general of their approach.

Schuyler gathered his family in one of the upper rooms of his house, and giving orders that the doors and windows should be barred, fired a pistol from a top-story window, to alarm the neighborhood.

The soldiers on guard, who had been lounging in the shade of a tree, started to their feet at the sound of the pistol; but, alas! too late, for they found themselves surrounded by a crowd of dusky forms, who bound them hand and foot, before they had time to resist.

In the room upstairs was the sturdy general, standing resolutely at the door, with gun in hand, while his black slaves were gathered about him, each with a weapon. At the other end of the room the women were huddled together, some weeping and some praying.

Suddenly a deafening crash was heard. The Indian band had broken into the house. With loud shouts they began to pillage and to destroy everything in sight. While they were yet busy downstairs, Mrs. Schuyler sprang to her feet and rushed to the door; for she had suddenly remembered that the baby, who was only a few months old, was asleep in its cradle in a room on the first floor.

The general caught his wife in his arms, and implored her not to go to certain death, saying that if any one was to go he would. While this generous struggle between husband and wife was going on, their young daughter, who had been standing near the door, glided by them, and descended the stairs.

All was dark in the hall, excepting where the light shone from the dining-room in which the Indians were pillaging the shelves and fighting over their booty. How to get past the dining-room door was the question, but the brave girl did not hesitate. Reaching the lower hall, she walked very deliberately forward, softly but quickly passing the door, and unobserved reached the room in which was the cradle.

She caught up the baby, crept back past the open door, and was just mounting the stairs, when one of the savages happened to see her. "*Whiz*" — and his sharp tomahawk struck the stair rail within a few inches of the baby's head. But the frightened girl hurried on, and in a few seconds was safe in her father's arms.

As for the Indians, fearing an attack from

the near-by garrison, they hastened away with the booty they had collected, and left General Schuyler and his family unharmed.

THE BOSTON TEA-PARTY

BY JOHN ANDREWS (ADAPTED) [1]

ON November 29, 1773, there arrived in Boston Harbor a ship carrying an hundred and odd chests of the detested tea. The people in the country roundabout, as well as the town's folk, were unanimous against allowing the landing of it; but the agents in charge of the consignment persisted in their refusal to take the tea back to London. The town bells were rung, for a general muster of the citizens. Handbills were stuck up calling on "Friends! Citizens! Countrymen!"

Mr. Rotch, the owner of the ship, found himself exposed not only to the loss of his ship, but to the loss of the money-value of the tea itself, if he should attempt to send her back without clearance papers from the custom-house; for the admiral kept a vessel in readiness to seize any ship which might leave without those papers. Therefore, Mr. Rotch declared that his ship should not carry back the tea without either the proper clearance or the promise of full indemnity for any losses he might incur.

[1] From a letter written to a friend in 1773.

Matters continued thus for some days, when a general muster was called of the people of Boston and of all the neighboring towns. They met, to the number of five or six thousand, at ten o'clock in the morning, in the Old South Meeting-House; where they passed a unanimous vote *that the tea should go out of the harbor that afternoon!*

A committee, with Mr. Rotch, was sent to the custom-house to demand a clearance. This the collector said he could not give without the duties first being paid. Mr. Rotch was then sent to ask for a pass from the governor, who returned answer that "consistent with the rules of government and his duty to the king he could not grant one without they produced a previous clearance from the office."

By the time Mr. Rotch returned to the Old South Meeting-House with this message, the candles were lighted and the house still crowded with people. When the governor's message was read a prodigious shout was raised, and soon afterward the moderator declared the meeting dissolved. This caused another general shout, outdoors and in, and what with the noise of breaking up the meeting, one might have thought that the inhabitants of the infernal regions had been let loose.

That night there mustered upon Fort Hill about two hundred strange figures, *said to be*

Indians from Narragansett. They were clothed in blankets, with heads muffled, and had copper-colored countenances. Each was armed with a hatchet or axe, and a pair of pistols. They spoke a strange, unintelligible jargon.

They proceeded two by two to Griffin's Wharf, where three tea-ships lay, each with one hundred and fourteen chests of the ill-fated article on board. And before nine o'clock in the evening every chest was knocked into pieces and flung over the sides.

Not the least insult was offered to any one, save one Captain Conner, who had ripped up the linings of his coat and waistcoat, and, watching his opportunity, had filled them with tea. But, being detected, he was handled pretty roughly. They not only stripped him of his clothes, but gave him a coat of mud, with a severe bruising into the bargain. Nothing but their desire not to make a disturbance prevented his being tarred and feathered.

The tea being thrown overboard, all the Indians disappeared in a most marvelous fashion.

The next day, if a stranger had walked through the streets of Boston, and had observed the calm composure of the people, he would hardly have thought that ten thousand pounds sterling of East India Company's tea had been destroyed the night before.

A GUNPOWDER STORY

BY JOHN ESTEN COOKE (ADAPTED)

IN the autumn of 1777 the English decided to attack Fort Henry, at Wheeling, in northwestern Virginia. This was an important border fort named in honor of Patrick Henry, and around which had grown up a small village of about twenty-five log houses.

A band of Indians, under the leadership of one Simon Girty, was supplied by the English with muskets and ammunition, and sent against the fort. This Girty was a white man, who, when a boy, had been captured by Indians, and brought up by them. He had joined their tribes, and was a ferocious and bloodthirsty leader of savage bands.

When the settlers at Wheeling heard that Simon Girty and his Indians were advancing on the town, they left their homes and hastened into the fort. Scarcely had they done so when the savages made their appearance.

The defenders of the fort knew that a desperate fight must now take place, and there seemed little probability that they would be able to hold out against their assailants. They had only forty-

[1] From *Stories of the Old Dominion*. Used by permission of the American Book Company, publishers.

two fighting men, including old men and boys, while the Indian force numbered about five hundred.

What was worse they had but a small amount of gunpowder. A keg containing the main supply had been left by accident in one of the village houses. This misfortune, as you will soon see, brought about the brave action of a young girl.

After several encounters with the savages, which took place in the village, the defenders withdrew to the fort. Then a number of Indians advanced with loud yells, firing as they came. The fire was returned by the defenders, each of whom had picked out his man, and taken deadly aim. Most of the attacking party were killed, and the whole body of Indians fell back into the near-by woods, and there awaited a more favorable opportunity to renew hostilities.

The men in the fort now discovered, to their great dismay, that their gunpowder was nearly gone. What was to be done? Unless they could get another supply, they would not be able to hold the fort, and they and their women and children would either be massacred or carried into captivity.

Colonel Shepherd, who was in command, explained to the settlers exactly how matters stood. He also told them of the forgotten keg of powder which was in a house standing about sixty yards from the gate of the fort.

It was plain to all that if any man should attempt to procure the keg, he would almost surely be shot by the lurking Indians. In spite of this three or four young men volunteered to go on the dangerous mission.

Colonel Shepherd replied that he could not spare three or four strong men, as there were already too few for the defense. Only one man should make the attempt and they might decide who was to go. This caused a dispute.

Just then a young girl stepped forward and said that *she* was ready to go. Her name was Elizabeth Zane, and she had just returned from a boarding-school in Philadelphia. This made her brave offer all the more remarkable, since she had not been bred up to the fearless life of the border.

At first the men would not hear of her running such a risk. She was told that it meant certain death. But she urged that they could not spare a man from the defense, and that the loss of one girl would not be an important matter. So after some discussion the settlers agreed that she should go for the powder.

The house, as has already been stated, stood about sixty yards from the fort, and Elizabeth hoped to run thither and bring back the powder in a few minutes. The gate was opened, and she passed through, running like a deer.

A few straggling Indians were dodging about the log houses of the town; they saw the fleeing girl, but for some reason they did not fire upon her. They may have supposed that she was returning to her home to rescue her clothes. Possibly they thought it a waste of good ammunition to fire at a woman, when they were so sure of taking the fort before long. So they looked on quietly while, with flying skirts, Elizabeth ran across the open, and entered the house.

She found the keg of powder, which was not large. She lifted it with both arms, and, holding the precious burden close to her breast, she darted out of the house and ran in the direction of the fort.

When the Indians saw what she was carrying they uttered fierce yells and fired. The bullets fell like hail about her, but not one so much as touched her garments. With the keg hugged to her bosom, she ran on, and reached the fort in safety. The gate closed upon her just as the bullets of the Indians buried themselves in its thick panels.

The rescued gunpowder enabled the little garrison to hold out until help arrived from the other settlements near Wheeling. And Girty, seeing that there were no further hopes of taking Fort Henry, withdrew his band.

Thus a weak but brave girl was the means of saving strong men with their wives and children. It was a heroic act, and Americans should never forget to honor the name of Elizabeth Zane.

THE CAPTURE OF FORT TICONDEROGA

BY WASHINGTON IRVING (ADAPTED)

SOME bold spirits in Connecticut conceived the project of surprising the old forts of Ticonderoga and Crown Point, already famous in the French War. Their situation on Lake Champlain gave them the command of the main route into Canada so that the possession of them would be all-important in case of hostilities. They were feebly garrisoned and negligently guarded, and abundantly furnished with artillery and military stores so needed by the patriot army.

At this juncture Ethan Allen stepped forward, a patriot, and volunteered with his "Green Mountain Boys." He was well fitted for the enterprise. During the border warfare over the New Hampshire Grants, he and his lieutenants had been outlawed by the Legislature of New York and rewards offered for their apprehension. He and his associates had armed themselves, set New York at defiance, and had sworn they would be the death of any one who should try to arrest them.

Thus Ethan Allen had become a kind of Robin Hood among the mountains. His experience as a frontier champion, his robustness of mind and body, and his fearless spirit made him a most desirable leader in the expedition against Fort Ticonderoga. Therefore he was appointed at the head of the attacking force.

Accompanied by Benjamin Arnold and two other officers, Allen and his party of soldiers who had been enlisted from several States, set out and arrived at Shoreham, opposite Fort Ticonderoga on the shore of Lake Champlain. They reached the place at night-time. There were only a few boats on hand, but the transfer of men began immediately. It was slow work. The night wore away; day was about to break, and but eighty-three men, with Allen and Arnold, had crossed. Should they wait for the rest to cross over, day would dawn, the garrison wake, and their enterprise might fail.

Allen drew up his men, addressed them in his own emphatic style, and announced his intention of making a dash at the fort without waiting for more force.

"It is a desperate attempt," said he, "and I ask no man to go against his will. I will take the lead, and be the first to advance. You that are willing to follow, poise your firelocks!"

Not a firelock but was poised!

They mounted the hill briskly but in silence, guided by a boy from the neighborhood.

The day dawned as Allen arrived at a sally-port. A sentry pulled trigger on him, but his piece missed fire. He retreated through a covered way. Allen and his men followed. Another sentry thrust at an officer with his bayonet, but was struck down by Allen, and begged for quarter. It was granted on condition of his leading the way instantly to the quarters of the commandant, Captain Delaplace, who was yet in bed.

Being arrived there, Allen thundered at the door, and demanded a surrender of the fort. By this time his followers had formed into two lines on the parade-ground, and given three hearty cheers.

The commandant appeared at the door half-dressed, the frightened face of his pretty wife peering over his shoulder. He gazed at Allen in bewildered astonishment.

"By whose authority do you act?" exclaimed he.

"In the name of the Continental Congress!" replied Allen, with a flourish of his sword, and an oath which we do not care to subjoin.

There was no disputing the point. The garrison, like the commandant, had been startled from sleep, and made prisoners as they rushed forth in their confusion. A surrender accordingly took place. The captain and forty-eight men who composed his garrison were sent prisoners to Hartford, in Connecticut.

And thus without the loss of a single man, one of the important forts, commanding the main route into Canada, fell into the hands of the patriots.

WASHINGTON AND THE COWARDS

BY WASHINGTON IRVING (ADAPTED)

DURING the evacuation of New York by Washington, two divisions of the enemy, encamped on Long Island, one British under Sir Henry Clinton, the other Hessian under Colonel Donop, emerged in boats from the deep wooded recesses of Newtown Inlet, and under cover of the fire from the ships began to land at two points between Turtle and Kip's Bays.

The breastworks were manned by patriot militia who had recently served in Brooklyn. Disheartened by their late defeat, they fled at the first advance of the enemy. Two brigades of Putnam's Connecticut troops, which had been sent that morning to support them, caught the panic, and, regardless of the commands and entreaties of their officers, joined in the general scamper.

At this moment Washington, who had mounted

his horse at the first sound of the cannonade, came galloping to the scene of confusion. Riding in among the fugitives he endeavored to rally and restore them to order. All in vain. At the first appearance of sixty or seventy redcoats, they broke again without firing a shot, and fled in headlong terror.

Losing all self-command at the sight of such dastardly conduct, Washington dashed his hat upon the ground in a transport of rage.

"Are these the men," exclaimed he, "with whom I am to defend America!"

In a paroxysm of passion and despair he snapped his pistols at some of them, threatened others with his sword, and was so heedless of his own danger that he might have fallen into the hands of the enemy, who were not eighty yards distant, had not an aide-de-camp seized the bridle of his horse, and absolutely hurried him away.

It was one of the rare moments of his life when the vehement element of his nature was stirred up from its deep recesses. He soon recovered his self-possession, and took measures against the general peril.

LABOR DAY

(FIRST MONDAY IN SEPTEMBER)

THE SMITHY

A HINDU FABLE

BY P. V. RAMASWAMI RAJU (ADAPTED)

ONCE words ran high in a smithy.

The furnace said: "If I cease to burn, the smithy must close."

The bellows said: "If I cease to blow, no fire, no smithy."

The hammer and anvil, also, each claimed the sole credit for keeping up the smithy.

The ploughshare that had been shaped by the furnace, the bellows, the hammer and the anvil, cried: "It is not each of you alone, that keeps up the smithy, but *all together*."

THE NAIL

BY THE BROTHERS GRIMM (TRANSLATED)[1]

A MERCHANT had done good business at the fair; he had sold his wares, and filled his bag with gold and silver. Then he set out at once on his journey home, for he wished to be in his own house before night.

At noon he rested in a town. When he wanted to go on, the stable-boy brought his horse, saying:

[1] From the Riverside Fourth Reader.

"A nail is wanting, sir, in the shoe of his left hind foot."

"Let it be wanting," answered the merchant; "the shoe will stay on for the six miles I have still to go. I am in a hurry."

In the afternoon he got down at an inn and had his horse fed. The stable-boy came into the room to him and said: "Sir, a shoe is wanting from your horse's left hind foot. Shall I take him to the blacksmith?"

"Let it still be wanting," said the man; "the horse can very well hold out for a couple of miles more. I am in a hurry."

So the merchant rode forth, but before long the horse began to limp. He had not limped long before he began to stumble, and he had not stumbled long before he fell down and broke his leg. The merchant had to leave the horse where he fell, and unstrap the bag, take it on his back, and go home on foot.

"That unlucky nail," said he to himself, "has made all this trouble."

THE ELVES AND THE SHOEMAKER

BY HORACE E. SCUDDER

THERE was once a shoemaker who worked very hard and was honest. Still, he could not earn enough to live on. At last, all he had in the world was gone except just leather enough to make one pair of shoes. He cut these out at night, and meant to rise early the next morning to make them up.

His heart was light in spite of his troubles, for his conscience was clear. So he went quietly to bed, left all his cares to God, and fell asleep. In the morning he said his prayers, and sat down to work, when, to his great wonder, there stood the shoes, already made, upon the table.

The good man knew not what to say or think. He looked at the work. There was not one false stitch in the whole job. All was neat and true.

That same day a customer came in, and the shoes pleased him so well that he readily paid a price higher than usual for them. The shoemaker took the money and bought leather enough to make two pairs more. He cut out the work in the evening, and went to bed early. He wished to be up with the sun and get to work.

He was saved all trouble, for when he got up in the morning, the work was done. Pretty soon buyers came in, who paid him well for his goods. So he bought leather enough for four pairs more.

He cut out the work again overnight, and found it finished in the morning as before. So it went on for some time. What was got ready at night was always done by daybreak, and the good man soon was well-to-do.

One evening, at Christmas-time, he and his wife sat over the fire, chatting, and he said: "I should like to sit up and watch to-night, that we may see who it is that comes and does my work for me." So they left the light burning, and hid themselves behind a curtain to see what would happen.

As soon as it was midnight, there came two little Elves. They sat upon the shoemaker's bench, took up all the work that was cut out, and began to ply their little fingers. They stitched and rapped and tapped at such a rate that the shoemaker was amazed, and could not take his eyes off them for a moment.

On they went till the job was done, and the shoes stood, ready for use, upon the table. This was long before daybreak. Then they ran away as quick as lightning.

The next day the wife said to the shoemaker: "These little Elves have made us rich, and we ought to be thankful to them, and do them some good in return. I am vexed to see them run about as they do. They have nothing upon their backs to keep off the cold. I'll tell you what we must do. I will make each of them a shirt, and a coat and waistcoat, and a pair of pantaloons into the bargain. Do you make each of them a little pair of shoes."

The good shoemaker liked the thought very

well. One evening he and his wife had the clothes ready, and laid them on the table instead of the work they used to cut out. Then they went and hid behind the curtain to watch what the little Elves would do.

At midnight the Elves came in and were going to sit down at their work as usual. But when they saw the clothes lying there for them, they laughed and were in high glee. They dressed themselves in the twinkling of an eye, and danced and capered and sprang about as merry as could be, till at last they danced out of the door, and over the green.

The shoemaker saw them no more, but everything went well with him as long as he lived.

THE HILLMAN AND THE HOUSEWIFE

BY JULIANA HORATIA EWING (ADAPTED)

IT is well known that the Fairy People cannot abide meanness. They like to be liberally dealt with when they beg or borrow of the human race; and, on the other hand, to those who come to them in need, they are invariably generous.

Now there once lived a certain housewife who had a sharp eye to her own interests, and gave alms of what she had no use for, hoping to get some reward in return. One day a Hillman knocked at her door.

"Can you lend us a saucepan, good mother?" said he. "There's a wedding in the hill, and all the pots are in use."

"Is he to have one?" asked the servant lass who had opened the door.

"Aye, to be sure," answered the housewife; "one must be neighborly."

But when the maid was taking a saucepan from the shelf, the housewife pinched her arm and whispered sharply: "Not that, you good-for-nothing! Get the old one out of the cupboard. It leaks, and the Hillmen are so neat, and such nimble workers, that they are sure to mend it before they send it home. So one obliges the Fairy People, and saves sixpence in tinkering!"

Thus bidden the maid fetched the saucepan, which had been laid by until the tinker's next visit, and gave it to the Hillman, who thanked her and went away.

In due time the saucepan was returned, and, as the housewife had foreseen, it was neatly mended and ready for use.

At supper-time the maid filled the pan with milk, and set it on the fire for the children's supper. But in a few minutes the milk was so burnt and smoked that no one could touch it, and even the pigs refused to drink it.

"Ah, good-for-nothing hussy!" cried the housewife, as she refilled the pan herself, "you would ruin the richest with your carelessness! There's a whole quart of good milk wasted at once!"

"*And that 's twopence!*" cried a voice that seemed to come from the chimney, in a whining tone, like some discontented old body going over her grievances.

The housewife had not left the saucepan for two minutes, when the milk boiled over, and it was all burnt and smoked as before.

"The pan must be dirty," muttered the good woman in vexation, "and there are two full quarts of milk as good as thrown to the dogs."

"*And that 's fourpence!*" added the voice in the chimney.

After a thorough cleaning the saucepan was once more filled and set on the fire, but with no better success. The milk boiled over again, and was hopelessly spoiled. The housewife shed tears of anger at the waste and cried: "Never before did such a thing befall me since I kept house! Three quarts of new milk burnt for one meal."

"*And that 's sixpence!*" cried the voice in the chimney. "You did n't save the tinkering after all, mother!"

With that the Hillman himself came tumbling down from the chimney, and went off laughing through the door.

But from then on the saucepan was as good as any other.

HOFUS THE STONE-CUTTER

A JAPANESE LEGEND

From the Riverside Third Reader (Adapted)

Once upon a time in Japan, there was a poor stone-cutter, named Hofus, who used to go every day to the mountain-side to cut great blocks of stone. He lived near the mountain in a little stone hut, and worked hard and was happy.

One day he took a load of stone to the house of a rich man. There he saw so many beautiful things that when he went back to his mountain he could think of nothing else. Then he began to wish that he too might sleep in a bed as soft as down, with curtains of silk, and tassels of gold. And he sighed: —

"Ah me! Ah me!
If Hofus only were rich as he!"

To his surprise, the voice of the Mountain Spirit answered: —

"Have thou thy wish!"

When Hofus returned home that evening his little hut was gone, and in its place stood a great palace. It was filled with beautiful things, and the best of all was a bed of down, with curtains of silk and tassels of gold.

Hofus decided to work no more. But he was

not used to being idle, and time passed slowly, — the days seemed very long.

One day as he sat by the window he saw a carriage dash past. It was drawn by snow-white horses. In it sat a prince, while before and behind were servants in suits of blue and white. One was holding a golden umbrella over the prince.

When the stone-cutter saw this, he began to feel unhappy, and he sighed: —

"Ah me! Ah me!
If Hofus only a prince might be!"

And again the same voice that he had heard on the mountain answered: —

"Be thou a prince!"

Straightway Hofus was a prince. He had servants dressed in crimson and gold, and he rode in a carriage with a golden umbrella over his head.

For a short time he was happy, but one day, as he walked in the garden, he saw that the flowers were drooping, the grass was dry and brown. And when he rode out he felt the hot sun burn him in spite of his umbrella.

"The sun is mightier than I," thought he, and then he sighed: —

"Ah me! Ah me!
If Hofus only the sun might be!"

And the voice answered: —

"Be thou the sun!"

Straightway the great sun he became. He burned the grass and rice-fields, he dried up the streams. Rich and poor alike suffered from the terrible heat.

One day a cloud came and rested in front of him, and hid the earth from his sight. He was angry and cried: —

"Ah me! Ah me!
If Hofus only a cloud might be!"

And the voice answered: —

"Be thou a cloud!"

Straightway a cloud he became. He floated before the face of the sun, and hid the earth from it.

Then day after day the cloud dropped rain. The rivers overflowed, and the rice-fields were covered with water. Towns were swept away. Only the great rocks on the mountain-side stood unmoved midst the flood.

The cloud looked at them in wonder, then he sighed: —

"Ah me! Ah me!
If Hofus only a rock might be!"

And the voice answered: —

"Be thou a rock!"

Straightway a rock he became. Proudly he stood. The sun could not burn him and the rain could not move him.

"Now, at last," he said, "no one is mightier than I."

But one day he was waked from his dreams by a noise, — tap! tap! tap! — down at his feet. He looked and there was a stone-cutter driving his tool into the rock. Another blow and the great rock shivered; a block of stone broke away.

"That man is mightier than I!" cried Hofus, and he sighed: —

> "Ah me! Ah me!
> If Hofus only the man might be!"

And the voice answered: —

> "Be thou thyself!"

And straightway Hofus was himself again, — a poor stone-cutter, working all day upon the mountain-side, and going home at night to his little hut. But he was content and happy, and never again did he wish to be other than Hofus the stone-cutter.

ARACHNE

BY JOSEPHINE PRESTON PEABODY

THERE was a certain maiden of Lydia, Arachne by name, renowned throughout the country for her skill as a weaver. She was as nimble with her fingers as Calypso, that Nymph who kept Odysseus for seven years in her enchanted island. She was as untiring as Penelope, the hero's wife, who wove day after day while she watched for his return. Day in and day out, Arachne wove too. The very Nymphs would gather about her loom, Naiads from the water and Dryads from the trees.

"Maiden," they would say, shaking the leaves or the foam from their hair, in wonder, "Pallas Athena must have taught you!"

But this did not please Arachne. She would not acknowledge herself a debtor, even to that goddess who protected all household arts, and by whose grace alone one had any skill in them.

"I learned not of Athena," said she. "If she can weave better, let her come and try."

The Nymphs shivered at this, and an aged woman, who was looking on, turned to Arachne.

"Be more heedful of your words, my daughter," said she. "The goddess may pardon you if you ask forgiveness, but do not strive for honors with the immortals."

Arachne broke her thread, and the shuttle stopped humming.

"Keep your counsel," she said. "I fear not Athena; no, nor any one else."

As she frowned at the old woman, she was amazed to see her change suddenly into one tall, majestic, beautiful, — a maiden of gray eyes and golden hair, crowned with a golden helmet. It was Athena herself.

The bystanders shrank in fear and reverence;

only Arachne was unawed and held to her foolish boast.

In silence the two began to weave, and the Nymphs stole nearer, coaxed by the sound of the shuttles, that seemed to be humming with delight over the two webs, — back and forth like bees.

They gazed upon the loom where the goddess stood plying her task, and they saw shapes and images come to bloom out of the wondrous colors, as sunset clouds grow to be living creatures when we watch them. And they saw that the goddess, still merciful, was spinning, as a warning for Arachne, the pictures of her own triumph over reckless gods and mortals.

In one corner of the web she made a story of her conquest over the sea-god Poseidon. For the first king of Athens had promised to dedicate the city to that god who should bestow upon it the most useful gift. Poseidon gave the horse. But Athena gave the olive, — means of livelihood, — symbol of peace and prosperity, and the city was called after her name. Again she pictured a vain woman of Troy, who had been turned into a crane for disputing the palm of beauty with a goddess. Other corners of the web held similar images, and the whole shone like a rainbow.

Meanwhile Arachne, whose head was quite turned with vanity, embroidered her web with stories against the gods, making light of Zeus himself and of Apollo, and portraying them as birds and beasts. But she wove with marvelous skill; the creatures seemed to breathe and speak, yet it was all as fine as the gossamer that you find on the grass before rain.

Athena herself was amazed. Not even her wrath at the girl's insolence could wholly overcome her wonder. For an instant she stood entranced; then she tore the web across, and three times she touched Arachne's forehead with her spindle.

"Live on, Arachne," she said. "And since it is your glory to weave, you and yours must weave forever." So saying, she sprinkled upon the maiden a certain magical potion.

Away went Arachne's beauty; then her very human form shrank to that of a spider, and so remained. As a spider she spent all her days weaving and weaving; and you may see something like her handiwork any day among the rafters.

THE METAL KING

A GERMAN FOLK-TALE

(ADAPTED)

ONCE long ago there was a high mountain whose rocks were veined with gold and silver and seamed with iron. At times, from a huge rent in the mountain-side, there shot out roaring, red flames, and clouds of black smoke. And when the village folk in the valley below saw this, they would say: "Look! the Metal King is at his forge." For they knew that in the gloomy heart of the mountain, the Metal King and his Spirits of the Mines wrought in gold and iron.

When the storm raged over the valley, the Metal King left his cavern and riding on the wings of the wind, with thundering shouts, hurled his red-hot bolts into the valley, now killing the peasants and their cattle, now burning houses and barns.

But when the weather was soft and mild, and the breezes blew gently about the mouth of his cavern, the Metal King returned to his forge in the depths of the mountain, and there shaped ploughshares and many other implements of iron. These he placed outside his cavern door, as gifts to the poor peasants.

It happened, on a time, there lived in that valley a lazy lad, who would neither till his fields nor ply a trade. He was avaricious, but he longed to win gold without mining, and wealth and fame without labor. So it came to pass that he set out one day to find the mountain treasure of the Metal King.

Taking a lighted lantern in one hand, a hatchet in the other, and a bundle of twigs under his arm, he entered the dark cavern. The dampness smote his cheek, bats flapped their wings in his face. Shivering with fear and cold, he pressed on through a long passage under an arched and blackened roof. As he passed along he dropped his twigs, one after another, so that they might guide him aright when he returned.

He came at last to a place where the passage branched off in two directions, — to the right and to the left. Choosing the right-hand path, he walked on and at length came to an iron door. He struck it twice with his hammer. It flew open, and a strong current of air rushing forth put out his light.

"Come in! Come in!" shouted a voice like the rolling of thunder, and the cavern echoes gave back the sounds.

Almost overcome by terror and shivering in every limb, the lad entered. As he stepped forward a dazzling light shone from the vaulted roof upheld by massive columns, and across the crystal side-walls flittered curious, shadowy figures.

The Metal King, huge and fierce-eyed, surrounded by the misshapen Spirits of the Mines, sat upon a block of pure silver, with a pile of shining gold lying before him.

"Come in, my friend!" he shouted again, and again the echoes rolled through the cavern. "Come near, and sit beside me."

The lad advanced, pale and trembling, and took his seat upon the silver block.

"Bring out more treasure," cried the Metal King, and at his command the Mountain Spirits fluttered away like dreams, only to return in a moment and pile high before the wondering lad bars of red gold, mounds of silver coin, and stacks of precious jewels.

And when the lad saw all that wealth he felt his heart burst with longing to grasp it, but when he tried to put out his hand, he found that he could not move his arm, nor could he lift his feet, nor turn his head.

"Thou seest these riches," said the Metal King; "they are but a handful compared with those thou mayest gain if thou wilt work with us in the mines. Hard is the service but rich the reward! Only say the word, and for a year and a day thou shalt be a Mountain Spirit."

"Nay," stammered the lad, in great terror, "nay, I came not to work. All I beg of thee is one bar of gold and a handful of the jewels that lie here. If they are mine I can dress better than the village lads, and ride in my own coach!"

"Lazy, ungrateful wretch!" cried the Metal King, rising from his seat, while his figure seemed to tower until his head touched the cavern roof, "wouldst thou seize without pay the treasures gained through the hard labor of my Mountain

Spirits! Hence! Get thee gone to thy place! Seek not here for unearned riches! Cast away thy discontented disposition and thou shalt turn stones into gold. Dig well thy garden and thy fields, sow them and tend them diligently, search the mountain-sides; and thou shalt gain through thine industry mines of gold and silver!"

Scarcely had the Metal King spoken when there was heard a screeching as of ravens, a crying as of night owls, and a mighty storm wind came rushing against the lad; and catching him up it drove him forth along the dark passage, and down the mountain-side, so that in a minute he found himself on the steps of his own house.

And from that time on a strange change came over the lad. He no longer idled and dreamed of sudden wealth, but morning, noon, and evening he labored diligently, sowing his fields, cultivating his garden, and mining on the mountain-side. Years came and went; all he touched prospered, and he grew to be the richest man in that country; but never again did he see the Metal King or the Spirits of the Mines.

THE CHOICE OF HERCULES

BY XENOPHON (ADAPTED)

LONG, long ago, when the world was young, there were many deeds waiting to be wrought by daring heroes. It was then that the mighty Hercules, who was yet a lad, felt an exceeding great and strong desire to go out into the wide world to seek his fortune.

One day, while wandering alone and thoughtful, he came to a place where two paths met. And sitting down he gravely considered which he should follow.

One path led over flowery meadows toward the darkening distance; the other, passing over rough stones and rugged, brown furrows, lost itself in the glowing sunset.

And as Hercules gazed into the distance, he saw two stately maidens coming toward him.

The first was tall and graceful, and wrapped round in a snow-white mantle. Her countenance was calm and beautiful. With gracious mien and modest glance she drew near the lad.

The other maiden made haste to outrun the first. She, too, was tall, but seemed taller than she really was. She, too, was beautiful, but her glance was bold. As she ran, a rosy garment like a cloud floated about her form, and she kept looking at her own round arms and shapely hands, and ever and anon she seemed to gaze admiringly at her shadow as it moved along the ground. And this fair one did outstrip the first maiden, and rushing forward held out her white hands to the lad, exclaiming: —

"I see thou art hesitating, O Hercules, by what path to seek thy fortune. Follow me along this flowery way, and I will make it a delightful and easy road. Thou shalt taste to the full of every kind of pleasure. No shadow of annoyance shall ever touch thee, nor strain nor stress of war and state disturb thy peace. Instead thou shalt tread upon carpets soft as velvet, and sit at golden tables, or recline upon silken couches. The fairest of maidens shall attend thee, music and perfume shall lull thy senses, and all that is delightful to eat and drink shall be placed before thee. Never shalt thou labor, but always live in joy and ease. Oh, come! I give my followers liberty and delight!"

And as she spoke the maiden stretched forth her arms, and the tones of her voice were sweet and caressing.

"What, O maiden," asked Hercules, "is thy name?"

"My friends," said she, "call me Happiness, but mine enemies name me Vice."

Even as she spoke, the white-robed maiden, who had drawn near, glided forward, and addressed the lad in gracious tones and with words stately and winning: —

"O beloved youth, who wouldst wander forth in search of Life, I too, would plead with thee! I, Virtue, have watched and tended thee from a child. I know the fond care thy parents have bestowed to train thee for a hero's part. Direct now thy steps along yon rugged path that leads to my dwelling. Honorable and noble mayest thou become through thy illustrious deeds.

"I will not seduce thee by promises of vain delights; instead will I recount to thee the things that really are. Lasting fame and true nobility come not to mortals save through pain and labor. If thou, O Hercules, seekest the gracious gifts of Heaven, thou must remain constant in prayer; if thou wouldst be beloved of thy friends, thou must serve thy friends; if thou desirest to be honored of the people thou must benefit the people; if thou art anxious to reap the fruits of the earth, thou must till the earth with labor; and if thou wishest to be strong in body and accomplish heroic deeds, thou must teach thy body to obey thy mind. Yea, all this and more also must thou do."

"Seest thou not, O Hercules," cried Vice, "over how difficult and tedious a road this Virtue would drive thee? I, instead, will conduct thy steps by a short and easy path to perfect Happiness."

"Wretched being!" answered Virtue, "wouldst thou deceive this lad! What lasting Happiness hast thou to offer! Thou pamperest thy followers with riches; thou deludest them with idleness;

thou surfeitest them with luxury; thou enfeeblest them with softness. In youth they grow slothful in body and weak in mind. They live without labor and wax fat. They come to a wretched old age, dissatisfied, and ashamed, and oppressed by the memory of their ill deeds; and, having run their course, they lay themselves down in melancholy death and their name is remembered no more.

"But those fortunate youths who follow me receive other counsel. I am the companion of virtuous men. Always I am welcome in the homes of artisans and in the cottages of tillers of the soil. I am the guardian of industrious households, and the rewarder of generous masters and faithful servants. I am the promoter of the labors of peace. No honorable deed is accomplished without me.

"My friends have sweet repose and the untroubled enjoyment of the fruits of their efforts. They remember their deeds with an easy conscience and contentment, and are beloved of their friends and honored by their country. And when they have run their course, and death overtakes them, their names are celebrated in song and praise, and they live in the hearts of their grateful countrymen.

"Come, then, O Hercules, thou son of noble parents, come, follow thou me, and by thy worthy and illustrious deeds secure for thyself exalted Happiness."

She ceased, and Hercules, withdrawing his gaze from the face of Vice, arose from his place, and followed Virtue along the rugged, brown path of Labor.

THE SPEAKING STATUE

FROM GESTA ROMANORUM (ADAPTED)

THERE was once a great emperor who made a law that whosoever worked on the birthday of his eldest son should be put to death. He caused this decree to be published throughout his empire, and, sending for his chief magician, said to him:—

"I wish you to devise an instrument which will tell me the name of each laborer who breaks my new law."

"Sire," answered the magician, "your will shall be accomplished." And he straightway constructed a wonderful, speaking statue, and placed it in the public square of the capital city. By its magic power this statue could discern all that went on in the empire on the birthday of the eldest prince, and it could tell the name of each laborer who worked in secret on that day. Thus things continued for some years, and many men were put to death.

Now, there was in the capital city a carpenter

named Focus. He was a diligent workman, laboring at his trade from early morning till late at night. One year, when the prince's birthday came round, he continued to work all that day.

The next morning he arose, dressed himself, and, before any one was astir in the streets, went to the magic statue and said: —

"O statue, statue! because you have denounced so many of our citizens, causing them to be put to death, I vow, if you accuse me, I will break your head!"

Shortly after this the emperor dispatched messengers to the statue to inquire if the law had been broken the day before. When the statue saw them, it exclaimed: —

"Friends, look up! What see ye written on my forehead?"

They looked up and beheld three sentences that ran thus: —

"Times are altered!
"Men grow worse!
"He who speaks the truth will have his head broken!"

"Go," said the statue, "declare to His Majesty what ye have seen and read."

The messenger accordingly departed and returned in haste to the emperor, and related to him all that had occurred.

The emperor ordered his guard to arm and to march instantly to the public square, where the statue was, and commanded that if any one had attempted to injure it, he should be seized, bound hand and foot, and dragged to the judgment hall.

The guard hastened to do the emperor's bidding. They approached the statue and said: —

"Our emperor commands you to tell who it is that threatened you."

The statue answered: "Seize Focus the carpenter. Yesterday he defied the emperor's edict; this morning he threatened to break my head."

The soldiers immediately arrested Focus, and dragged him to the judgment hall.

"Friend," said the emperor, "what do I hear of you? Why do you work on my son's birthday?"

"Your Majesty," answered Focus, "it is impossible for me to keep your law. I am obliged to earn eight pennies every day, therefore was I forced to work yesterday."

"And why eight pennies?" asked the emperor.

"Every day through the year," answered Focus, "I am bound to repay two pennies I borrowed in my youth; two I lend; two I lose; and two I spend."

"How is this?" said the emperor; "explain yourself further."

"Your Majesty," replied Focus, "listen to me. I am bound each day to repay two pennies to my old father, for when I was a boy he expended upon me daily the like sum. Now he is poor and needs my assistance, and I return what I formerly borrowed. Two other pennies I lend my son, who is pursuing his studies, in order that, if by chance I should fall into poverty, he may restore the loan to me, just as I am now doing to his grandfather. Again, I lose two pennies on my wife, who is a scold and has an evil temper. On account of her bad disposition I consider whatever I give her entirely lost. Lastly, two other pennies I spend on myself for meat and drink. I cannot do all this without working every day. You now know the truth, and, I pray you, give a righteous judgment."

"Friend," said the emperor, "you have answered well. Go and work diligently at your calling."

That same day the emperor annulled the law forbidding labor on his son's birthday. Not long after this he died, and Focus the carpenter, on account of his singular wisdom, was elected emperor in his stead. He governed wisely, and after his death there was deposited in the royal archives a portrait of Focus wearing a crown adorned with eight pennies.

THE CHAMPION STONE-CUTTER

BY HUGH MILLER

DAVID FRASER was a famous Scotch hewer. On hearing that it had been remarked among a party of Edinburgh masons that, though regarded as the first of Glasgow stone-cutters, he would find in the eastern capital at least his equals, he attired himself most uncouthly in a long-tailed coat of tartan, and, looking to the life the untamed, untaught, conceited little Celt, he presented himself on Monday morning, armed with a letter of introduction from a Glasgow builder, before the foreman of an Edinburgh squad of masons engaged upon one of the finer buildings at that time in the course of erection.

The letter specified neither his qualifications nor his name. It had been written merely to secure for him the necessary employment, and the necessary employment it did secure.

The better workmen of the party were engaged, on his arrival, in hewing columns, each of which was deemed sufficient work for a week; and David was asked somewhat incredulously, by the foreman, if he could hew.

"Oh, yes, *he thought* he could hew."

"Could he hew columns such as these?"

"Oh, yes, *he thought* he could hew columns such as these."

A mass of stone, in which a possible column lay hid, was accordingly placed before David, not under cover of the shed, which was already occupied by workmen, but. agreeably to David's own request, directly in front of it, where he might be seen by all, and where he straightway commenced a most extraordinary course of antics.

Buttoning his long tartan coat fast around him, he would first look along the stone from the one end, anon from the other, and then examine it in front and rear; or, quitting it altogether for the time, he would take up his stand beside the other workmen, and, after looking at them with great attention, return and give it a few taps with the mallet, in a style evidently imitative of theirs, but monstrously a caricature.

The shed all that day resounded with roars of laughter; and the only thoroughly grave man on the ground was he who occasioned the mirth of all the others.

Next morning David again buttoned his coat; but he got on much better this day than the former. He was less awkward and less idle, though not less observant than before; and he succeeded ere evening in tracing, in workmanlike fashion, a few draughts along the future column. He was evidently greatly improving!

On the morning of Wednesday he threw off his coat; and it was seen that, though by no means in a hurry, he was seriously at work. There were no more jokes or laughter; and it was whispered in the evening that the strange Highlander had made astonishing progress during the day.

By the middle of Thursday he had made up for

his two days' trifling, and was abreast of the other workmen. Before night he was far ahead of them; and ere the evening of Friday, when they had still a full day's work on each of their columns, David's was completed in a style that defied criticism; and, his tartan coat again buttoned around him, he sat resting himself beside it.

The foreman went out and greeted him. "Well," he said, "you have beaten us all. You certainly *can* hew!"

"Yes," said David, "I *thought* I could hew columns. Did the other men take much more than a week to learn?"

"Come, come, *David Fraser*," replied the foreman, "we all guess who you are. You have had your week's joke out; and now, I suppose, we must give you your week's wages, and let you go away!"

"Yes," said David, "work waits for me in Glasgow; but I just thought it might be well to know how you hewed on this east side of the country."

BILL BROWN'S TEST

BY CLEVELAND MOFFETT

ALL firemen have courage, but it cannot be known until the test how many have this particular kind — Bill Brown's kind.

What happened was this: Engine 29, pumping and pounding her prettiest, stood at the northwest corner of Greenwich and Warren streets, so close to the blazing drug-house that Driver Marks thought it was n't safe there for the three horses, and led them away. That was fortunate, but it left Brown alone, right against the cheek of the fire, watching his boiler, stoking in coal, keeping his steam-gauge at 75. As the fire gained, chunks of red-hot sandstone began to smash down on the engine. Brown ran his pressure up to 80, and watched the door anxiously where the boys had gone in.

Then the explosion came, and a blue flame, wide as a house, curled its tongues halfway across the street, enwrapping engine and man, setting fire to the elevated railway station overhead, or such wreck of it as the shock had left.

Bill Brown stood by his engine, with a wall of fire before him and a sheet of fire above him. He heard quick footsteps on the pavements, and voices, that grew fainter and fainter, crying, "Run for your lives!" He heard the hose-wagon horses somewhere back in the smoke go plunging away, mad with fright and their burns. He was alone with the fire, and the skin was hanging in shreds on his hands, face, and neck. Only a fireman knows how one blast of flame can shrivel up a man, and the pain over the bared surfaces was, — well, there is no pain worse than that of fire scorching in upon the quick flesh seared by fire.

Here, I think, was a crisis to make a very brave man quail. Bill Brown knew perfectly well why every one was running; there was going to be another explosion in a couple of minutes, maybe sooner, out of this hell in front of him. And the order had come for every man to save himself, and every man had done it except the lads inside. And the question was, Should he run or should he stay and die? It was tolerably certain that he would die if he stayed. On the other hand, the boys of old 29 were in there. Devanny and McArthur, and Gillon and Merron, his friends, his chums. He 'd seen them drag the hose in through that door, — there it was now, a long, throbbing snake of it, — and they had n't come out. Perhaps they were dead. Yes, but perhaps they were n't. If they were alive, they needed water now more than they ever needed anything before. And they could n't get water if he quit his engine.

Bill Brown pondered this a long time, perhaps four seconds; then he fell to stoking in coal, and he screwed her up another notch, and he eased her running parts with the oiler. Explosion or not, pain or not, alone or not, he was going to stay and make that engine hum. He had done the greatest thing a man can do, — had offered his life for his friends.

It is pleasant to know that this sacrifice was averted. A quarter of a minute or so before the second and terrible explosion, Devanny and his men came staggering from the building. Then it was that Merron fell, and McArthur checked his flight to save him. Then it was, but not until then, that Bill Brown left Engine 29 to her fate (she was crushed by the falling walls), and ran for his life with his comrades. He had waited for them, he had stood the great test.

COLUMBUS DAY

(OCTOBER 12)

COLUMBUS AND THE EGG

BY JAMES BALDWIN (ADAPTED)[1]

ONE day Columbus was at a dinner which a Spanish gentleman had given in his honor, and several persons were present who were jealous of the great admiral's success. They were proud, conceited fellows, and they very soon began to try to make Columbus uncomfortable.

"You have discovered strange lands beyond the seas," they said, "but what of that? We do not see why there should be so much said about it. Anybody can sail across the ocean; and anybody can coast along the islands on the other side, just as you have done. It is the simplest thing in the world."

Columbus made no answer; but after a while he took an egg from a dish and said to the company: —

"Who among you, gentlemen, can make this egg stand on end?"

One by one those at the table tried the experiment. When the egg had gone entirely around and none had succeeded, all said that it could not be done.

[1] From *Thirty More Famous Stories Retold.* Copyright, 1905, by American Book Company.

Then Columbus took the egg and struck its small end gently upon the table so as to break the shell a little. After that there was no trouble in making it stand upright.

"Gentlemen," said he, "what is easier than to do this which you said was impossible? It is the simplest thing in the world. Anybody can do it, — *after he has been shown how!*"

COLUMBUS AT LA RABIDA

BY WASHINGTON IRVING (ADAPTED)

ABOUT half a league from the little seaport of Palos de Moguer, in Andalusia, there stood, and continues to stand at the present day, an ancient convent of Franciscan friars, dedicated to Santa Maria de Rabida.

One day a stranger on foot, in humble guise, but of a distinguished air, accompanied by a small boy, stopped at the gate of the convent and asked of the porter a little bread and water for his child. While receiving this humble refreshment, the prior of the convent, Juan Perez de Marchena, happened to pass by, and was struck with the appearance of the stranger. Observing from his air and accent that he was a foreigner, he entered into conversation with him and soon learned the particulars of his story.

That stranger was Columbus.

Accompanied by his little son Diego, he was on his way to the neighboring town of Huelva, to seek a brother-in-law, who had married a sister of his deceased wife.

The prior was a man of extensive information. His attention had been turned in some measure to geographical and nautical science. He was greatly interested by the conversation of Columbus, and struck with the grandeur of his views. When he found, however, that the voyager was on the point of abandoning Spain to seek the patronage of the court of France, the good friar took the alarm.

He detained Columbus as his guest, and sent for a scientific friend to converse with him. That friend was Garcia Fernandez, a physician of Palos. He was equally struck with the appearance and conversation of the stranger. Several conferences took place at the convent, at which veteran mariners and pilots of Palos were present.

Facts were related by some of these navigators in support of the theory of Columbus. In a word, his project was treated with a deference in the quiet cloisters of La Rabida and among the seafaring men of Palos which had been sought in vain among sages and philosophers.

Among the navigators of Palos was one Martin Alonzo Pinzon, the head of a family of wealth, members of which were celebrated for their adventurous expeditions. He was so convinced of the feasibility of Columbus's plan that he offered to engage in it with purse and person, and to bear the expenses of Columbus in an application to court.

Fray Juan Perez, being now fully persuaded of the importance of the proposed enterprise, advised Columbus to repair to the court, and make his propositions to the Spanish sovereigns, offering to give him a letter of recommendation to his friend, the Prior of the Convent of Prado and confessor to the queen, and a man of great political influence; through whose means he would, without doubt, immediately obtain royal audience and favor. Martin Alonzo Pinzon, also, generously furnished him with money for the journey, and the Friar took charge of his youthful son, Diego, to maintain and educate him in the convent.

Thus aided and encouraged and elated with fresh hopes, Columbus took leave of the little *junto* at La Rabida, and set out, in the spring of 1486, for the Castilian court, which had just assembled at Cordova, where the sovereigns were fully occupied with their chivalrous enterprise for the conquest of Granada. But alas! success was not yet! for Columbus met with continued disappointments and discouragements, while his projects were opposed by many eminent prelates and Spanish scientists, as being against religion and unscientific. Yet in spite of this opposition, by degrees the theory of Columbus began to obtain proselytes. He appeared in the presence of the king with modesty, yet self-possession, inspired by a consciousness of the dignity and importance of his errand; for he felt himself, as he afterwards declared in his letters, animated as if by a sacred fire from above, and considered himself an instrument in the hand of Heaven to accomplish its great designs. For nearly seven years of apparently fruitless solicitation, Columbus followed the royal court from place to place, at times encouraged by the sovereigns, and at others neglected.

At last he looked round in search of some other source of patronage, and feeling averse to subjecting himself to further tantalizing delays and disappointments of the court, determined to repair to Paris. He departed, therefore, and went to the Convent of La Rabida to seek his son Diego. When the worthy Friar Juan Perez de Marchena beheld Columbus arrive once more at the gate of his convent after nearly seven years of fruitless effort at court, and saw by the humility of his garb the poverty he had experienced, he was greatly moved; but when he found that he was about to carry his proposition to another country, his patriotism took alarm.

The Friar had once been confessor to the queen, and knew that she was always accessible to persons of his sacred calling. He therefore wrote a letter to her, and at the same time entreated Columbus to remain at the convent until an answer could be received. The latter was easily persuaded, for he felt as if on leaving Spain he was again abandoning his home.

The little council at La Rabida now cast round their eyes for an ambassador to send on this momentous mission. They chose one Sebastian Rodriguez, a pilot of Lepe, one of the most shrewd and important personages in this maritime neighborhood. He so faithfully and successfully conducted his embassy that he returned shortly with an answer.

Isabella had always been favorably disposed to the proposition of Columbus. She thanked Juan Perez for his timely services and requested him to repair immediately to the court, leaving Columbus in confident hope until he should hear further from her. This royal letter, brought back by the pilot at the end of fourteen days, spread great joy in the little *junto* at the convent.

No sooner did the warm-hearted friar receive it than he saddled his mule, and departed, privately, before midnight to the court. He journeyed through the countries of the Moors, and rode into the new city of Santa Fé where

Ferdinand and Isabella were engaged in besieging the capital of Granada.

The sacred office of Juan Perez gained him a ready admission into the presence of the queen. He pleaded the cause of Columbus with enthusiasm. He told of his honorable motives, of his knowledge and experience, and his perfect capacity to fulfill the undertaking. He showed the solid principles upon which the enterprise was founded, and the advantage that must attend its success, and the glory it must shed upon the Spanish Crown.

Isabella, being warm and generous of nature and sanguine of disposition, was moved by the representations of Juan Perez, and requested that Columbus might be again sent to her. Bethinking herself of his poverty and his humble plight, she ordered that money should be forwarded to him, sufficient to bear his traveling expenses, and to furnish him with decent raiment.

The worthy friar lost no time in communicating the result of his mission. He transmitted the money, and a letter, by the hand of an inhabitant of Palos, to the physician, Garcia Fernandez, who delivered them to Columbus. The latter immediately changed his threadbare garb for one more suited to the sphere of a court, and purchasing a mule, set out again, reanimated by hopes, for the camp before Granada.

This time, after some delay, his mission was attended with success. The generous spirit of Isabella was enkindled, and it seemed as if the subject, for the first time, broke upon her mind in all its real grandeur. She declared her resolution to undertake the enterprise, but paused for a moment, remembering that King Ferdinand looked coldly on the affair, and that the royal treasury was absolutely drained by the war.

Her suspense was but momentary. With an enthusiasm worthy of herself and of the cause, she exclaimed: "I undertake the enterprise for my own crown of Castile, and will pledge my jewels to raise the necessary funds." This was the proudest moment in the life of Isabella. It stamped her renown forever as the patroness of the discovery of the New World.

THE MUTINY

BY A. DE LAMARTINE (ADAPTED)

WHEN Columbus left the Canaries to pass with his three small ships into the unknown seas, the eruptions of Teneriffe illuminated the heavens and were reflected in the sea. This cast terror into the minds of his seamen. They thought that it was the flaming sword of the angel who expelled the first man from Eden, and who now was trying to drive back in anger those presumptuous ones who were seeking entrance to the forbidden and unknown seas and lands. But the admiral passed from ship to ship explaining to his men, in a simple way, the action of volcanoes, so that the sailors were no longer afraid.

But as the peak of Teneriffe sank below the horizon, a great sadness fell upon the men. It was their last beacon, the farthest sea-mark of the Old World. They were seized with a nameless terror and loneliness.

Then the admiral called them around him in his own ship, and told them many stories of the things they might hope to find in the wonderful new world to which they were going, — of the lands, the islands, the seas, the kingdoms, the riches, the vegetation, the sunshine, the mines of gold, the sands covered with pearls, the mountains shining with precious stones, the plains loaded with spices. These stories, tinged with the brilliant colors of their leader's rich imagination, filled the discouraged sailors with hope and good spirits.

But as they passed over the trackless ocean, and saw day by day the great billows rolling between them and the mysterious horizon, the sailors were again filled with dread. They lacked the courage to sail onward into the unknown distance. The compass began to vacillate, and no longer pointed toward the north; this confused both Columbus and his pilots. The men fell into a panic, but the resolute and patient admiral encouraged them once more. So buoyed up by his faith and hope, they continued to sail onwards over the pathless waters.

The next day a heron and a tropical bird flew about the masts of the ships, and these seemed to the wondering sailors as two witnesses come to confirm the reasoning of Columbus.

The weather was mild and serene, the sky clear, the waves transparent, the dolphins played across the bows, the airs were warm, and the perfumes, which the waves brought from afar, seemed to exhale from their foam. The brilliancy of the stars and the deep beauty of the night breathed a feeling of calm security that comforted and sustained the sailors.

The sea also began to bring its messages. Unknown vegetations floated upon its surface. Some were rock-plants, that had been swept off the cliffs by the waves; some were fresh-water plants; and others, recently torn from their roots, were still full of sap. One of them carried a live crab, — a little sailor afloat on a tuft of grass. These plants and living things could not have passed many days in the water without fading and dying. And all encouraged the sailors to believe that they were nearing land.

At eve and morning the distant waning clouds,

like those that gather round the mountain-tops, took the form of cliffs and hills skirting the horizon. The cry of "land" was on the tip of every tongue. But Columbus by his reckoning knew that they must still be far from any land, but fearing to discourage his men he kept his thoughts to himself, for he found no trustworthy friend among his companions whose heart was firm enough to bear his secret.

During the long passage Columbus conversed with his own thoughts, and with the stars, and with God whom he felt was his protector. He occupied his days in making notes of what he observed. The nights he passed on deck with his pilots, studying the stars and watching the seas. He withdrew into himself, and his thoughtful gravity impressed his companions sometimes with respect and sometimes with mistrust and awe.

Each morning the bows of the vessels plunged through the fantastic horizon which the evening mist had made the sailors mistake for a shore. They kept rolling on through the boundless and bottomless abyss. Gradually terror and discontent once more took possession of the crews. They began to imagine that the steadfast east wind that drove them westward prevailed eternally in this region, and that when the time came to sail homeward, the same wind would prevent their return. For surely their provisions and water could not hold out long enough for them to beat their way eastward over those wide waters!

Then the sailors began to murmur against the admiral and his seeming fruitless obstinacy, and they blamed themselves for obeying him, when it might mean the sacrifice of the lives of one hundred and twenty sailors.

But each time the murmurs threatened to break out into mutiny, Providence seemed to send more encouraging signs of land. And these for the time being changed the complaints to hopes. At evening little birds of the most delicate species, that build their nests in the shrubs of the garden and orchard, hovered warbling about the masts. Their delicate wings and joyous notes bore no signs of weariness or fright, as of birds swept far away to sea by a storm. These signs again aroused hope.

The green weeds on the surface of the ocean looked like waving corn before the ears are ripe. The vegetation beneath the water delighted the eyes of the sailors tired of the endless expanse of blue. But the seaweed soon became so thick that they were afraid of entangling their rudders and keels, and of remaining prisoners forever in the forests of the ocean, as ships of the northern seas are shut in by ice. Thus each joy soon turned to fear, — so terrible to man is the unknown.

The wind ceased, the calms of the tropics

alarmed the sailors. An immense whale was seen sleeping on the waters. They fancied there were monsters in the deep which would devour their ships. The roll of the waves drove them upon currents which they could not stem for want of wind. They imagined they were approaching the cataracts of the ocean, and that they were being hurried toward the abysses into which the deluge had poured its world of waters.

Fierce and angry faces crowded round the mast. The murmurs rose louder and louder. They talked of compelling the pilots to put about and of throwing the admiral into the sea. Columbus, to whom their looks and threats revealed these plans, defied them by his bold bearing or disconcerted them by his coolness.

Again nature came to his assistance, by giving him fresh breezes from the east, and a calm sea under his bows. Before the close of the day came the first cry of "Land ho!" from the lofty poop. All the crews, repeating this cry of safety, life, and triumph, fell on their knees on the decks, and struck up the hymn, "Glory be to God in heaven and upon earth." When it was over, all climbed as high as they could up the masts, yards, and rigging to see with their own eyes the new land that had been sighted.

But the sunrise destroyed this new hope all too quickly. The imaginary land disappeared with the morning mist, and once more the ships seemed to be sailing over a never-ending wilderness of waters.

Despair took possession of the crews. Again the cry of "Land ho!" was heard. But the sailors found as before that their hopes were but a passing cloud. Nothing wearies the heart so much as false hopes and bitter disappointments.

Loud reproaches against the admiral were heard from every quarter. Bread and water were beginning to fail. Despair changed to fury. The men decided to turn the heads of the vessels toward Europe, and to beat back against the winds that had favored the admiral, whom they intended to chain to the mast of his own vessel and to give up to the vengeance of Spain should they ever reach the port of their own country.

These complaints now became clamorous. The admiral restrained them by the calmness of his countenance. He called upon Heaven to decide between himself and the sailors. He flinched not. He offered his life as a pledge, if they would but trust and wait for three days more. He swore that, if, in the course of the third day, land was not visible on the horizon, he would yield to their wishes and steer for Europe.

The mutinous men reluctantly consented and allowed him three days of grace.

. . . .

At sunrise on the second day rushes recently torn up were seen floating near the vessels. A plank hewn by an axe, a carved stick, a bough of hawthorn in blossom, and lastly a bird's nest built on a branch which the wind had broken, and full of eggs on which the parent-bird was sitting, were seen swimming past on the waters. The sailors brought on board these living witnesses of their approach to land. They were like a message from the shore, confirming the promises of Columbus.

The overjoyed and repentant mutineers fell on their knees before the admiral whom they had insulted but the day before, and craved pardon for their mistrust.

As the day and night advanced many other sights and sounds showed that land was very near. Toward day delicious and unknown perfumes borne on a soft land breeze reached the vessels, and there was heard the roar of the waves upon the reefs.

The dawn, as it spread over the sky, gradually raised the shores of an island from the waves. Its distant extremities were lost in the morning mist. As the sun rose it shone on the land ascending from a low yellow beach to the summit of hills whose dark-green covering contrasted strongly with the clear blue of the heavens. The foam of the waves broke on the yellow sand, and forests of tall and unknown trees stretched away, one above another, over successive terraces of the island. Green valleys, and bright clefts in the hollows afforded a half glimpse into these mysterious wilds. And thus the land of golden promises, the land of future greatness, first appeared to Christopher Columbus, the Admiral of the Ocean, and thus he gave a New World to the nations to come.

THE FIRST LANDING OF COLUMBUS IN THE NEW WORLD

BY WASHINGTON IRVING (ADAPTED)

It was on Friday morning, the 12th of October, that Columbus first beheld the New World. As the day dawned he saw before him an island, several leagues in extent, and covered with trees like a continual orchard. Though apparently uncultivated it was populous, for the inhabitants were seen issuing from all parts of the woods and running to the shore. They were perfectly naked, and, as they stood gazing at the ships, appeared by their attitudes and gestures to be lost in astonishment.

Columbus made signals for the ships to cast anchor and the boats to be manned and armed. He entered his own boat, richly attired in scarlet, and holding the royal standard; while Martin Alonzo Pinzon and his brother put off in company in their boats, each with a banner of the enterprise emblazoned with a green cross, having on either side the letters "F." and "Y.," the initials of the Castilian monarchs Fernando and Ysabel, surmounted by crowns.

As he approached the shore, Columbus was delighted with the purity and suavity of the atmosphere, the crystal transparency of the sea, and the extraordinary beauty of the vegetation. He beheld also fruits of an unknown kind upon the trees which overhung the shores.

On landing he threw himself on his knees, kissed the earth, and returned thanks to God with tears of joy. His example was followed by the rest.[1]

"Almighty and Eternal God," prayed Columbus, "who by the energy of Thy creative word hast made the firmament, the earth and the sea; blessed and glorified be thy name in all places! May thy majesty and dominion be exalted for ever and ever, as Thou hast permitted thy holy name to be made known and spread by the most humble of thy servants, in this hitherto unknown portion of Thine empire."

Columbus, then rising, drew his sword, displayed the royal standard, and assembling around him the two captains and the rest who had landed, he took solemn possession in the name of the Castilian sovereigns, giving the island the name of San Salvador.

[1] This prayer is taken from Lamartine.

HALLOWEEN

(OCTOBER 31)

THE OLD WITCH

BY THE BROTHERS GRIMM (TRANSLATED)

THERE was once a little girl who was very willful and who never obeyed when her elders spoke to her; so how could she be happy?

One day she said to her parents: "I have heard so much of the old witch that I will go and see her. People say she is a wonderful old woman, and has many marvelous things in her house, and I am very curious to see them."

But her parents forbade her going, saying: "The witch is a wicked old woman, who performs many godless deeds; and if you go near her, you are no longer a child of ours."

The girl, however, would not turn back at her parents' command, but went to the witch's house. When she arrived there the old woman asked her:—

"Why are you so pale?"

"Ah," she replied, trembling all over, "I have frightened myself so with what I have just seen."

"And what did you see?" inquired the old witch.

"I saw a black man on your steps."

"That was a collier," replied she.

"Then I saw a gray man."

"That was a sportsman," said the old woman.

"After him I saw a blood-red man."

"That was a butcher," replied the old woman.

"But, oh, I was most terrified," continued the girl, "when I peeped through your window, and saw not you, but a creature with a fiery head."

"Then you have seen the witch in her proper dress," said the old woman. "For you I have long waited, and now you shall give me light."

So saying the witch changed the little girl into a block of wood, and then threw it on the fire; and when it was fully alight, she sat down on the hearth and warmed herself, saying: —

"How good I feel! The fire has not burned like this for a long time!"

SHIPPEITARO

A JAPANESE FOLK-TALE

BY MARY F. NIXON-ROULET (ADAPTED) [1]

ONCE upon a time there was a brave soldier lad who was seeking his fortune in the wide, wide world. One day he lost his way in a pathless forest, and wandered about until he came at length to a small clearing in the midst of which stood a ruined temple. The huge trees waved above its walls, and the leaves in the thicket whispered

[1] From *Japanese Folk-Stories and Fairy Tales*. Copyright, 1908 by American Book Company.

around them. No sun ever shone there, and no human being lived there.

A storm was coming up, and the soldier lad took refuge among the ruins.

"Here is all I want," said he. "Here I shall have shelter from the storm-god's wrath, and a comfortable place to sleep in."

So he wrapped himself in his cloak, and, lying down, was soon fast asleep. But his slumbers did not last long. At midnight he was wakened by fearful shrieks, and springing to his feet, he looked out at the temple door.

The storm was over. Moonlight shone on the clearing. And there he saw what seemed to be a troop of monstrous cats, who like huge phantoms marched across the open space in front of the temple. They broke into a wild dance, uttering shrieks, howls, and wicked laughs. Then they all sang together: —

"Whisper not to Shippeitaro
That the Phantom Cats are near;
Whisper not to Shippeitaro,
Lest he soon appear!"

The soldier lad crouched low behind the door, for brave as he was he did not wish these fearful creatures to see him. But soon, with a chorus of wild yells, the Phantom Cats disappeared as quickly as they had come, and all was quiet as before.

Then the soldier lad lay down and went to sleep again, nor did he waken till the sun peered into the temple and told him that it was morning. He quickly found his way out of the forest and walked on until he came to the cottage of a peasant.

As he approached he heard sounds of bitter weeping. A beautiful young maiden met him at the door, and her eyes were red with crying. She greeted him kindly.

"May I have some food?" said he.

"Enter and welcome," she replied. "My parents are just having breakfast. You may join them, for no one passes our door hungry."

Thanking her the lad entered, and her parents greeted him courteously but sadly, and shared their breakfast with him. He ate heartily, and, when he was finished, rose to go.

"Thank you many times for this good meal, kind friends," said he, "and may happiness be yours."

"Happiness can never again be ours!" answered the old man, weeping.

"You are in trouble, then," said the lad. "Tell me about it; perhaps I can help you in some way."

"Alas!" replied the old man, "There is within yonder forest a ruined temple. It is the abode of horrors too terrible for words. Each year a demon, whom no one has ever seen, demands that the people of this land give him a beautiful maiden to devour. She is placed in a cage and carried to the temple just at sunset. This year it is my daughter's turn to be offered to the fiend!" And the old man buried his face in his hands and groaned.

The soldier lad paused to think for a moment, then he said: —

"It is terrible, indeed! But do not despair. I think I know a way to help you. Who is Shippeitaro?"

"Shippeitaro is a beautiful dog, owned by our lord, the prince," answered the old man.

"That is just the thing!" cried the lad. "Only keep your daughter closely at home. Do not let her out of your sight. Trust me and she shall be saved."

Then the soldier lad hurried away, and found the castle of the prince. He begged that he might borrow Shippeitaro just for one night.

"You may take him upon the condition that you bring him back safely," said the prince.

"To-morrow he shall return in safety," answered the lad.

Taking Shippeitaro with him, he hurried to the peasant's cottage, and, when evening was come, he placed the dog in the cage which was to have carried the maiden. The bearers then took the cage to the ruined temple, and, placing it on the ground, ran away as fast as their legs would carry them.

The lad, laughing softly to himself, hid inside the temple as before, and so quiet was the spot that he fell asleep. At midnight he was aroused by the same wild shrieks he had heard the night before. He rose and looked out at the temple door.

Through the darkness, into the moonlight, came the troop of Phantom Cats. This time they were led by a fierce, black Tomcat. As they came nearer they chanted with unearthly screeches: —

"Whisper not to Shippeitaro
That the Phantom Cats are near;
Whisper not to Shippeitaro,
Lest he soon appear!"

With that the great Tomcat caught sight of the cage and, uttering a fearful yowl, sprang upon it. With one blow of his claws he tore open the lid, when, instead of the dainty morsel he expected, out jumped Shippeitaro!

The dog sprang upon the Tomcat, and caught him by the throat; while the Phantom Cats stood still in amazement. Drawing his sword the lad hurried to Shippeitaro's side, and what with Shippeitaro's teeth and the lad's hard blows, in an instant the great Tomcat was torn and cut into pieces. When the Phantom Cats saw this, they uttered one wild shriek and fled away, never to return again.

Then the soldier lad, leading Shippeitaro, returned in triumph to the peasant's cottage. There in terror the maiden awaited his arrival, but great was the joy of herself and her parents when they knew that the Tomcat was no more.

"Oh, sir," cried the maiden, "I can never thank you! I am the only child of my parents, and no one would have been left to care for them if I had been the monster's victim."

"Do not thank me," answered the lad. "Thank the brave Shippeitaro. It was he who sprang upon the great Tomcat and chased away the Phantom Creatures."

HANSEL AND GRETHEL

BY THE BROTHERS GRIMM (ADAPTED)

HARD-BY a great forest dwelt a poor wood-cutter with his two children and his wife who was their stepmother. The boy was called Hansel and the girl Grethel. The wood-cutter had little to bite and to break, and once when a great famine fell on the land he could no longer get daily bread. Now when he thought over this by night in his bed, and tossed about in his trouble, he groaned, and said to his wife: —

"What is to become of us? How are we to feed our poor children, when we no longer have anything even for ourselves?"

"I'll tell you what, husband," answered the woman; "early to-morrow morning we will take the children out into the woods where it is the thickest; there we will light a fire for them, and give each of them one piece of bread more, and then we will go to our work and leave them alone. They will not find the way home again, and we shall be rid of them."

"No, wife," said the man, "I will not do that; how can I bear to leave my children alone in the woods? — the wild beasts would soon come and tear them to pieces."

"Oh, you fool!" said she. "Then we must all four die of hunger; you may as well plane the planks for our coffins." And she left him no peace until he said he would do as she wished.

"But I feel very sorry for the poor children, all the same," said the man.

The two children had also not been able to sleep for hunger, and had heard what their father's wife had said to their father.

Grethel wept bitter tears, and said to Hansel, "Now all is over with us."

"Be quiet, Grethel," said Hansel, "do not be troubled; I will soon find a way to help us."

And when the old folks had fallen asleep, he got up, put on his little coat, opened the door below, and crept outside. The moon shone brightly, and the white pebbles which lay in front of the house shone like real silver pennies. Hansel stooped and put as many of them in the little pocket of his coat as he could make room for. Then he went back, and said to Grethel, "Be at ease, dear little sister, and sleep in peace; God will not forsake us." And he lay down again in his bed.

When the day dawned, but before the sun had risen, the woman came and awoke the two children, saying: —

"Get up, you lazy things! we are going into the forest to fetch wood." She gave each a little piece of bread, and said, "There is something for your dinner, but do not eat it up before then, for you will get nothing else."

Grethel took the bread under her apron, as Hansel had the stones in his pocket. Then they all set out together on the way to the forest, and Hansel threw one after another of the white pebble-stones out of his pocket on the road.

When they had reached the middle of the forest, the father said, "Now, children, pile up some wood and I will light a fire that you may not be cold."

Hansel and Grethel drew brushwood together till it was as high as a little hill.

The brushwood was lighted, and when the flames were burning very high the woman said: —

"Now, children, lie down by the fire and rest; we will go into the forest and cut some wood. When we have done, we will come back and fetch you away."

Hansel and Grethel sat by the fire, and when

noon came, each ate a little piece of bread, and as they heard the strokes of the wood-axe they were sure their father was near. But it was not the axe, it was a branch which he had tied to a dry tree, and the wind was blowing it backward and forward. As they had been sitting such a long time they were tired, their eyes shut, and they fell fast asleep. When at last they awoke, it was dark night.

Grethel began to cry, and said, "How are we to get out of the forest now?"

But Hansel comforted her, saying, "Just wait a little, until the moon has risen, and then we will soon find the way."

And when the full moon had risen, Hansel took his little sister by the hand, and followed the pebbles, which shone like bright silver pieces, and showed them the way.

They walked the whole night long, and by break of day came once more to their father's house.

They knocked at the door, and when the woman opened it, and saw that it was Hansel and Grethel, she said, "You naughty children, why have you slept so long in the forest? we thought you were never coming back at all!"

The father, however, was glad, for it had cut him to the heart to leave them behind alone.

Not long after, there was once more a great lack

of food in all parts, and the children heard the woman saying at night to their father: —

"Everything is eaten again; we have one half-loaf left, and after that there is an end. The children must go; we will take them farther into the wood, so that they will not find their way out again; there is no other means of saving ourselves!"

The man's heart was heavy, and he thought, "It would be better to share our last mouthful with the children."

The woman, however, would listen to nothing he had to say, but scolded him. He who says A must say B, too, and as he had given way the first time, he had to do so a second time also.

The children were still awake and had heard the talk. When the old folks were asleep, Hansel again got up, and wanted to go and pick up pebbles, but the woman had locked the door, and he could not get out.

So he comforted his little sister, and said: —

"Do not cry, Grethel; go to sleep quietly, the good God will help us."

Early in the morning came the woman, and took the children out of their beds. Their bit of bread was given to them, but it was still smaller than the time before. On the way into the forest Hansel crumbled his in his pocket, and often threw a morsel on the ground until little by little, he had thrown all the crumbs on the path.

The woman led the children still deeper into the forest, where they had never in their lives been before. Then a great fire was again made, and she said: —

"Just sit there, you children, and when you are tired you may sleep a little; we are going into the forest to cut wood, and in the evening when we are done, we will come and fetch you away."

When it was noon, Grethel shared her piece of bread with Hansel, who had scattered his by the way. Then they fell asleep, and evening came and went, but no one came to the poor children.

They did not awake until it was dark night, and Hansel comforted his little sister, and said: —

"Just wait, Grethel, until the moon rises, and then we shall see the crumbs of bread which I have scattered about; they will show us our way home again."

When the moon came they set out, but they found no crumbs, for the many thousands of birds which fly about in the woods and fields had picked them all up.

Hansel said to Grethel, "We shall soon find the way."

But they did not find it. They walked the whole night and all the next day, too, from morning till evening, but they did not get out of the forest; they were very hungry, for they had nothing to eat but two or three berries which grew on the ground. And as they were so tired that their legs would carry them no longer, they lay down under a tree and fell asleep.

It was now three mornings since they had left their father's house. They began to walk again, but they always got deeper into the forest, and if help did not come soon, they must die of hunger and weariness. When it was midday, they saw a beautiful snow-white bird sitting on a bough. It sang so sweetly that they stood still and listened to it. And when it had done, it spread its wings and flew away before them, and they followed it until they reached a little house, on the roof of which it perched; and when they came quite up to the little house, they saw it was built of bread and covered with cakes, but that the windows were of clear sugar.

"We will set to work on that," said Hansel, "and have a good meal. I will eat a bit of the roof, and you, Grethel, can eat some of the window, it will taste sweet."

Hansel reached up, and broke off a little of the roof to try how it tasted, and Grethel leaned against the window and nibbled at the panes.

Then a soft voice cried from the room, —

"Nibble, nibble, gnaw,
Who is nibbling at my little house?"

The children answered: —

"The wind, the wind,
The wind from heaven";

and went on eating. Hansel, who thought the roof tasted very nice, tore down a great piece of it; and Grethel pushed out the whole of one round window-pane, sat down, and went to eating it.

All at once the door opened, and a very, very old woman, who leaned on crutches, came creeping out. Hansel and Grethel were so scared that they let fall what they had in their hands.

The old woman, however, nodded her head, and said, "Oh, you dear children, who has brought you here? Do come in, and stay with me. No harm shall happen to you."

She took them both by the hand, and led them into her little house. Then good food was set before them, milk and pancakes, with sugar, apples, and nuts. Afterwards two pretty little beds were covered with clean white linen, and Hansel and Grethel lay down in them, and thought they were in heaven.

The old woman had only pretended to be so kind; she was in reality a wicked witch, who lay in wait for children, and had built the little bread house in order to coax them there.

Early in the morning, before the children were awake, she was already up, and when she saw both of them sleeping and looking so pretty, with their plump red cheeks, she muttered to herself, "That will be a dainty mouthful!"

Then she seized Hansel, carried him into a little

stable, and shut him in behind a grated door. He might scream as he liked, it was of no use. Then she went to Grethel, shook her till she awoke and cried: "Get up, lazy thing; fetch some water, and cook something good for your brother; he is in the stable outside, and is to be made fat. When he is fat, I will eat him."

Grethel began to weep, but it was all in vain; she was forced to do what the wicked witch told her.

And now the best food was cooked for poor Hansel, but Grethel got nothing but crab-shells.

Every morning the woman crept to the little stable, and cried, "Hansel, stretch out your finger that I may feel if you will soon be fat."

Hansel, however, stretched out a little bone to her, and the old woman, who had dim eyes, could not see it; she thought it was Hansel's finger, and wondered why he grew no fatter. When four weeks had gone by, and Hansel still was thin, she could wait no longer.

"Come, Grethel," she cried to the girl, "fly round and bring some water. Let Hansel be fat or lean, to-morrow I will kill him, and cook him."

Ah, how sad was the poor little sister when she had to fetch the water, and how her tears did flow down over her cheeks!

"Dear God, do help us," she cried. "If the wild beasts in the forest had but eaten us, we should at any rate have died together."

"Just keep your noise to yourself," said the old woman; "all that won't help you at all."

Early in the morning, Grethel had to go out and hang up the kettle with the water, and light the fire.

"We will bake first," said the old woman. "I have already heated the oven, and got the dough ready."

She pushed poor Grethel out to the oven, from which the flames of fire were already darting.

"Creep in," said the witch, "and see if it is heated, so that we can shut the bread in." And when once Grethel was inside, she meant to shut the oven and let her bake in it, and then she would eat her, too.

But Grethel saw what she had in her mind, and said, "I do not know how I am to do it; how do you get in?"

"Silly goose," said the old woman. "The door is big enough; just look, I can get in myself!" and she crept up and thrust her head into the oven. Then Grethel gave her a push that drove her far into it, and shut the iron door, tight.

Grethel ran as quick as lightning to Hansel, opened his little stable, and cried, "Hansel, we are saved! The old witch is dead!"

Then Hansel sprang out like a bird from its cage when the door is opened for it. How they did dance about and kiss each other. And as they had no longer any need to fear her, they went

SHE THOUGHT IT WAS HANSEL'S FINGER

into the witch's house, and in every corner there stood chests full of pearls and jewels.

"These are far better than pebbles!" said Hansel, and filled his pockets; and Grethel said, "I, too, will take something home with me," and filled her pinafore.

"But now we will go away," said Hansel, "that we may get out of the witch's forest." When they had walked for two hours, they came to a great piece of water. "We cannot get over," said Hansel; "I see no foot-plank and no bridge."

"And no boat crosses, either," answered Grethel, "but a white duck is swimming there; if I ask her, she will help us over." Then she cried, —

"Little duck, little duck, dost thou see,
Hansel and Grethel are waiting for thee?
There's never a plank or bridge in sight,
Take us across on thy back so white."

The duck came to them, and Hansel sat on its back, and told his sister to sit by him.

"No," replied Grethel, "that will be too heavy for the little duck; she shall take us across, one after the other."

The good little duck did so, and when they were once safely across and had walked for a short time, they knew where they were, and at last they saw from afar their father's house.

Then they began to run, rushed in, and threw themselves into their father's arms. The man had not known one happy hour since he had left the children in the forest; the woman, however, was dead. Grethel emptied her pinafore until pearls and precious stones rolled about the floor, and Hansel threw one handful after another out of his pocket to add to them. Then all care was at an end, and they lived happily together ever after.

My tale is done; there runs a mouse; whosoever catches it may make himself a big fur cap out of it.

BURG HILL'S ON FIRE

A CELTIC FAIRY TALE

BY ELIZABETH W. GRIERSON (ADAPTED)

ONCE upon a time there was a rich farmer who had a thrifty wife. She used to go out and gather all the little bits of wool which she could find on the hillsides, and bring them home. Then, after her family had gone to bed, she would sit up and card the wool and spin it into yarn, then she would weave the yarn into cloth to make garments for her children.

But all this work made her feel very tired, so that one night, sitting at her loom, she laid down her shuttle and cried: —

"Oh, that some one would come from far or near, from land or sea, to help me!"

No sooner had the words left her lips than she heard some one knocking at the door.

"Who is there?" cried she.

"Tell Quary, good housewife," answered a wee, wee voice. "Open the door to me. As long as I have you'll get."

She opened the door and there on the threshold stood a queer, little woman, dressed in a green gown and wearing a white cap on her head.

The good housewife was so astonished that she stood and stared at her strange visitor; but without a word the little woman ran past her, and seated herself at the spinning-wheel.

The good housewife shut the door, but just then she heard another knock.

"Who is there?" said she.

"Tell Quary, good housewife. Open the door to me," said another wee, wee voice. "As long as I have you'll get."

And when she opened the door there was another queer, little woman, in a lilac frock and a green cap, standing on the threshold.

She, too, ran into the house without waiting to say, "By your leave," and picking up the distaff, began to put some wool on it.

Then before the housewife could get the door shut, a funny little manikin, with green trousers and a red cap, came running in, and followed the tiny women into the kitchen, seized hold of a handful of wool, and began to card it. Another wee, wee woman followed him, and then another tiny manikin, and another, and another, until it seemed to the good housewife that all the fairies and pixies in Scotland were coming into her house.

The kitchen was alive with them. Some of them hung the great pot over the fire to boil water to wash the wool that was dirty. Some teased the clean wool, and some carded it. Some spun it into yarn, and some wove the yarn into great webs of cloth.

And the noise they made was like to make her head run round. "Splash! splash! Whirr! whirr! Clack! clack!" The water in the pot bubbled over. The spinning-wheel whirred. The shuttle in the loom flew backwards and forwards.

And the worst of it was that all the Fairies cried out for something to eat, and although the good housewife put on her griddle and baked bannocks as fast as she could, the bannocks were eaten up the moment they were taken off the fire, and yet the Fairies shouted for more.

At last the poor woman was so troubled that she went into the next room to wake her husband. But although she shook him with all her might, she could not wake him. It was very plain to see that he was bewitched.

Frightened almost out of her senses, and leaving

the Fairies eating her last batch of bannocks, she stole out of the house and ran as fast as she could to the cottage of the Wise Man who lived a mile away.

She knocked at his door till he got up and put his head out of the window, to see who was there; then she told him the whole story.

"Thou foolish woman," said he, "let this be a lesson to thee never to pray for things thou dost not need! Before thy husband can be loosed from the spell the Fairies must be got out of the house and the fulling-water, which they have boiled, must be thrown over him. Hurry to the little hill that lies behind thy cottage, climb to the top of it, and set the bushes on fire; then thou must shout three times: '*Burg Hill 's on fire!*' Then will all the little Fairies run out to see if this be true, for they live under the hill. When they are all out of the cottage, do thou slip in as quickly as thou canst, and turn the kitchen upside down. Upset everything the Fairies have worked with, else the things their fingers have touched will open the door to them, and let them in, in spite of thee."

So the good housewife hurried away. She climbed to the top of the little hill back of her cottage, set the bushes on fire, and cried out three times as loud as she was able: "*Burg Hill 's on fire!*"

And sure enough, the door of the cottage was

flung wide open, and all the little Fairies came running out, knocking each other over in their eagerness to be first at the hill.

In the confusion the good housewife slipped away, and ran as fast as she could to her cottage; and when she was once inside, it did not take her long to bar the door, and turn everything upside down.

She took the band off the spinning-wheel, and twisted the head of the distaff the wrong way. She lifted the pot of fulling-water off the fire, and turned the room topsy-turvy, and threw down the carding-combs.

Scarcely had she done so, when the Fairies returned, and knocked at the door.

"Good housewife! let us in," they cried.

"The door is shut and bolted, and I will not open it," answered she.

"Good spinning-wheel, get up and open the door," they cried.

"How can I," answered the spinning-wheel, "seeing that my band is undone?"

"Kind distaff, open the door for us," said they.

"That would I gladly do," said the distaff, "but I cannot walk, for my head is turned the wrong way."

"Weaving-loom, have pity, and open the door."

"I am all topsy-turvy, and cannot move," sighed the loom.

"Fulling-water, open the door," they implored.

"I am off the fire," growled the fulling-water, "and all my strength is gone."

"Oh! Is there nothing that will come to our aid, and open the door?" they cried.

"I will," said a little barley-bannock, that had lain hidden, toasting on the hearth; and it rose and trundled like a wheel quickly across the floor.

But luckily the housewife saw it, and she nipped it between her finger and thumb, and, because it was only half-baked, it fell with a "splatch" on the cold floor.

Then the Fairies gave up trying to get into the kitchen, and instead they climbed up by the windows into the room where the good housewife's husband was sleeping, and they swarmed upon his bed and tickled him until he tossed about and muttered as if he had a fever.

Then all of a sudden the good housewife remembered what the Wise Man had said about the fulling-water. She ran to the kitchen and lifted a cupful out of the pot, and carried it in, and threw it over the bed where her husband was.

In an instant he woke up in his right senses. Then he jumped out of bed, ran across the room and opened the door, and the Fairies vanished. And they have never been seen from that day to this.

THE KING OF THE CATS

AN ENGLISH FOLK-TALE

BY ERNEST RHYS

ONCE upon a time there were two brothers who lived in a lonely house in a very lonely part of Scotland. An old woman used to do the cooking, and there was no one else, unless we count her cat and their own dogs, within miles of them.

One autumn afternoon the elder of the two, whom we will call Elshender, said he would not go out; so the younger one, Fergus, went alone to follow the path where they had been shooting the day before, far across the mountains.

He meant to return home before the early sunset; however, he did not do so, and Elshender became very uneasy as he watched and waited in vain till long after their usual supper-time. At last Fergus returned, wet and exhausted, nor did he explain why he was so late.

But after supper when the two brothers were seated before the fire, on which the peat crackled cheerfully, the dogs lying at their feet, and the old woman's black cat sitting gravely with half-shut eyes on the hearth between them, Fergus recovered himself and began to tell his adventures.

"You must be wondering," said he, "what made me so late. I have had a very, very strange adventure to-day. I hardly know what to say about it. I went, as I told you I should, along our yesterday's track. A mountain fog came on just as I was about to turn homewards, and I completely lost my way. I wandered about for a long time not knowing where I was, till at last I saw a light, and made for it, hoping to get help.

"As I came near it, it disappeared, and I found myself close to an old oak tree. I climbed into the branches the better to look for the light, and, behold! there it was right beneath me, inside the hollow trunk of the tree. I seemed to be looking down into a church, where a funeral was taking place. I heard singing, and saw a coffin surrounded by torches, all carried by — But I know you won't believe me, Elshender, if I tell you!"

His brother eagerly begged him to go on, and threw a dry peat on the fire to encourage him. The dogs were sleeping quietly, but the cat was sitting up, and seemed to be listening just as carefully and cannily as Elshender himself Both brothers, indeed, turned their eyes on the cat as Fergus took up his story.

"Yes," he continued, "it is as true as I sit here. The coffin and the torches were both carried by *cats*, and upon the coffin were marked a crown and a scepter!"

He got no farther, for the black cat started up, shrieking: —

"My stars! old Peter's dead, and I'm the King o' the Cats!" — Then rushed up the chimney, and was seen no more.

THE STRANGE VISITOR

AN ENGLISH FOLK-TALE

BY JOSEPH JACOBS

A WOMAN was sitting at her reel one night; and still she sat, and still she reeled, and still she wished for company.

In came a pair of broad, broad soles, and sat down at the fireside!

And still she sat, and still she reeled, and still she wished for company.

In came a pair of small, small legs, and sat down on the broad, broad soles!

And still she sat, and still she reeled, and still she wished for company.

In came a pair of thick, thick knees, and sat down on the small, small legs!

And still she sat, and still she reeled, and still she wished for company.

In came a pair of thin, thin thighs, and sat down on the thick, thick knees!

And still she sat, and still she reeled, and still she wished for company.

In came a pair of huge, huge hips, and sat down on the thin, thin thighs!

And still she sat, and still she reeled, and still she wished for company.

In came a wee, wee waist, and sat down on the huge, huge hips!

And still she sat, and still she reeled, and still she wished for company.

In came a pair of broad, broad shoulders, and sat down on the wee, wee waist!

And still she sat, and still she reeled, and still she wished for company.

In came a pair of small, small arms, and sat down on the broad, broad shoulders!

And still she sat, and still she reeled, and still she wished for company.

In came a pair of huge, huge hands, and sat down on the small, small arms!

And still she sat, and still she reeled, and still she wished for company.

In came a small, small neck, and sat down on the broad, broad shoulders!

And still she sat, and still she reeled, and still she wished for company.

In came a huge, huge head, and sat down on the small, small neck!

. . . .

"How did you get such broad, broad feet?" quoth the Woman.

"Much tramping, much tramping!" (*gruffly.*)

"How did you get such small, small legs?"
"*Aih-h-h!* — late — and *wee-e-e*-moul!" (*whiningly.*)

"How did you get such thick, thick knees?"
"Much praying, much praying!" (*piously.*)

"How did you get such thin, thin thighs?"
"Aih-h-h! — late — and wee-e-e-moul!" (*whiningly.*)

"How did you get such big, big hips?"
"Much sitting, much sitting!" (*gruffly.*)

"How did you get such a wee, wee waist?"
"Aih-h-h! — late — and wee-e-e-moul!" (*whiningly.*)

"How did you get such broad, broad shoulders?"
"With carrying broom, with carrying broom!" (*gruffly.*)

"How did you get such small arms?"
"Aih-h-h! — late — and wee-e-e-moul!" (*whiningly.*)

"How did you get such huge, huge hands?"
"Threshing with an iron flail! Threshing with an iron flail!" (*gruffly.*)

"How did you get such a small, small neck?"
"Aih-h-h! — late — and wee-e-e-moul!" (*piti-fully.*)

"How did you get such a huge, huge head?"
"Much knowledge, much knowledge!" (*keenly.*)

"What do you come for?"
"FOR YOU ! ! !" (*at the top of the voice, with a wave of the arms and a stamp of the feet.*)

THE BENEVOLENT GOBLIN

FROM GESTA ROMANORUM (ADAPTED)

IN the kingdom of England there is a hillock in the midst of a dense wood. Thither in old days knights and their followers were wont to repair when tired and thirsty after the chase. When one of their number called out, "I thirst!" there immediately started up a Goblin with a cheerful countenance, clad in a crimson robe, and bearing in his outstretched hand a large drinking-horn richly ornamented with gold and precious jewels, and full of the most delicious, unknown beverage.

The Goblin presented the horn to the thirsty knight, who drank and instantly felt refreshed and cool. After the drinker had emptied the horn, the Goblin offered a silken napkin to wipe the mouth. Then, without waiting to be thanked, the strange creature vanished as suddenly as he had come.

Now once there was a knight of churlish nature, who was hunting alone in those parts. Feeling thirsty and fatigued, he visited the hillock and cried out: —

"I thirst!"

Instantly the Goblin appeared and presented the horn.

When the knight had drained it of its delicious beverage, instead of returning the horn, he thrust it into his bosom, and rode hastily away.

He boasted far and wide of his deed, and his feudal lord hearing thereof caused him to be bound and cast into prison; then fearing lest he, too, might become partaker in the theft and ingratitude of the knight, the lord presented the jeweled horn to the King of England, who carefully preserved it among the royal treasures. But never again did the benevolent Goblin return to the hillock in the wood.

THE PHANTOM KNIGHT OF THE VANDAL CAMP

FROM GESTA ROMANORUM (ADAPTED)

THERE was once in Great Britain, a knight named Albert, strong in arms and adorned with every virtue. One day as he was seeking for adventure, he chanced to wander into a castle where he was hospitably entertained.

At night, after supper, as was usual in great families during the winter, the household gathered about the hearth and occupied the time in relating divers tales.

At last they told how in the near-by plain of Wandlesbury there was a haunted mound. There in old days the Vandals, who laid waste the land and slaughtered Christians, had pitched their camp and built about it a great rampart. And it was further related that in the hush of the night, if any one crossed the plain, ascended the mound, and called out in a loud voice, "Let my adversary appear!" there immediately started up from the ruined ramparts a huge, ghostly figure, armed and mounted for battle. This phantom then attacked the knight who had cried out and speedily overcame him.

Now, when Albert heard this marvelous tale, he greatly doubted its truth, and was determined to put the matter to a test. As the moon was shining brightly, and the night was quiet, he armed, mounted, and immediately hastened to the plain of Wandlesbury, accompanied by a squire of noble blood.

He ascended the mound, dismissed his attendant, and shouted: —

"Let my adversary appear!"

Instantly there sprang from the ruins a huge, ghostly knight completely armed and mounted on an enormous steed.

This phantom rushed upon Albert, who spurred his horse, extended his shield, and drove at his antagonist with his lance. Both knights were shaken by the encounter. Albert, however, so resolutely and with so strong an arm pressed his adversary that the latter was thrown violently to the ground. Seeing this Albert hastily seized the steed of the fallen knight, and started to leave the mound.

But the phantom, rising to his feet, and seeing his horse led away, flung his lance and cruelly wounded Albert in the thigh. This done he vanished as suddenly as he had appeared.

Our knight, overjoyed at his victory, returned in triumph to the castle, where the household crowded around him and praised his bravery. But when he put off his armor he found the cuish from his right thigh filled with clots of blood from an angry wound in his side. The family, alarmed, hastened to apply healing herbs and bandages.

The captured horse was then brought forward. He was prodigiously large, and black as jet. His eyes were fierce and flashing, his neck proudly arched, and he wore a glittering war-saddle upon his back.

As the first streaks of dawn began to appear, the animal reared wildly, snorted as if with pain and anger, and struck the ground so furiously with his hoofs that the sparks flew. The black cock of the castle crew and the horse, uttering a terrible cry, instantly disappeared.

And every year, on the selfsame night, at the selfsame hour, the wounds of the knight Albert broke out afresh, and tormented him with agony. Thus till his dying day he bore in his body a yearly reminder of his encounter with the Phantom Knight of the Vandal Camp.

THANKSGIVING DAY

(LAST THURSDAY IN NOVEMBER)

THE FIRST HARVEST-HOME IN PLYMOUTH

BY W. DE LOSS LOVE, JR. (ADAPTED)

AFTER prayer and fasting and a farewell feast, the Pilgrim Fathers left the City of Leyden, and sought the new and unknown land. "So they lefte y^t goodly & pleasante citie," writes their historian Bradford, "which had been ther resting place near 12 years, but they knew they were pilgrimes & looked not much on those things, but lift up their eyes to ye Heavens their dearest cuntrie, and quieted their spirits."

When, after many vexing days upon the deep, the pilgrims first sighted the New World, they were filled with praise and thanksgiving. Going ashore they fell upon their knees and blessed the God of Heaven. And after that, whenever they were delivered from accidents or despair, they gave God "solemne thanks and praise." Such were the Pilgrims and such their habit day by day.

The first winter in the New World was marked by great suffering and want. Hunger and illness thinned the little colony, and caused many graves to be made on the near-by hillside.

The spring of 1621 opened. The seed was sown in the fields. The colonists cared for it without ceasing, and watched its growth with anxiety; for well they knew that their lives depended upon a full harvest.

The days of spring and summer flew by, and the autumn came. Never in Holland or England had the Pilgrims seen the like of the treasures bounteous Nature now spread before them. The woodlands were arrayed in gorgeous colors, brown, crimson, and gold, and swarmed with game of all kinds, that had been concealed during the summer. The little farm-plots had been blessed by the sunshine and showers, and now plentiful crops stood ready for the gathering. The Pilgrims, rejoicing, reaped the fruit of their labors, and housed it carefully for the winter. Then, filled with the spirit of thanksgiving, they held the first harvest-home in New England.

For one whole week they rested from work, feasted, exercised their arms, and enjoyed various recreations. Many Indians visited the colony, amongst these their greatest king, Massasoit, with ninety of his braves. The Pilgrims entertained them for three days. And the Indians went out into the woods and killed fine deer, which they brought to the colony and presented to the governor and the captain and others. So all made merry together.

And bountiful was the feast. Oysters, fish and wild turkey, Indian maize and barley bread, geese and ducks, venison and other savory meats, decked the board. Kettles, skillets, and spits were overworked, while knives and spoons, kindly assisted by fingers, made merry music on pewter plates. Wild grapes, "very sweete and strong," added zest to the feast. As to the vegetables, why, the good governor describes them thus: —

> "All sorts of grain which our own land doth yield,
> Was hither brought, and sown in every field;
> As wheat and rye, barley, oats, beans, and pease
> Here all thrive and they profit from them raise;
> All sorts of roots and herbs in gardens grow, —
> Parsnips, carrots, turnips, or what you'll sow,
> Onions, melons, cucumbers, radishes,
> Skirets, beets, coleworts and fair cabbages."

Thus a royal feast it was the Pilgrims spread that first golden autumn at Plymouth, a feast worthy of their Indian guests.

All slumbering discontents they smothered with common rejoicings. When the holiday was over, they were surely better, braver men because they had turned aside to rest awhile and be thankful together. So the exiles of Leyden claimed the harvests of New England.

This festival was the bursting into life of a new conception of man's dependence on God's gifts in Nature. It was the promise of autumnal Thanksgivings to come.

THE MASTER OF THE HARVEST

BY MRS. ALFRED GATTY (ADAPTED)

THE Master of the Harvest walked by the side of his cornfields in the springtime. A frown was on his face, for there had been no rain for several weeks, and the earth was hard from the parching of the east winds. The young wheat had not been able to spring up.

So as he looked over the long ridges that stretched in rows before him, he was vexed and began to grumble and say:—

"The harvest will be backward, and all things will go wrong."

Then he frowned more and more, and uttered complaints against Heaven because there was no rain; against the earth because it was so dry; against the corn because it had not sprung up.

And the Master's discontent was whispered all over the field, and along the ridges where the corn-seed lay. And the poor little seeds murmured:—

"How cruel to complain! Are we not doing our best? Have we let one drop of moisture pass by unused? Are we not striving every day to be ready for the hour of breaking forth? Are we idle? How cruel to complain!"

But of all this the Master of the Harvest heard

nothing, so the gloom did not pass from his face. Going to his comfortable home he repeated to his wife the dark words, that the drought would ruin the harvest, for the corn was not yet sprung up.

Then his wife spoke cheering words, and taking her Bible she wrote some texts upon the flyleaf, and after them the date of the day.

And the words she wrote were these: "The eyes of all wait upon Thee; and Thou givest them their meat in due season. Thou openest Thine hand and satisfiest the desire of every living thing. How excellent is Thy loving-kindness, O God! therefore the children of men put their trust under the shadow of Thy wings. Thou hast put gladness in my heart, more than in the time that their corn and their wine increased."

And so a few days passed as before, and the house was gloomy with the discontent of the Master. But at last one evening there was rain all over the land, and when the Master of the Harvest went out the next morning for his early walk by the cornfields, the corn had sprung up at last.

The young shoots burst out at once, and very soon all along the ridges were to be seen rows of tender blades, tinting the whole field with a delicate green. And day by day the Master of the Harvest saw them, and was satisfied, but he spoke of other things and forgot to rejoice.

Then a murmur rose among the corn-blades.

"The Master was angry because we did not come up; now that we have come forth why is he not glad? Are we not doing our best? From morning and evening dews, from the glow of the sun, from the juices of the earth, from the freshening breezes, even from clouds and rain, are we not taking food and strength, warmth and life? Why does he not rejoice?"

And when the Master's wife asked him if the wheat was doing well he answered, "Fairly well," and nothing more.

But the wife opened her Book, and wrote again on the flyleaf: "Who hath divided a watercourse for the overflowing of waters, or a way for the lightning of thunder, to cause it to rain on the earth where no man is, on the wilderness wherein there is no man, to satisfy the desolate and waste ground, and to cause the bud of the tender herb to spring forth? For He maketh small the drops of water; they pour down rain according to the vapor thereof, which the clouds do drop and distil upon man abundantly. Also can any understand the spreadings of the clouds, or the noise of his tabernacle?"

Very peaceful were the next few weeks. All nature seemed to rejoice in the fine weather. The corn-blades shot up strong and tall. They burst into flowers and gradually ripened into ears of grain. But alas! the Master of the Harvest had still some fault to find. He looked at the ears and saw that they were small. He grumbled and said: —

"The yield will be less than it ought to be. The harvest will be bad."

And the voice of his discontent was breathed over the cornfield where the plants were growing and growing. They shuddered and murmured: "How thankless to complain! Are we not growing as fast as we can? If we were idle would we bear wheat-ears at all? How thankless to complain!"

Meanwhile a few weeks went by and a drought settled on the land. Rain was needed, so that the corn-ears might fill. And behold, while the wish for rain was yet on the Master's lips, the sky became full of heavy clouds, darkness spread over the land, a wild wind arose, and the roaring of thunder announced a storm. And such a storm! Along the ridges of corn-plants drove the rain-laden wind, and the plants bent down before it and rose again like the waves of the sea. They bowed down and they rose up. Only where the whirlwind was the strongest they fell to the ground and could not rise again.

And when the storm was over, the Master of the Harvest saw here and there patches of over-weighted corn, yet dripping from the thunder-shower, and he grew angry with them, and forgot to think of the long ridges where the corn-plants were still standing tall and strong, and where the corn-ears were swelling and rejoicing.

His face grew darker than ever. He railed against the rain. He railed against the sun because it did not shine. He blamed the wheat because it might perish before the harvest.

"But why does he always complain?" moaned the corn-plants. "Have we not done our best from the first? Has not God's blessing been with us? Are we not growing daily more beautiful in strength and hope? Why does not the Master trust, as we do, in the future richness of the harvest?"

Of all this the Master of the Harvest heard nothing. But his wife wrote on the flyleaf of her Book: "He watereth the hills from his chambers, the earth is satisfied with the fruit of thy works. He causeth the grass to grow for the cattle and herb for the service of man, that he may bring forth food out of the earth, and wine that maketh glad the heart of man, and oil to make his face to shine, and bread which strengtheneth man's heart."

And day by day the hours of sunshine were more in number. And by degrees the green corn-ears ripened into yellow, and the yellow turned into gold, and the abundant harvest was ready, and the laborers were not wanting.

Then the bursting corn broke out into songs of rejoicing. "At least we have not labored and watched in vain! Surely the earth hath yielded her increase! Blessed be the Lord who daily loadeth us with benefits! Where now is the Master of the Harvest? Come, let him rejoice with us!"

And the Master's wife brought out her Book and her husband read the texts she had written even from the day when the corn-seeds were held back by the first drought, and as he read a new heart seemed to grow within him, a heart that was thankful to the Lord of the Great Harvest. And he read aloud from the Book: —

"Thou visitest the earth and waterest it; thou greatly enrichest it with the river of God which is full of water; thou preparest them corn, when thou hast so provided for it. Thou waterest the ridges thereof abundantly; thou settlest the furrows thereof; thou makest it soft with showers; thou blessest the springing thereof. Thou crownest the year with thy goodness, and thy paths drop fatness. They drop upon the pastures of the wilderness, and the little hills rejoice on every side. The pastures are clothed with flocks. The valleys also are covered over with corn; they shout for joy, they also sing. — O that men would praise the Lord for His goodness, and for his wonderful works to the children of men!"

SAINT CUTHBERT'S EAGLE

BY THE VENERABLE BEDE (ADAPTED)

ONCE upon a time, the good Saint Cuthbert of Lindesfarne, went forth from his monastery to preach to the poor. He took with him a young lad as his only attendant. Together they walked along the dusty way. The heat of the noonday sun beat upon their heads, and fatigue overcame them.

"Son," said Saint Cuthbert, "do you know any one on the road, whom we may ask for food and a place in which to rest?"

"I was just thinking the same thing," answered the lad, "but I know nobody on the road who will entertain us. Alas! why did we not bring along provisions? How can we proceed on our long journey without them?"

"My son," answered the saint, "learn to have trust in God, who never will suffer those to perish of hunger who believe in Him."

Then looking up and seeing an eagle flying in the air, he added, "Do you see the eagle yonder? It is possible for God to feed us by means of this bird."

While they were talking thus, they came to a river, and, lo! the eagle stood on the bank.

"Son," said Saint Cuthbert, "run and see what

provision God has made for us by his handmaid the bird."

The lad ran, and found a good-sized fish that the eagle had just caught. This he brought to the saint.

"What have you done?" exclaimed the good man, "why have you not given a part to God's handmaid? Cut the fish in two pieces, and give her one, as her service well deserves."

The lad did as he was bidden, and the eagle, taking the half fish in her beak, flew away.

Then entering a neighboring village, Saint Cuthbert gave the other half to a peasant to cook, and while the lad and the villagers feasted, the good saint preached to them the Word of God

THE EARS OF WHEAT

BY THE BROTHERS GRIMM (TRANSLATED)

AGES upon ages ago, says the German grandmother, when angels used to wander on earth, the ground was more fruitful than it is now. Then the stalks of wheat bore not fifty or sixty fold, but four times five hundred fold. Then the wheat-ears grew from the bottom to the top of the stalk. But the men of the earth forgot that this blessing came from God, and they became idle and selfish.

One day a woman went through a wheat-field, and her little child, who accompanied her, fell into a puddle and soiled her frock. The mother tore off a handful of the wheat-ears and cleaned the child's dress with them.

Just then an angel passed by and saw her. Wrathfully he spoke: —

"Wasteful woman, no longer shall the wheat-stalks produce ears. You mortals are not worthy of the gifts of Heaven!"

Some peasants who were gathering wheat in the fields heard this, and falling on their knees, prayed and entreated the angel to leave the wheat alone, not only on their account, but for the sake of the little birds who otherwise must perish of hunger.

The angel pitied their distress, and granted a part of the prayer. And from that day to this the ears of wheat have grown as they do now.

HOW INDIAN CORN CAME INTO THE WORLD

AN OJIBBEWAY LEGEND

BY HENRY R. SCHOOLCRAFT (ADAPTED)

LONG, long ago, in a beautiful part of this country, there lived an Indian with his wife and children. He was poor and found it hard to provide food enough for his family. But though needy he was kind and contented, and always gave thanks to the Great Spirit for everything that he received.

His eldest son, Wunzh, was likewise kind and gentle and thankful of heart, and he longed greatly to do something for his people.

The time came that Wunzh reached the age when every Indian boy fasts so that he may see in a vision the Spirit that is to be his guide through life. Wunzh's father built him a little lodge apart, so that the boy might rest there undisturbed during his days of fasting. Then Wunzh withdrew to begin the solemn rite.

On the first day he walked alone in the woods looking at the flowers and plants, and filling his mind with the beautiful images of growing things so that he might see them in his night-dreams. He saw how the flowers and herbs and berries grew, and he knew that some were good for food, and that others healed wounds and cured sickness. And his heart was filled with even a greater longing to do something for his family and his tribe.

"Truly," thought he, "the Great Spirit made all things. To Him we owe our lives. But could He not make it easier for us to get our food than by hunting and catching fish? I must try to find this out in my vision."

So Wunzh returned to his lodge and fasted and slept. On the third day he became weak and faint. Soon he saw in a vision a young brave coming down from the sky and approaching the lodge. He was clad in rich garments of green and yellow colors. On his head was a tuft of nodding green plumes, and all his motions were graceful and swaying.

"I am sent to you, O Wunzh," said the sky-stranger, "by that Great Spirit who made all things in sky and earth. He has seen your fasting, and knows how you wish to do good to your people, and that you do not seek for strength in war nor for the praise of warriors. I am sent to tell you how you may do good to your kindred. Arise and wrestle with me, for only by overcoming me may you learn the secret."

Wunzh, though he was weak from fasting, felt courage grow in his heart, and he arose and wrestled with the stranger. But soon he became weaker and exhausted, and the stranger, seeing this, smiled gently on him and said: "My friend, this is enough for once, I will come again to-morrow." And he vanished as suddenly as he had appeared.

The next day the stranger came, and Wunzh felt himself weaker than before; nevertheless he rose and wrestled bravely. Then the stranger spoke a second time. "My friend," he said, "have courage! To-morrow will be your last trial." And he disappeared from Wunzh's sight.

On the third day the stranger came as before, and the struggle was renewed. And Wunzh, though fainter in body, grew strong in mind and will, and he determined to win or perish in the attempt. He exerted all his powers, and, lo! in a while, he prevailed and overcame the stranger.

"O Wunzh, my friend," said the conquered one, "you have wrestled manfully. You have met your trial well. To-morrow I shall come again and you must wrestle with me for the last time. You will prevail. Do you then strip off my garments, throw me down, clean the earth of roots and weeds, and bury me in that spot. When you have done so, leave my body in the ground. Come often to the place and see whether I have come to life, but be careful not to let weeds or grass grow on my grave. If you do all this well, you will soon discover how to benefit your fellow creatures." Having said this the stranger disappeared.

In the morning Wunzh's father came to him with food. "My son," he said, "you have fasted long. It is seven days since you have tasted food, and you must not sacrifice your life. The Master of Life does not require that."

"My father," replied the boy, "wait until the sun goes down to-morrow. For a certain reason I wish to fast until that hour."

"Very well," said the old man, "I shall wait until the time arrives when you feel inclined to eat." And he went away.

The next day, at the usual hour, the sky-stranger came again. And, though Wunzh had fasted seven days, he felt a new power arise within him. He grasped the stranger with superhuman strength, and threw him down. He took from him his beautiful garments, and, finding him dead, buried him in the softened earth, and did all else as he had been directed.

He then returned to his father's lodge, and partook sparingly of food. There he abode for some time. But he never forgot the grave of his friend. Daily he visited it, and pulled up the weeds and grass, and kept the earth soft and moist. Very soon, to his great wonder, he saw the tops of green plumes coming through the ground.

Weeks passed by, the summer was drawing to a close. One day Wunzh asked his father to follow him. He led him to a distant meadow. There, in the place where the stranger had been buried, stood a tall and graceful plant, with bright-colored, silken hair, and crowned by nodding green plumes. Its stalk was covered with waving leaves, and there grew from its sides clusters of milk-filled ears of corn, golden and sweet, each ear closely wrapped in its green husks.

"It is my friend!" shouted the boy joyously; "it is Mondawmin, the Indian Corn! We need no longer depend on hunting, so long as this gift is planted and cared for. The Great Spirit has heard my voice and has sent us this food."

Then the whole family feasted on the ears of corn and thanked the Great Spirit who gave it. So Indian Corn came into the world.

THE NUTCRACKER DWARF

BY COUNT FRANZ POCCI (TRANSLATED)

Two boys gathered some hazelnuts in the woods. They sat down under a tree and tried to eat them, but they did not have their knives, and could not bite open the nuts with their teeth.

"Oh," they complained, "if only some one would come and open the nuts for us!"

Hardly had they said this when a little man came through the woods. And such a strange little man! He had a great, great head, and from the back of it a slender pigtail hung down to his heels. He wore a golden cap, a red coat and yellow stockings.

As he came near he sang: —

"Hight! hight! Bite! bite!
Hans hight I! Nuts bite I!
I chase the squirrels through the trees,
I gather nuts just as I please,
I place them 'twixt my jaws so strong,
And crack and eat them all day long!"

The boys almost died of laughter when they saw this funny little man, who they knew was a Wood Dwarf.

They called out to him: "If you know how to crack nuts, why, come here and open ours."

But the little man grumbled through his long white beard: —

"If I crack the nuts for you,
Promise that you'll give me two."

"Yes, yes," cried the boys, "you shall have all the nuts you wish, only crack some for us, and be quick about it!"

The little man stood before them, for he could not sit down because of his long, stiff pigtail that hung down behind, and he sang: —

"Lift my pigtail, long and thin,
Place your nuts my jaws within,
Pull the pigtail down, and then
I'll crack your nuts, my little men."

The boys did as they were told, laughing hard all the time. Whenever they pulled down the pigtail, there was a sharp *crack*, and a broken nut sprang out of the Nutcracker's mouth.

Soon all the hazelnuts were opened, and the little man grumbled again: —

"Hight! hight! Bite! bite!
Your nuts are cracked, and now my pay
I'll take and then I'll go away."

Now one of the boys wished to give the little man his promised reward, but the other, who was a bad boy, stopped him, saying: —

"Why do you give that old fellow our nuts? There are only enough for us. As for you, Nutcracker, go away from here and find some for yourself."

Then the little man grew angry, and he grumbled horribly: —

"If you do not pay my fee,
Why, then, you've told a lie to me!
I am hungry, you're well fed,
Quick, or I'll bite off your head!"

But the bad boy only laughed and said: "You'll bite off my head, will you! Go away from here just as fast as you can, or you shall feel these nutshells," and he shook his fist at the little man.

The Nutcracker grew red with rage. He pulled up his pigtail, snapping his jaws together, — *crack*, — and the bad boy's head was off.

THE PUMPKIN PIRATES

A TALE FROM LUCIAN

BY ALFRED J. CHURCH (ADAPTED)

ONCE upon a time, one Lucian the Greek was filled with a desire to see strange countries, and especially to discover whether there was any opposite shore to the ocean by which he lived.

So having purchased a vessel, he strengthened it for a voyage, that he knew would without doubt be long and stormy. Then he chose fifty stout young fellows having the same love of adventure as himself, and next he hired the best captain that could be got for money, and put a store of provisions and water on board.

All this being done, he set sail. For many days he and his companions voyaged on deep waters and in strange seas. At times the wind was fair and gentle, and at others it blew so hard that the sea rose in a terrible manner.

One day there came a violent whirlwind which twisted the ship about, and, lifting it into the air, carried it upward into the sky, until it reached the Moon. There Lucian and his comrades disembarked and visited the inhabitants of Moonland. They took part in a fierce battle between the Moon-Folk, the Sun-Folk, and an army of Vulture-Horsemen; and, after many other wonderful adventures, they departed from Moonland, and sailing through the sky, visited the Morning Star. Then the wind dropping, the ship settled once more upon the sea, and they sailed on the water.

One morning the wind began to blow vehemently, and they were driven by storm for days. On the third day they fell in with the Pumpkin Pirates. These were savages who were wont to sally forth from the islands that lay in the seas thereabouts, and plunder them that sailed by.

For ships they had large pumpkins, each being not less than ninety feet in length. These pumpkins they dried, and afterward dug out all the inner part of them till they were quite hollow. For masts they had reeds, and for sails, in the place of canvas, pumpkin leaves.

These savages attacked Lucian's vessel with two ships' or rather two pumpkins' crews, and wounded many of his company. For stones they used the pumpkin-seeds, which were about the bigness of a large apple.

Lucian's company fought for some time, without gaining the advantage, when about noon they saw coming toward them, in the rear of the Pumpkin Pirates, the Nut-Shell Sailors. These two tribes were at war with each other.

As soon as the Pumpkin Pirates saw the others approaching, they left off fighting Lucian's crew, and prepared to give battle to the Nut-Shell Sailors. When Lucian saw this he ordered the captain to set all sails; and they departed with speed. But looking back he could see that the Nut-Shell Sailors had the best of the battle, being superior in numbers, having five crews against two of the Pumpkin Pirates, and also because their ships were stronger. As for their ships, they were the shells of nuts which had been split in half, each measuring fifteen fathoms, or thereabouts.

As soon as the Pumpkin Pirates and the Nut-Shell Sailors were out of sight, Lucian set himself to dressing the wounds of his injured companions.

And from that time on both Lucian and his crew wore their armor continually, not knowing when another strange enemy might come upon them.

THE SPIRIT OF THE CORN

AN IROQUOIS LEGEND

BY HARRIET MAXWELL CONVERSE (ADAPTED)

THERE was a time, says the Iroquois grandmother, when it was not needful to plant the corn-seed nor to hoe the fields, for the corn sprang up of itself, and filled the broad meadows. Its stalks grew strong and tall, and were covered with leaves like waving banners, and filled with ears of pearly grain wrapped in silken green husks.

In those days Onatah, the Spirit of the Corn, walked upon the earth. The sun lovingly touched her dusky face with the blush of the morning, and her eyes grew soft as the gleam of the stars on dark streams. Her night-black hair was spread before the breeze like a wind-driven cloud.

As she walked through the fields, the corn, the Indian maize, sprang up of itself from the earth, and filled the air with its fringed tassels and whispering leaves. With Onatah walked her two sisters, the Spirits of the Squash and the Bean. As they passed by, squash-vines and bean-plants grew from the corn-hills.

One day Onatah wandered away alone in search

of early dew. Then the Evil One of the earth, Hahgwehdaetgah, followed swiftly after. He grasped her by the hair and dragged her beneath the ground down to his gloomy cave. Then, sending out his fire-breathing monsters, he blighted Onatah's grain. And when her sisters, the Spirits of the Squash and the Bean, saw the flame-monsters raging through the fields, they flew far away in terror.

As for poor Onatah, she lay a trembling captive in the dark prison-cave of the Evil One. She mourned the blight of her cornfields, and sorrowed over her runaway sisters.

"O warm, bright sun!" she cried, "if I may walk once more upon the earth, never again will I leave my corn!"

And the little birds of the air heard her cry, and winging their way upward they carried her vow and gave it to the sun as he wandered through the blue heavens.

The sun, who loved Onatah, sent out many searching beams of light. They pierced through the damp earth, and entering the prison-cave, guided her back again to her fields.

And ever after that she watched her fields alone, for no more did her sisters, the Spirits of the Squash and Bean, watch with her. If her fields thirsted, no longer could she seek the early dew. If the flame-monsters burned her corn, she could not search the skies for cooling winds. And when the great rains fell and injured her harvest, her voice grew so faint that the friendly sun could not hear it.

But ever Onatah tenderly watched her fields and the little birds of the air flocked to her service. They followed her through the rows of corn, and made war on the tiny enemies that gnawed at the roots of the grain.

And at harvest-time the grateful Onatah scattered the first gathered corn over her broad lands, and the little birds, fluttering and singing, joyfully partook of the feast spread for them on the meadow-ground.

THE HORN OF PLENTY

BY OVID (ADAPTED)

ÆNEUS, King of Ætolia, had a daughter whose name was Deïanira. So beautiful was the maiden that her fame spread throughout the world, and many princes came to woo her. Among these were two strangers, who drove all the other suitors from the hall of King Æneus.

One was Hercules, huge of limb and broad of shoulder. He was clad in the skins of beasts, and carried in his hand a knotted club. His tangled hair hung down upon his brawny neck, and his fierce eyes gleamed from behind his shaggy brows.

The other stranger was Acheloüs, god of the Calydonian River. Slender and graceful was he, and clad in flowing green raiment. In his hand he carried a staff of plaited reeds, and on his head was a crown of water-lilies. His voice was soft and caressing, like the gentle murmur of summer brooks.

"O King Æneus," said Acheloüs, standing before the throne, "behold I am the King of Waters. If thou wilt receive me as thy son-in-law I will make the beautiful Deïanira queen of my river kingdom."

"King Æneus," said the mighty Hercules, stepping forward, "Deïanira is mine, and I will not yield her to this river-god."

"Impertinent stranger!" cried Acheloüs, turning toward the hero, while his voice rose till it sounded like the thunder of distant cataracts, and his green garment changed to the blackness of night, — "impertinent stranger! how darest thou claim this maiden, — thou who hast mortal blood in thy veins! Behold me, the god Acheloüs, the powerful King of the Waters! I wind with majesty through the rich lands of my wide realms. I make all fields through which I flow beautiful with grass and flowers. By my right divine I claim this maiden."

But with scowling eye and rising wrath Hercules made answer. "Thou wouldst fight with words, like a woman, while I would win by my strength! My right hand is better than my tongue. If thou wouldst have the maiden, then must thou first overcome me in combat."

Thereupon Acheloüs threw off his raiment and began to prepare himself for the struggle. Hercules took off his garment of beasts' skins, and cast aside his club. The two then anointed their bodies with oil, and threw yellow sand upon themselves.

They took their places, they attacked, they retired, they rushed again to the conflict. They stood firm, and they yielded not. Long they bravely wrestled and fought; till at length Hercules by his might overcame Acheloüs and bore him to the ground. He pressed him down, and, while the fallen river-god lay panting for breath, the hero seized him by the neck.

Then did Acheloüs have recourse to his magic arts. Transforming himself into a serpent he escaped from the hero. He twisted his body into winding folds, and darted out his forked tongue with frightful hissings.

But Hercules laughed mockingly, and cried out: "Ah, Acheloüs! While yet in my cradle I strangled two serpents! And what art thou compared to the Hydra whose hundred heads I cut off? Every time I cut off one head two others grew in its place. Yet did I conquer that horror, in spite of its branching serpents that darted from every wound! Thinkest thou, then, that I fear thee, thou mimic snake?" And even as he spake he gripped, as with a pair of pincers, the back of the river-god's head.

And Acheloüs struggled in vain to escape. Then, again having recourse to his magic, he became a raging bull, and renewed the fight. But Hercules, that mighty hero, threw his huge arms over the brawny neck of the bull, and dragged him about. Then seizing hold of his horns, he bent his head to one side, and bearing down fastened them into the ground. And that was not enough, but with relentless hand he broke one of the horns, and tore it from Acheloüs's forehead.

The river-god returned to his own shape. He roared aloud with rage and pain, and hiding his mutilated head in his mantle, rushed from the hall and plunged into the swirling waters of his stream.

Then the goddess of Plenty, and all the Wood-Nymphs and Water-Nymphs came forward to greet the conqueror with song and dance. They took the huge horn of Acheloüs and heaped it high with the rich and glowing fruits and flowers of autumn. They wreathed it with vines and with clustering grapes, and bearing it aloft presented it to Hercules and his beautiful bride Deïanira.

And ever since that day has the Horn of Plenty gladdened men's hearts at Harvest-Time.

CHRISTMAS DAY

(DECEMBER 25)

LITTLE PICCOLA

AFTER CELIA THAXTER

IN the sunny land of France there lived many years ago a sweet little maid named Piccola.

Her father had died when she was a baby, and her mother was very poor and had to work hard all day in the fields for a few sous.

Little Piccola had no dolls and toys, and she was often hungry and cold, but she was never sad nor lonely.

What if there were no children for her to play with! What if she did not have fine clothes and beautiful toys! In summer there were always the birds in the forest, and the flowers in the fields and meadows, — the birds sang so sweetly, and the flowers were so bright and pretty!

In the winter when the ground was covered with snow, Piccola helped her mother, and knit long stockings of blue wool.

The snow-birds had to be fed with crumbs, if she could find any, and then, there was Christmas Day.

But one year her mother was ill and could not earn any money. Piccola worked hard all the day long, and sold the stockings which she knit, even when her own little bare feet were blue with the cold.

As Christmas Day drew near she said to her mother, "I wonder what the good Saint Nicholas will bring me this year. I cannot hang my stocking in the fireplace, but I shall put my wooden shoe on the hearth for him. He will not forget me, I am sure."

"Do not think of it this year, my dear child," replied her mother. "We must be glad if we have bread enough to eat."

But Piccola could not believe that the good saint would forget her. On Christmas Eve she put her little wooden patten on the hearth before the fire, and went to sleep to dream of Saint Nicholas.

As the poor mother looked at the little shoe, she thought how unhappy her dear child would be to find it empty in the morning, and wished that she had something, even if it were only a tiny cake, for a Christmas gift. There was nothing in the house but a few sous, and these must be saved to buy bread.

When the morning dawned Piccola awoke and ran to her shoe.

Saint Nicholas had come in the night. He had not forgotten the little child who had thought of him with such faith.

See what he had brought her. It lay in the

wooden patten, looking up at her with its two bright eyes, and chirping contentedly as she stroked its soft feathers.

A little swallow, cold and hungry, had flown into the chimney and down to the room, and had crept into the shoe for warmth.

Piccola danced for joy, and clasped the shivering swallow to her breast.

She ran to her mother's bedside. "Look, look!" she cried. "A Christmas gift, a gift from the good Saint Nicholas!" And she danced again in her little bare feet.

Then she fed and warmed the bird, and cared for it tenderly all winter long; teaching it to take crumbs from her hand and her lips, and to sit on her shoulder while she was working.

In the spring she opened the window for it to fly away, but it lived in the woods near by all summer, and came often in the early morning to sing its sweetest songs at her door.

THE STRANGER CHILD

A LEGEND

BY COUNT FRANZ POCCI (TRANSLATED)

THERE once lived a laborer who earned his daily bread by cutting wood. His wife and two children, a boy and girl, helped him with his work. The boy's name was Valentine, and the girl's,

Marie. They were obedient and pious and the joy and comfort of their poor parents.

One winter evening, this good family gathered about the table to eat their small loaf of bread, while the father read aloud from the Bible. Just as they sat down there came a knock on the window, and a sweet voice called: —

"O let me in! I am a little child, and I have nothing to eat, and no place to sleep in. I am so cold and hungry! Please, good people, let me in!"

Valentine and Marie sprang from the table and ran to open the door, saying: —

"Come in, poor child, we have but very little ourselves, not much more than thou hast, but what we have we will share with thee."

The stranger Child entered, and going to the fire began to warm his cold hands.

The children gave him a portion of their bread, and said: —

"Thou must be very tired; come, lie down in our bed, and we will sleep on the bench here before the fire."

Then answered the stranger Child: "May God in Heaven reward you for your kindness."

They led the little guest to their small room, laid him in their bed, and covered him closely, thinking to themselves: —

"Oh! how much we have to be thankful for! We have our nice warm room and comfortable bed, while this Child has nothing but the sky for a roof, and the earth for a couch."

When the parents went to their bed, Valentine and Marie lay down on the bench before the fire, and said one to the other: —

"The stranger Child is happy now, because he is so warm! Good-night!"

Then they fell asleep.

They had not slept many hours, when little Marie awoke, and touching her brother lightly, whispered: —

"Valentine, Valentine, wake up! wake up! Listen to the beautiful music at the window."

Valentine rubbed his eyes and listened. He heard the most wonderful singing and the sweet notes of many harps.

"Blessed Child,
Thee we greet,
With sound of harp
And singing sweet.

"Sleep in peace,
Child so bright,
We have watched thee
All the night.

"Blest the home
That holdeth Thee,
Peace, and love,
Its guardians be."

The children listened to the beautiful singing, and it seemed to fill them with unspeakable happiness. Then creeping to the window they looked out.

They saw a rosy light in the east, and, before the house in the snow, stood a number of little children holding golden harps and lutes in their hands, and dressed in sparkling, silver robes.

Full of wonder at this sight, Valentine and Marie continued to gaze out at the window, when they heard a sound behind them, and turning saw the stranger Child standing near. He was clad in a golden garment, and wore a glistening, golden crown upon his soft hair. Sweetly he spoke to the children: —

"I am the Christ Child, who wanders about the world seeking to bring joy and good things to loving children. Because you have lodged me this night I will leave with you my blessing."

As the Christ Child spoke He stepped from the door, and breaking off a bough from a fir tree that grew near, planted it in the ground, saying: —

"This bough shall grow into a tree, and every year it shall bear Christmas fruit for you."

Having said this He vanished from their sight, together with the silver-clad, singing children — the angels.

And, as Valentine and Marie looked on in wonder, the fir bough grew, and grew, and grew, into a stately Christmas Tree laden with golden apples, silver nuts, and lovely toys. And after that, every year at Christmas time, the Tree bore the same wonderful fruit.

And you, dear boys and girls, when you gather around your richly decorated trees, think of the two poor children who shared their bread with a stranger child, and be thankful.

SAINT CHRISTOPHER

A GOLDEN LEGEND

ENGLISHED BY WILLIAM CAXTON (ADAPTED)

CHRISTOPHER was a Canaanite, and he was of a right great stature, twelve cubits in height, and had a terrible countenance. And it is said that as he served and dwelled with the King of Canaan, it came in his mind that he would seek the greatest prince that was in the world, and him would he serve and obey.

So he went forth and came to a right great king, whom fame said was the greatest of the world. And when the king saw him he received him into his service, and made him to dwell in his court.

Upon a time a minstrel sang before him a song in which he named oft the devil. And the king, who was a Christian, when he heard him name the devil, made anon the sign of the cross.

And when Christopher saw that he marveled, and asked what the sign might mean. And because the king would not say, he said: "If thou tell me not, I shall no longer dwell with thee."

And then the King told him, saying: "Alway when I hear the devil named make I this sign lest he grieve or annoy me."

Then said Christopher to him: "Fearest thou the devil? Then is the devil more mighty and greater than thou art. I am then deceived, for I had supposed that I had found the most mighty and the most greatest lord in all the world! Fare thee well, for I will now go seek the devil to be my lord and I his servant."

So Christopher departed from this king and hastened to seek the devil. And as he went by a great desert he saw a company of knights, and one of them, a knight cruel and horrible, came to him and demanded whither he went.

And Christopher answered: "I go to seek the devil for to be my master."

Then said the knight: "I am he that thou seekest."

And then Christopher was glad and bound himself to be the devil's servant, and took him for his master and lord.

Now, as they went along the way they found there a cross, erect and standing. And anon as the devil saw the cross he was afeared and fled. And when Christopher saw that he marveled and demanded why he was afeared, and why he fled away. And the devil would not tell him in no wise.

Then Christopher said to him: "If thou wilt not tell me, I shall anon depart from thee and shall serve thee no more."

Wherefore the devil was forced to tell him and said: "There was a man called Christ, which was hanged on the cross, and when I see his sign I am sore afraid and flee from it."

To whom Christopher said: "Then he is greater and more mightier than thou, since thou art afraid of his sign, and I see well that I have labored in vain, and have not founden the greatest lord of the world. I will serve thee no longer, but I will go seek Christ."

And when Christopher had long sought where he should find Christ, at last he came into a great desert, to a hermit that dwelt there. And he inquired of him where Christ was to be found.

Then answered the hermit: "The king whom thou desirest to serve, requireth that thou must often fast."

Christopher said: "Require of me some other thing and I shall do it, but fast I may not."

And the hermit said: "Thou must then wake and make many prayers."

And Christopher said: "I do not know how to pray, so this I may not do."

And the hermit said: "Seest thou yonder deep

and wide river, in which many people have perished? Because thou art noble, and of high stature and strong of limb, so shalt thou live by the river and thou shalt bear over all people who pass that way. And this thing will be pleasing to our Lord Jesu Christ, whom thou desirest to serve, and I hope he shall show himself to thee."

Then said Christopher: "Certes, this service may I well do, and I promise Him to do it."

Then went Christopher to this river, and built himself there a hut. He carried a great pole in his hand, to support himself in the water, and bore over on his shoulders all manner of people to the other side. And there he abode, thus doing many days.

And on a time, as he slept in his hut, he heard the voice of a child which called him: —

"Christopher, Christopher, come out and bear me over."

Then he awoke and went out, but he found no man. And when he was again in his house he heard the same voice, crying: —

"Christopher, Christopher, come out and bear me over."

And he ran out and found nobody.

And the third time he was called and ran thither, and he found a Child by the brink of the river, which prayed him goodly to bear him over the water.

And then Christopher lifted up the Child on his shoulders, and took his staff, and entered into the river for to pass over. And the water of the river arose and swelled more and more; and the Child was heavy as lead, and always as Christopher went farther the water increased and grew more, and the Child more and more waxed heavy, insomuch that Christopher suffered great anguish and was afeared to be drowned.

And when he was escaped with great pain, and passed over the water, and set the Child aground, he said: —

"Child, thou hast put me in great peril. Thou weighest almost as I had all the world upon me. I might bear no greater burden."

And the Child answered: "Christopher, marvel thee nothing, for thou hast not only borne all the world upon thee, but thou hast borne Him that created and made all the world, upon thy shoulders. I am Jesu Christ the King whom thou servest. And that thou mayest know that I say the truth, set thy staff in the earth by thy house, and thou shalt see to-morn that it shall bear flowers and fruit."

And anon the Child vanished from his eyes.

And then Christopher set his staff in the earth, and when he arose on the morn, he found his staff bearing flowers, leaves, and dates.

THE CHRISTMAS ROSE

AN OLD LEGEND

BY LIZZIE DEAS (Adapted)

When the Magi laid their rich offerings of myrrh, frankincense, and gold, by the bed of the sleeping Christ Child, legend says that a shepherd maiden stood outside the door quietly weeping.

She, too, had sought the Christ Child. She, too, desired to bring him gifts. But she had nothing to offer, for she was very poor indeed. In vain she had searched the countryside over for one little flower to bring Him, but she could find neither bloom nor leaf, for the winter had been cold.

And as she stood there weeping, an angel passing saw her sorrow, and stooping he brushed aside the snow at her feet. And there sprang up on the spot a cluster of beautiful winter roses, — waxen white with pink tipped petals.

"Nor myrrh, nor frankincense, nor gold," said the angel, "is offering more meet for the Christ Child than these pure Christmas Roses."

Joyfully the shepherd maiden gathered the flowers and made her offering to the Holy Child.

THE WOODEN SHOES OF LITTLE WOLFF

BY FRANÇOIS COPPÉE (ADAPTED)

ONCE upon a time, — so long ago that the world has forgotten the date, — in a city of the North of Europe, — the name of which is so hard to pronounce that no one remembers it, — there was a little boy, just seven years old, whose name was Wolff. He was an orphan and lived with his aunt, a hard-hearted, avaricious old woman, who never kissed him but once a year, on New Year's Day; and who sighed with regret every time she gave him a bowlful of soup.

The poor little boy was so sweet-tempered that he loved the old woman in spite of her bad treatment, but he could not look without trembling at the wart, decorated with four gray hairs, which grew on the end of her nose.

As Wolff's aunt was known to have a house of her own and a woolen stocking full of gold, she did not dare to send her nephew to the school for the poor. But she wrangled so that the schoolmaster of the rich boys' school was forced to lower his price and admit little Wolff among his pupils. The bad schoolmaster was vexed to have a boy so meanly clad and who paid so little, and he punished little Wolff severely without cause, ridiculed him, and even incited against him his comrades, who were the sons of rich citizens. They made the orphan their drudge and mocked at him so much that the little boy was as miserable as the stones in the street, and hid himself away in corners to cry — when the Christmas season came.

On the Eve of the great Day the schoolmaster was to take all his pupils to the midnight mass, and then to conduct them home again to their parents' houses.

Now as the winter was very severe, and a quantity of snow had fallen within the past few days, the boys came to the place of meeting warmly wrapped up, with fur-lined caps drawn down over their ears, padded jackets, gloves and knitted mittens, and good strong shoes with thick soles. Only little Wolff presented himself shivering in his thin everyday clothes, and wearing on his feet socks and wooden shoes.

His naughty comrades tried to annoy him in every possible way, but the orphan was so busy warming his hands by blowing on them, and was suffering so much from chilblains, that he paid no heed to the taunts of the others. Then the band of boys, marching two by two, started for the parish church.

It was comfortable inside the church, which was brilliant with lighted tapers. And the pupils, made lively by the gentle warmth, the sound of the organ, and the singing of the choir, began to chatter in low tones. They boasted of the midnight treats awaiting them at home. The son of the Mayor had seen, before leaving the house, a monstrous goose larded with truffles so that it looked like a black-spotted leopard. Another boy told of the fir tree waiting for him, on the branches of which hung oranges, sugar-plums, and punchinellos. Then they talked about what the Christ Child would bring them, or what he would leave in their shoes which they would certainly be careful to place before the fire when they went to bed. And the eyes of the little rogues, lively as a crowd of mice, sparkled with delight as they thought of the many gifts they would find on waking, — the pink bags of burnt almonds, the bonbons, lead soldiers standing in rows, menageries, and magnificent jumping-jacks, dressed in purple and gold.

Little Wolff, alas! knew well that his miserly old aunt would send him to bed without any supper; but as he had been good and industrious all the year, he trusted that the Christ Child would not forget him, so he meant that night to set his wooden shoes on the hearth.

The midnight mass was ended. The worshipers hurried away, anxious to enjoy the treats awaiting them in their homes. The band of pupils, two by two, following the schoolmaster, passed out of the church.

Now, under the porch, seated on a stone bench, in the shadow of an arched niche, was a child asleep, — a little child dressed in a white garment and with bare feet exposed to the cold. He was not a beggar, for his dress was clean and new, and beside him upon the ground, tied in a cloth, were the tools of a carpenter's apprentice.

Under the light of the stars, his face, with its closed eyes, shone with an expression of divine sweetness, and his soft, curling blond hair seemed to form an aureole of light about his forehead. But his tender feet, blue with the cold on this cruel night of December, were pitiful to see!

The pupils so warmly clad and shod, passed with indifference before the unknown child. Some, the sons of the greatest men in the city, cast looks of scorn on the barefooted one. But little Wolff, coming last out of the church, stopped deeply moved before the beautiful, sleeping child.

"Alas!" said the orphan to himself, "how dreadful! This poor little one goes without stockings in weather so cold! And, what is worse, he has no shoe to leave beside him while he sleeps, so that the Christ Child may place something in it to comfort him in all his misery."

And carried away by his tender heart, little Wolff drew off the wooden shoe from his right foot, placed it before the sleeping child; and as best as he was able, now hopping, now limping,

DREW OFF THE WOODEN SHOE

and wetting his sock in the snow, he returned to his aunt.

"You good-for-nothing!" cried the old woman, full of rage as she saw that one of his shoes was gone. "What have you done with your shoe, little beggar?"

Little Wolff did not know how to lie, and, though shivering with terror as he saw the gray hairs on the end of her nose stand upright, he tried, stammering, to tell his adventure.

But the old miser burst into frightful laughter. "Ah! the sweet young master takes off his shoe for a beggar! Ah! master spoils a pair of shoes for a barefoot! This is something new, indeed! Ah! well, since things are so, I will place the shoe that is left in the fireplace, and to-night the Christ Child will put in a rod to whip you when you wake. And to-morrow you shall have nothing to eat but water and dry bread, and we shall see if the next time you will give away your shoe to the first vagabond that comes along."

And saying this the wicked woman gave him a box on each ear, and made him climb to his wretched room in the loft. There the heart-broken little one lay down in the darkness, and, drenching his pillow with tears, fell asleep.

But in the morning, when the old woman, awakened by the cold and shaken by her cough, descended to the kitchen, oh! wonder of wonders!

she saw the great fireplace filled with bright toys, magnificent boxes of sugar-plums, riches of all sorts, and in front of all this treasure, the wooden shoe which her nephew had given to the vagabond, standing beside the other shoe which she herself had placed there the night before, intending to put in it a handful of switches.

And as little Wolff, who had come running at the cries of his aunt, stood in speechless delight before all the splendid Christmas gifts, there came great shouts of laughter from the street.

The old woman and the little boy went out to learn what it was all about, and saw the gossips gathered around the public fountain. What could have happened? Oh, a most amusing and extraordinary thing! The children of all the rich men of the city, whose parents wished to surprise them with the most beautiful gifts, had found nothing but switches in their shoes!

Then the old woman and little Wolff remembered with alarm all the riches that were in their own fireplace, but just then they saw the pastor of the parish church arriving with his face full of perplexity.

Above the bench near the church door, in the very spot where the night before a child, dressed in white, with bare feet exposed to the great cold, had rested his sleeping head, the pastor had seen a golden circle wrought into the old stones. Then all the people knew that the beautiful, sleeping child, beside whom had lain the carpenter's tools, was the Christ Child himself, and that he had rewarded the faith and charity of little Wolff.

THE PINE TREE

BY HANS CHRISTIAN ANDERSEN (TRANSLATED)

I

WHEN IT WAS LITTLE

OUT in the woods stood such a nice little Pine Tree: he had a good place; the sun could get at him; there was fresh air enough; and round him grew many big comrades, both pines and firs. But the little Pine wanted so very much to be a grown-up tree.

He did not think of the warm sun and of the fresh air, he did not care for the little cottage-children who ran about and prattled when they were looking for wild strawberries and raspberries. Often they came with a whole jug full, or had their strawberries strung on a straw, and sat down near the little Tree and said, "Oh, what a nice little fellow!" This was what the Tree could not bear to hear.

The year after he had shot up a good deal, and the next year after he was still bigger; for with pine trees one can always tell by the shoots how many years old they are.

"Oh, were I but such a big tree as the others are," sighed the little Tree. "Then I could spread my branches so far, and with the tops look out into the wide world! Birds would build nests among my branches; and when there was a breeze, I could nod as grandly as the others there."

He had no delight at all in the sunshine, or in the birds, or the red clouds which morning and evening sailed above him.

When now it was winter and the snow all around lay glittering white, a hare would often come leaping along, and jump right over the little Tree. Oh, that made him so angry! But two winters went by, and with the third the Tree was so big that the hare had to go round it. "Oh, to grow, to grow, to become big and old, and be tall," thought the Tree: "that, after all, is the most delightful thing in the world!"

In autumn the wood-cutters always came and felled some of the largest trees. This happened every year, and the young Pine Tree, that was now quite well grown, trembled at the sight; for the great stately trees fell to the earth with noise and cracking, the branches were lopped off, and the trees looked quite bare, they were so long and thin; you would hardly know them for trees, and then they were laid on carts, and horses dragged them out of the wood.

Where did they go to? What became of them?

In spring, when the Swallow and the Stork came, the Tree asked them, "Don't you know where they have been taken? Have you not met them anywhere?"

The Swallow did not know anything about it; but the Stork looked doubtful, nodded his head, and said, "Yes; I have it; I met many new ships as I was flying from Egypt; on the ships were splendid masts, and I dare say it was they that smelt so of pine. I wish you joy, for they lifted themselves on high in fine style!"

"Oh, were I but old enough to fly across the sea! How does the sea really look? and what is it like?"

"Aye, that takes a long time to tell," said the Stork, and away he went.

"Rejoice in thy youth!" said the Sunbeams, "rejoice in thy hearty growth, and in the young life that is in thee!"

And the Wind kissed the Tree, and the Dew wept tears over him, but the Pine Tree understood it not.

II

CHRISTMAS IN THE WOODS

When Christmas came, quite young trees were cut down; trees which were not even so large or of the same age as this Pine Tree, who had no rest or peace, but always wanted to be off. These young trees, and they were always the finest looking, always kept their branches; they were laid on carts, and the horses drew them out of the wood.

"Where are they going to?" asked the Pine Tree. "They are not taller than I; there was one, indeed, that was much shorter; — and why do they keep all their branches? Where are they carrying them to?"

"We know! we know!" chirped the Sparrows. "We have peeped in at the windows down there in the town. We know where they are carrying them to. Oh, they are going to where it is as bright and splendid as you can think! We peeped through the windows, and saw them planted in the middle of the warm room, and dressed with the most splendid things, — with gilded apples, with gingerbread, with toys and many hundred lights!"

"And then?" asked the Pine Tree, and he trembled in every bough. "And then? What happens then?"

"We did not see anything more: it beat everything!"

"I wonder if I am to sparkle like that!" cried the Tree, rejoicing. "That is still better than to go over the sea! How I do suffer for very longing! Were Christmas but come! I am now tall, and stretch out like the others that were carried off last year! Oh, if I were already on the cart! I wish I were in the warm room with all the splendor and brightness. And then? Yes; then will come something better, something still grander, or why should they dress me out so? There must come something better, something still grander, — but what? Oh, how I long, how I suffer! I do not know myself what is the matter with me!"

"Rejoice in us!" said the Air and the Sunlight; "rejoice in thy fresh youth out here in the open air!"

But the Tree did not rejoice at all; he grew and grew; and he stood there in all his greenery; rich green was he winter and summer. People that saw him said, "That's a fine tree!" and toward Christmas he was the first that was cut down. The axe struck deep into the very pith; the Tree fell to the earth with a sigh: he felt a pang — it was like a swoon; he could not think of happiness, for he was sad at being parted from his home, from the place where he had sprung up. He well knew that he should never see his dear old comrades, the little bushes and flowers around him, any more; perhaps not even the birds! The setting off was not at all pleasant.

The Tree only came to himself when he was unloaded in a courtyard with other trees, and heard a man say, "That one is splendid! we don't want the others." Then two servants came in rich livery and carried the Pine Tree into a large and splendid room. Portraits were hanging on the walls, and near the white porcelain stove stood two large Chinese vases with lions on the covers. There, too, were large easy-chairs, silken sofas, large tables full of picture-books, and full of toys worth a hundred times a hundred dollars — at least so the children said. And the Pine Tree was stuck upright in a cask filled with sand: but no one could see that it was a cask, for green cloth was hung all around it, and it stood on a gayly colored carpet. Oh, how the Tree quivered! What was to happen? The servants, as well as the young ladies, dressed it. On one branch there hung little nets cut out of colored paper; each net was filled with sugar-plums; gilded apples and walnuts hung as though they grew tightly there, and more than a hundred little red, blue, and white tapers were stuck fast into the branches. Dolls that looked for all the world like men — the Tree had never seen such things before — fluttered among the leaves, and at the very top a large star of gold tinsel was fixed. It was really splendid — splendid beyond telling.

"This evening!" said they all; "how it will shine this evening!"

"Oh," thought the Tree, "if it were only evening! If the tapers were but lighted! And then I wonder what will happen! I wonder if the other trees from the forest will come to look at me!

I wonder if the sparrows will beat against the window-panes! I wonder if I shall take root here, and stand dressed so winter and summer!"

Aye, aye, much he knew about the matter! but he had a real back-ache for sheer longing, and a back-ache with trees is the same thing as a headache with us.

III

CHRISTMAS IN THE HOUSE

The candles were now lighted. What brightness! What splendor! The Tree trembled so in every bough that one of the tapers set fire to a green branch. It blazed up splendidly.

Now the Tree did not even dare to tremble. That was a fright! He was so afraid of losing something of all his finery, that he was quite confused amidst the glare and brightness; and now both folding-doors opened, and a troop of children rushed in as if they would tip the whole Tree over. The older folks came quietly behind; the little ones stood quite still, but only for a moment; then they shouted so that the whole place echoed their shouts, they danced round the Tree, and one present after another was pulled off.

"What are they about?" thought the Tree. "What is to happen now?" And the lights burned down to the very branches, and as they burned down they were put out one after the other, and then the children had leave to plunder the Tree. Oh, they rushed upon it so that it cracked in all its limbs; if its tip-top with the gold star on it had not been fastened to the ceiling, it would have tumbled over.

The children danced about with their pretty toys; no one looked at the Tree except the old nurse, who peeped in among the branches; but it was only to see if there was a fig or an apple that had been forgotten.

"A story! a story!" cried the children, and they dragged a little fat man toward the Tree. He sat down under it, and said, "Now we are in the shade, and the Tree can hear very well too. But I shall tell only one story. Now which will you have: that about Ivedy-Avedy, or about Klumpy-Dumpy who tumbled downstairs, and came to the throne after all, and married the princess?"

"Ivedy-Avedy," cried some; "Klumpy-Dumpy," cried the others. There was such a bawling and screaming! — the Pine Tree alone was silent, and he thought to himself, "Am I not to bawl with the rest? — am I to do nothing whatever?" — for he was one of them, and he had done what he had to do.

And the man told about Klumpy-Dumpy who tumbled downstairs, and came to the throne after all, and married the princess. And the children clapped their hands, and cried out, "Go on, go on!" They wanted to hear about Ivedy-Avedy too, but the little man only told them about Klumpy-Dumpy. The Pine Tree stood quite still and thoughtful: the birds in the wood had never told anything like this. "Klumpy-Dumpy fell downstairs, and yet he married the princess! Yes, yes, that's the way of the world!" thought the Pine Tree, and he believed it all, because it was such a nice man who told the story.

"Well, well! who knows, perhaps I may fall downstairs, too, and so get a princess!" And he looked forward with joy to the next day when he should be decked out with lights and toys, fruits and tinsel.

"To-morrow I won't tremble!" thought the Pine Tree. "I will enjoy to the full all my splendor! To-morrow I shall hear again the story of Klumpy-Dumpy, and perhaps that of Ivedy-Avedy too." And the whole night the Tree stood still in deep thought.

In the morning the servant and the maid came in.

IV

IN THE ATTIC

"Now all the finery will begin again," thought the Pine. But they dragged him out of the room, and up the stairs into the attic; and here in a dark corner, where no daylight could enter, they left him. "What's the meaning of this?" thought the Tree. "What am I to do here? What shall I see and hear now, I wonder?" And he leaned against the wall and stood and thought and thought. And plenty of time he had, for days and nights passed, and nobody came up; and when at last somebody did come, it was only to put some great trunks in the corner. There stood the Tree quite hidden; it seemed as if he had been entirely forgotten.

"'T is now winter out-of-doors!" thought the Tree. "The earth is hard and covered with snow; men cannot plant me now; therefore I have been put up here under cover till spring! How thoughtful that is! How good men are, after all! If it were not so dark here, and so terribly lonely! Not even a hare. Out there it was so pleasant in the woods, when the snow was on the ground, and the hare leaped by; yes — even when he jumped over me; but I did not like it then. It is terribly lonely here!"

"Squeak! squeak!" said a little Mouse at the same moment, peeping out of his hole. And then another little one came. They snuffed about the Pine Tree, and rustled among the branches.

"It is dreadfully cold," said the little Mouse. "But for that, it would be delightful here, old Pine, would n't it!"

"I am by no means old," said the Pine Tree. "There are many a good deal older than I am."

"Where do you come from?" asked the Mice; "and what can you do?" They were so very curious. "Tell us about the most beautiful spot on earth. Have you been there? Were you ever in the larder, where cheeses lie on the shelves, and hams hang from above; where one dances about on tallow candles; where one goes in lean and comes out fat?"

"I don't know that place," said the Tree. "But I know the wood where the sun shines, and where the little birds sing."

And then he told his story from his youth up; and the little Mice had never heard the like before; and they listened and said, —

"Well, to be sure! How much you have seen! How happy you must have been!"

"I!" said the Pine Tree, and he thought over what he had himself told. "Yes, really those were happy times." And then he told about Christmas Eve, when he was decked out with cakes and candles.

"Oh," said the little Mice, "how lucky you have been, old Pine Tree!"

"I am not at all old," said he. "I came from the wood this winter; I am in my prime, and am only rather short of my age."

"What delightful stories you know!" said the

Mice: and the next night they came with four other little Mice, who were to hear what the Tree had to tell; and the more he told, the more plainly he remembered all himself; and he thought: "That was a merry time! But it can come! it can come! Klumpy-Dumpy fell down stairs, and yet he got a princess! Maybe I can get a princess too!" And all of a sudden he thought of a nice little Birch Tree growing out in the woods: to the Pine, that would be a really charming princess.

"Who is Klumpy-Dumpy?" asked the little Mice.

So then the Pine Tree told the whole fairy tale, for he could remember every single word of it; and the little Mice jumped for joy up to the very top of the Tree. Next night two more Mice came, and on Sunday two Rats, even; but they said the stories were not amusing, which vexed the little Mice, because they, too, now began to think them not so very amusing either.

"Do you know only that one story?" asked the Rats.

"Only that one!" answered the Tree. "I heard it on my happiest evening; but I did not then know how happy I was."

"It is a very stupid story! Don't you know one about bacon and tallow candles? Can't you tell any larder-stories?"

"No," said the Tree.

"Thank you, then," said the Rats; and they went home.

At last the little Mice stayed away also; and the Tree sighed: "After all, it was very pleasant when the sleek little Mice sat round me and heard what I told them. Now that too is over. But I will take good care to enjoy myself when I am brought out again."

But when was that to be? Why, it was one morning when there came a number of people and set to work in the loft. The trunks were moved, the tree was pulled out and thrown down; they knocked him upon the floor, but a man drew him at once toward the stairs, where the daylight shone.

V

OUT OF DOORS AGAIN

"Now life begins again," thought the Tree. He felt the fresh air, the first sunbeam, — and now he was out in the courtyard. All passed so quickly that the Tree quite forgot to look to himself, there was so much going on around him. The court adjoined a garden, and all was in flower; the roses hung over the fence, so fresh and smelling so sweetly; the lindens were in blossom, the Swallows flew by, and said, "Quirre-virre-vit! my husband is come!" But it was not the Pine Tree that they meant.

"Now, I shall really live," said he with joy, and spread out his branches; dear! dear! they were all dry and yellow. It was in a corner among weeds and nettles that he lay. The golden star of tinsel was still on top of the Tree, and shone in the bright sunshine.

In the courtyard a few of the merry children were playing who had danced at Christmas round the Tree, and were so glad at the sight of him. One of the littlest ran and tore off the golden star.

"See what is still on the ugly old Christmas Tree!" said he, and he trampled on the branches, so that they cracked under his feet.

And the Tree saw all the beauty of the flowers, and the freshness in the garden; he saw himself, and he wished he had stayed in his dark corner in the attic: he thought of his fresh youth in the wood, of the merry Christmas Eve, and of the little Mice who had heard so gladly the story of Klumpy-Dumpy.

"Gone! gone!" said the poor Tree. "Had I but been happy when I could be. Gone! gone!"

And the gardener's boy came and chopped the Tree into small pieces; there was a whole heap lying there. The wood flamed up finely under the large brewing kettle, and it sighed so deeply! Each sigh was like a little shot. So the children ran to where it lay and sat down before the fire, and peeped in at the blaze, and shouted "Piff! paff!" But at every snap there was a deep sigh. The Tree was thinking of summer days in the wood, and of winter nights when the stars shone; it was thinking of Christmas Eve and Klumpy-Dumpy, the only fairy tale it had heard and knew how to tell, — and so the Tree burned out.

The boys played about in the court, and the youngest wore the gold star on his breast which the Tree had worn on the happiest evening of his life. Now, that was gone, the Tree was gone, and gone too was the story. All, all was gone, and that's the way with all stories.

THE CHRISTMAS CUCKOO

BY FRANCES BROWNE (ADAPTED)

ONCE upon a time there stood in the midst of a bleak moor, in the North Country, a certain village. All its inhabitants were poor, for their fields were barren, and they had little trade; but the poorest of them all were two brothers called Scrub and Spare, who followed the cobbler's craft. Their hut was built of clay and wattles. The door was low and always open, for there was no window. The roof did not entirely keep out the rain and the only thing comfortable was a wide fireplace, for which the brothers could never find wood enough to make sufficient fire. There they worked in most brotherly friendship, though with little encouragement.

On one unlucky day a new cobbler arrived in the village. He had lived in the capital city of the kingdom and, by his own account, cobbled for the queen and the princesses. His awls were sharp, his lasts were new; he set up his stall in a neat cottage with two windows. The villagers soon found out that one patch of his would outwear two of the brothers'. In short, all the mending left Scrub and Spare, and went to the new cobbler.

The season had been wet and cold, their barley did not ripen well, and the cabbages never half-closed in the garden. So the brothers were poor that winter, and when Christmas came they had nothing to feast on but a barley loaf and a piece of rusty bacon. Worse than that, the snow was very deep and they could get no firewood.

Their hut stood at the end of the village; beyond it spread the bleak moor, now all white and silent. But that moor had once been a forest; great roots of old trees were still to be found in it, loosened from the soil and laid bare by the winds and rains. One of these, a rough, gnarled log, lay hard by their door, the half of it above the snow, and Spare said to his brother: —

"Shall we sit here cold on Christmas while the great root lies yonder? Let us chop it up for fire wood, the work will make us warm."

"No," said Scrub, "it's not right to chop wood on Christmas; besides, that root is too hard to be broken with any hatchet."

"Hard or not, we must have a fire," replied Spare. "Come, brother, help me in with it. Poor as we are there is nobody in the village will have such a yule log as ours."

Scrub liked a little grandeur, and, in hopes of having a fine yule log, both brothers strained and strove with all their might till, between pulling and pushing, the great old root was safe on the hearth, and beginning to crackle and blaze with the red embers.

In high glee the cobblers sat down to their bread and bacon. The door was shut, for there was nothing but cold moonlight and snow outside; but the hut, strewn with fir boughs and ornamented with holly, looked cheerful as the ruddy blaze flared up and rejoiced their hearts.

Then suddenly from out the blazing root they heard: "Cuckoo! cuckoo!" as plain as ever the spring-bird's voice came over the moor on a May morning.

"What is that?" said Scrub, terribly frightened; "it is something bad!"

"Maybe not," said Spare.

And out of the deep hole at the side of the root, which the fire had not reached, flew a large, gray cuckoo, and lit on the table before them. Much as the cobblers had been surprised, they were still more so when it said: —

"Good gentlemen, what season is this?"

"It's Christmas," said Spare.

"Then a merry Christmas to you!" said the cuckoo. "I went to sleep in the hollow of that old root one evening last summer, and never woke till the heat of your fire made me think it was summer again. But now since you have burned my lodging, let me stay in your hut till the spring comes round, — I only want a hole to sleep in, and when I go on my travels next summer be assured I will bring you some present for your trouble."

"Stay and welcome," said Spare, while Scrub sat wondering if it were something bad or not.

"I'll make you a good warm hole in the thatch," said Spare. "But you must be hungry after that long sleep, — here is a slice of barley bread. Come help us to keep Christmas!"

The cuckoo ate up the slice, drank water from a brown jug, and flew into a snug hole which Spare scooped for it in the thatch of the hut.

Scrub said he was afraid it would n't be lucky; but as it slept on and the days passed he forgot his fears.

So the snow melted, the heavy rains came, the cold grew less, the days lengthened, and one sunny morning the brothers were awakened by the cuckoo shouting its own cry to let them know the spring had come.

"Now I'm going on my travels," said the bird, "over the world to tell men of the spring. There is no country where trees bud, or flowers bloom, that I will not cry in before the year goes round. Give me another slice of barley bread to help me on my journey, and tell me what present I shall bring you at the twelvemonth's end."

Scrub would have been angry with his brother for cutting so large a slice, their store of barley being low, but his mind was occupied with what present it would be most prudent to ask for.

"There are two trees hard by the well that lies at the world's end," said the cuckoo; "one of them is called the golden tree, for its leaves are all of beaten gold. Every winter they fall into the well with a sound like scattered coin, and I know not what becomes of them. As for the other, it is always green like a laurel. Some call it the wise, and some the merry, tree. Its leaves never fall, but they that get one of them keep a blithe heart in spite of all misfortunes, and can make themselves as merry in a hut as in a palace."

"Good master cuckoo, bring me a leaf off that tree!" cried Spare.

"Now, brother, don't be a fool!" said Scrub; "think of the leaves of beaten gold! Dear master cuckoo, bring me one of them!"

Before another word could be spoken the cuckoo had flown out of the open door, and was shouting its spring cry over moor and meadow.

The brothers were poorer than ever that year. Nobody would send them a single shoe to mend, and Scrub and Spare would have left the village but for their barley-field and their cabbage-garden. They sowed their barley, planted their cabbage, and, now that their trade was gone, worked in the rich villagers' fields to make out a scanty living.

So the seasons came and passed; spring, summer, harvest, and winter followed each other as they have done from the beginning. At the end of the latter Scrub and Spare had grown so poor and ragged that their old neighbors forgot to invite them to wedding feasts or merrymakings, and the brothers thought the cuckoo had forgotten them, too, when at daybreak on the first of April they heard a hard beak knocking at their door, and a voice crying: —

"Cuckoo! cuckoo! Let me in with my presents!"

Spare ran to open the door, and in came the cuckoo, carrying on one side of its bill a golden leaf larger than that of any tree in the North Country; and in the other side of its bill, one like that of the common laurel, only it had a fresher green.

"Here," it said, giving the gold to Scrub and the green to Spare, "it is a long carriage from the world's end. Give me a slice of barley bread, for I must tell the North Country that the spring has come."

Scrub did not grudge the thickness of that slice, though it was cut from their last loaf. So much gold had never been in the cobbler's hands before, and he could not help exulting over his brother.

"See the wisdom of my choice," he said, holding up the large leaf of gold. "As for yours, as good might be plucked from any hedge, I wonder a sensible bird would carry the like so far."

"Good master cobbler," cried the cuckoo, finishing its slice, "your conclusions are more hasty than courteous. If your brother is disappointed this time, I go on the same journey every year, and for your hospitable entertainment will think it no trouble to bring each of you whichever leaf you desire."

"Darling cuckoo," cried Scrub, "bring me a golden one."

And Spare, looking up from the green leaf on which he gazed as though it were a crown-jewel, said: —

"Be sure to bring me one from the merry tree."

And away flew the cuckoo.

"This is the feast of All Fools, and it ought to be your birthday," said Scrub. "Did ever man fling away such an opportunity of getting rich? Much good your merry leaves will do in the midst of rags and poverty!"

But Spare laughed at him, and answered with quaint old proverbs concerning the cares that come with gold, till Scrub, at length getting angry, vowed his brother was not fit to live with a respectable man; and taking his lasts, his awls, and his golden leaf, he left the wattle hut, and went to tell the villagers.

They were astonished at the folly of Spare, and charmed with Scrub's good sense, particularly when he showed them the golden leaf, and told that the cuckoo would bring him one every spring.

The new cobbler immediately took him into partnership; the greatest people sent him their shoes to mend. Fairfeather, a beautiful village maiden, smiled graciously upon him; and in the course of that summer they were married, with a grand wedding feast, at which the whole village danced except Spare, who was not invited, because the bride could not bear his low-mindedness, and his brother thought him a disgrace to the family.

As for Scrub he established himself with Fairfeather in a cottage close by that of the new cobbler, and quite as fine. There he mended shoes to everybody's satisfaction, had a scarlet coat and a fat goose for dinner on holidays. Fairfeather, too, had a crimson gown, and fine blue ribbons; but neither she nor Scrub was content, for to buy this grandeur the golden leaf had to be broken and parted with piece by piece, so the last morsel was gone before the cuckoo came with another.

Spare lived on in the old hut, and worked in the cabbage-garden. (Scrub had got the barley-field because he was the elder.) Every day his coat grew more ragged, and the hut more weather-beaten; but people remarked that he never looked sad or sour. And the wonder was that, from the time any one began to keep his company, he or she grew kinder, happier, and content.

Every first of April the cuckoo came tapping at their doors with the golden leaf for Scrub, and the green for Spare. Fairfeather would have entertained it nobly with wheaten bread and honey, for she had some notion of persuading it to bring two golden leaves instead of one; but the cuckoo flew away to eat barley bread with Spare, saying it was not fit company for fine people, and liked the old hut where it slept so snugly from Christmas till spring.

Scrub spent the golden leaves, and remained always discontented; and Spare kept the merry ones.

I do not know how many years passed in this manner, when a certain great lord, who owned that village, came to the neighborhood. His castle stood on the moor. It was ancient and strong, with high towers and a deep moat. All the country as far as one could see from the highest turret belonged to its lord; but he had not been there for twenty years, and would not have come then only he was melancholy. And there he lived in a very bad temper. The servants said nothing would please him, and the villagers put on their worst clothes lest he should raise their rents.

But one day in the harvest-time His Lordship chanced to meet Spare gathering water-cresses at a meadow stream, and fell into talk with the cobbler. How it was nobody could tell, but from that hour the great lord cast away his melancholy. He forgot all his woes, and went about with a noble train, hunting, fishing, and making merry in his hall, where all travelers were entertained, and all the poor were welcome.

This strange story spread through the North Country, and great company came to the cobbler's hut, — rich men who had lost their money, poor men who had lost their friends, beauties who had grown old, wits who had gone out of fashion, — all came to talk with Spare, and, whatever their troubles had been, all went home merry.

The rich gave him presents, the poor gave him thanks. Spare's coat ceased to be ragged, he had bacon with his cabbage, and the villagers began to think there was some sense in him.

By this time his fame had reached the capital city, and even the court. There were a great many discontented people there; and the king had lately fallen into ill humor because a neighboring princess, with seven islands for her dowry, would not marry his eldest son.

So a royal messenger was sent to Spare, with a velvet mantle, a diamond ring, and a command that he should repair to court immediately.

"To-morrow is the first of April," said Spare, "and I will go with you two hours after sunrise."

The messenger lodged all night at the castle, and the cuckoo came at sunrise with the merry leaf.

"Court is a fine place," it said, when the cobbler told it he was going, "but I cannot come there; they would lay snares and catch me; so be careful of the leaves I have brought you, and give me a farewell slice of barley bread."

Spare was sorry to part with the cuckoo, little as he had of its company, but he gave it a slice which would have broken Scrub's heart in former times, it was so thick and large. And having sewed up the leaves in the lining of his leather doublet, he set out with the messenger on his way to court.

His coming caused great surprise there. Everybody wondered what the king could see in such a common-looking man; but scarcely had His

Majesty conversed with him half an hour, when the princess and her seven islands were forgotten and orders given that a feast for all comers should be spread in the banquet hall.

The princes of the blood, the great lords and ladies, the ministers of state, after that discoursed with Spare, and the more they talked the lighter grew their hearts, so that such changes had never been seen at court.

The lords forgot their spites and the ladies their envies, the princes and ministers made friends among themselves, and the judges showed no favor.

As for Spare, he had a chamber assigned him in the palace, and a seat at the king's table. One sent him rich robes, and another costly jewels; but in the midst of all his grandeur he still wore the leathern doublet, and continued to live at the king's court, happy and honored, and making all others merry and content.

THE CHRISTMAS FAIRY OF STRASBURG

A GERMAN FOLK-TALE

BY J. STIRLING COYNE (ADAPTED)

ONCE, long ago, there lived near the ancient city of Strasburg, on the river Rhine, a young and handsome count, whose name was Otto. As the years flew by he remained unwed, and never so much as cast a glance at the fair maidens of the country round; for this reason people began to call him "Stone-Heart."

It chanced that Count Otto, on one Christmas Eve, ordered that a great hunt should take place in the forest surrounding his castle. He and his guests and his many retainers rode forth, and the chase became more and more exciting. It led through thickets, and over pathless tracts of forest, until at length Count Otto found himself separated from his companions.

He rode on by himself until he came to a spring of clear, bubbling water, known to the people around as the "Fairy Well." Here Count Otto dismounted. He bent over the spring and began to lave his hands in the sparkling tide, but to his wonder he found that though the weather was cold and frosty, the water was warm and delightfully caressing. He felt a glow of joy pass through his veins, and, as he plunged his hands deeper, he fancied that his right hand was grasped by another, soft and small, which gently slipped from his finger the gold ring he always wore. And, lo! when he drew out his hand, the gold ring was gone.

Full of wonder at this mysterious event, the count mounted his horse and returned to his castle, resolving in his mind that the very next day he would have the Fairy Well emptied by his servants.

He retired to his room, and, throwing himself just as he was upon his couch, tried to sleep; but the strangeness of the adventure kept him restless and wakeful.

Suddenly he heard the hoarse baying of the watch-hounds in the courtyard, and then the creaking of the drawbridge, as though it were being lowered. Then came to his ear the patter of many small feet on the stone staircase, and next he heard indistinctly the sound of light footsteps in the chamber adjoining his own.

Count Otto sprang from his couch, and as he did so there sounded a strain of delicious music, and the door of his chamber was flung open. Hurrying into the next room, he found himself in the midst of numberless Fairy beings, clad in gay and sparkling robes. They paid no heed to him, but began to dance, and laugh, and sing, to the sound of mysterious music.

In the center of the apartment stood a splendid Christmas Tree, the first ever seen in that country. Instead of toys and candles there hung on its lighted boughs diamond stars, pearl necklaces, bracelets of gold ornamented with colored jewels, aigrettes of rubies and sapphires, silken belts embroidered with Oriental pearls, and daggers mounted in gold and studded with the rarest gems. The whole tree swayed, sparkled, and glittered in the radiance of its many lights.

Count Otto stood speechless, gazing at all this wonder, when suddenly the Fairies stopped dancing and fell back, to make room for a lady of dazzling beauty who came slowly toward him.

She wore on her raven-black tresses a golden diadem set with jewels. Her hair flowed down upon a robe of rosy satin and creamy velvet. She stretched out two small, white hands to the count and addressed him in sweet, alluring tones: —

"Dear Count Otto," said she, "I come to return your Christmas visit. I am Ernestine, the Queen of the Fairies. I bring you something you lost in the Fairy Well."

And as she spoke she drew from her bosom a golden casket, set with diamonds, and placed it in his hands. He opened it eagerly and found within his lost gold ring.

Carried away by the wonder of it all, and overcome by an irresistible impulse, the count pressed the Fairy Ernestine to his heart, while she, holding him by the hand, drew him into the magic mazes of the dance. The mysterious music floated through the room, and the rest of that Fairy company circled and whirled around the Fairy Queen and Count Otto, and then gradually dissolved into a mist of many colors, leaving the count and his beautiful guest alone.

Then the young man, forgetting all his former coldness toward the maidens of the country round about, fell on his knees before the Fairy and besought her to become his bride. At last she consented on the condition that he should never speak the word "death" in her presence.

The next day the wedding of Count Otto and Ernestine, Queen of the Fairies, was celebrated with great pomp and magnificence, and the two continued to live happily for many years.

Now it happened on a time, that the count and his Fairy wife were to hunt in the forest around the castle. The horses were saddled and bridled, and standing at the door, the company waited, and the count paced the hall in great impatience; but still the Fairy Ernestine tarried long in her chamber. At length she appeared at the door of the hall, and the count addressed her in anger.

"You have kept us waiting so long," he cried, "that you would make a good messenger to send for Death!"

Scarcely had he spoken the forbidden and fatal word, when the Fairy, uttering a wild cry, vanished from his sight. In vain Count Otto, overwhelmed with grief and remorse, searched the castle and the Fairy Well, no trace could he find of his beautiful, lost wife but the imprint of her delicate hand set in the stone arch above the castle gate.

Years passed by, and the Fairy Ernestine did not return. The count continued to grieve.

Every Christmas Eve he set up a lighted tree in the room where he had first met the Fairy, hoping in vain that she would return to him.

Time passed and the count died. The castle fell into ruins. But to this day may be seen above the massive gate, deeply sunken in the stone arch the impress of a small and delicate hand.

And such, say the good folk of Strasburg, was the origin of the Christmas Tree.

THE THREE PURSES

A LEGEND

BY WILLIAM S. WALSH (ADAPTED)

WHEN Saint Nicholas was Bishop of Myra, there were among his people three beautiful maidens, daughters of a nobleman. Their father was so poor that he could not afford to give them dowries, and as in that land no maid might marry without a dowry, so these three maidens could not wed the youths who loved them.

At last the father became so very poor that he no longer had money with which to buy food or clothes for his daughters, and he was overcome by shame and sorrow. As for the daughters they wept continually, for they were both cold and hungry.

One day Saint Nicholas heard of the sad state of this noble family. So at night, when the maidens were asleep, and the father was watching, sorrowful and lonely, the good saint took a handful of gold, and, tying it in a purse, set off for the nobleman's house. Creeping to the open window he threw the purse into the chamber, so that it fell on the bed of the sleeping maidens.

The father picked up the purse, and when he opened it and saw the gold, he rejoiced greatly, and awakened his daughters. He gave most of the gold to his eldest child for a dowry, and thus she was enabled to wed the young man whom she loved.

A few days later Saint Nicholas filled another purse with gold, and, as before, went by night to the nobleman's house, and tossed the purse through the open window. Thus the second daughter was enabled to marry the young man whom she loved.

Now, the nobleman felt very grateful to the unknown one who threw purses of gold into his room and he longed to know who his benefactor was and to thank him. So the next night he watched beneath the open window. And when all was dark, lo! good Saint Nicholas came for the third time, carrying a silken purse filled with gold, and as he was about to throw it on the youngest maiden's bed, the nobleman caught him by his robe, crying: —

"Oh, good Saint Nicholas! why do you hide yourself thus?"

And he kissed the saint's hands and feet, but Saint Nicholas, overcome with confusion at having his good deed discovered, begged the nobleman to tell no man what had happened.

Thus the nobleman's third daughter was enabled to marry the young man whom she loved; and she and her father and her two sisters lived happily for the remainder of their lives.

THE THUNDER OAK

A SCANDINAVIAN LEGEND

WILLIAM S. WALSH AND OTHER SOURCES

WHEN the heathen raged through the forests of the ancient Northland there grew a giant tree branching with huge limbs toward the clouds. It was the Thunder Oak of the war-god Thor.

Thither, under cover of night, heathen priests were wont to bring their victims — both men and beasts — and slay them upon the altar of the thunder-god. There in the darkness was wrought many an evil deed, while human blood was poured forth and watered the roots of that gloomy tree, from whose branches depended the mistletoe, the fateful plant that sprang from the blood-fed veins of the oak. So gloomy and terror-ridden was the spot on which grew the tree that no beasts of field or forest would lodge beneath its dark branches, nor would birds nest or perch among its gnarled limbs.

Long, long ago, on a white Christmas Eve, Thor's priests held their winter rites beneath the Thunder Oak. Through the deep snow of the dense forest hastened throngs of heathen folk, all intent on keeping the mystic feast of the mighty Thor. In the hush of the night the folk gathered in the glade where stood the tree. Closely they pressed around the great altar-stone under the overhanging boughs where stood the white-robed priests. Clearly shone the moonlight on all.

Then from the altar flashed upward the sacrificial flames, casting their lurid glow on the straining faces of the human victims awaiting the blow of the priest's knife.

But the knife never fell, for from the silent avenues of the dark forest came the good Saint Winfred and his people. Swiftly the saint drew from his girdle a shining axe. Fiercely he smote the Thunder Oak, hewing a deep gash in its trunk. And while the heathen folk gazed in horror and wonder, the bright blade of the axe circled faster and faster around Saint Winfred's head, and the flakes of wood flew far and wide from the deepening cut in the body of the tree.

Suddenly there was heard overhead the sound of a mighty, rushing wind. A whirling blast struck the tree. It gripped the oak from its foundations. Backward it fell like a tower, groaning as it split into four pieces.

But just behind it, unharmed by the ruin, stood a young fir tree, pointing its green spire to heaven.

Saint Winfred dropped his axe, and turned to speak to the people. Joyously his voice rang out through the crisp, winter air: —

"This little tree, a young child of the forest, shall be your holy tree to-night. It is the tree of peace, for your houses are built of fir. It is the sign of endless life, for its leaves are forever green. See how it points upward to heaven! Let this be called the tree of the Christ Child. Gather about it, not in the wildwood, but in your own homes. There it will shelter no deeds of blood, but loving gifts and rites of kindness. So shall the peace of the White Christ reign in your hearts!"

And with songs of joy the multitude of heathen folk took up the little fir tree and bore it to the house of their chief, and there with good will and peace they kept the holy Christmastide.

THE CHRISTMAS THORN OF GLASTONBURY

A LEGEND OF ANCIENT BRITAIN

ADAPTED FROM WILLIAM OF MALMESBURY AND OTHER SOURCES

THERE is a golden Christmas legend and it relates how Joseph of Arimathea — that good man and just, who laid our Lord in his own sepulcher, was persecuted by Pontius Pilate, and how he fled from Jerusalem carrying with him the Holy Grail hidden beneath a cloth of samite, mystical and white.

For many moons he wandered, leaning on his staff cut from a white-thorn bush. He passed over raging seas and dreary wastes, he wandered through trackless forests, climbed rugged mountains, and forded many floods. At last he came to Gaul where the Apostle Philip was preaching the glad tidings to the heathen. And there Joseph abode for a little space.

Now, upon a night while Joseph lay asleep in his hut, he was wakened by a radiant light. And as he gazed with wondering eyes he saw an angel standing by his couch, wrapped in a cloud of incense.

"Joseph of Arimathea," said the angel, "cross thou over into Britain and preach the glad tidings to King Arvigarus. And there, where a Christmas miracle shall come to pass, do thou build the first Christian church in that land."

And while Joseph lay perplexed and wondering in his heart what answer he should make, the angel vanished from his sight.

Then Joseph left his hut and calling the Apostle Philip, gave him the angel's message. And, when morning dawned, Philip sent him on his way, accompanied by eleven chosen followers. To the water's side they went, and embarking in a little ship, they came unto the coasts of Britain.

And they were met there by the heathen who carried them before Arvigarus their king. To him and to his people did Joseph of Arimathea preach the glad tidings; but the king's heart, though moved, was not convinced. Nevertheless he gave to Joseph and his followers Avalon, the happy isle, the isle of the blessed, and he bade them depart straightway and build there an altar to their God.

And a wonderful gift was this same Avalon, sometimes called the Island of Apples, and also known to the people of the land as Ynis-witren, the Isle of Glassy Waters. Beautiful and peaceful was it. Deep it lay in the midst of a green valley, and the balmy breezes fanned its apple orchards, and scattered afar the sweet fragrance of rosy blossoms or ripened fruit. Soft grew the green grass beneath the feet. The smooth waves gently lapped the shore, and water-lilies floated on the surface of the tide; while in the blue sky above sailed the fleecy clouds.

And it was on the holy Christmas Eve that Joseph and his companions reached the Isle of Avalon. With them they carried the Holy Grail hidden beneath its cloth of snow-white samite. Heavily they toiled up the steep ascent of the hill called Weary-All. And when they reached the top Joseph thrust his thorn-staff into the ground.

And, lo! a miracle! the thorn-staff put forth roots, sprouted and budded, and burst into a mass of white and fragrant flowers! And on the spot where the thorn had bloomed, there Joseph built the first Christian church in Britain. And he made it "wattled all round" of osiers gathered from the water's edge. And in the chapel they placed the Holy Grail.

And so, it is said, ever since at Glastonbury Abbey — the name by which that Avalon is known to-day — on Christmas Eve the white thorn buds and blooms.

THE THREE KINGS OF COLOGNE

A LEGEND OF THE MIDDLE AGES

BY JOHN OF HILDESHEIM — MODERNIZED BY H. S. MORRIS (ADAPTED)

THE STAR

Now, when the Children of Israel were gone out of Egypt, and had won and made subject to them Jerusalem and all the land lying about, there was in the Kingdom of Ind a tall hill called the Hill of Vaws, or the Hill of Victory. On this hill were stationed sentinels of Ind, who watched day and night against the Children of Israel, and afterward against the Romans.

And if an enemy approached, the keepers of the Hill of Vaws made a great fire to warn the inhabitants of the land so that the men might make ready to defend themselves.

Now in the time when Balaam prophesied of the Star that should betoken the birth of Christ, all the great lords and the people of Ind and in the East desired greatly to see this Star of which he spake; and they gave gifts to the keepers of the Hill of Vaws, and bade them, if they saw by night or by day any star in the air, that had not been seen aforetime, that they, the keepers, should send anon word to the people of Ind.

And thus was it that for so long a time the fame of this Star was borne throughout the lands of the East. And the more the Star was sought for, and the more its fame increased, so much the more all the people of the Land of Ind desired to see it. So they ordained twelve of the wisest and greatest of the clerks of astronomy, that were in all that country about, and gave them great hire to keep watch upon the Hill of Vaws for the Star that was prophesied of Balaam.

Now, when Christ was born in Bethlehem of Judea, His Star began to rise in the manner of a sun, bright shining. It ascended above the Hill of Vaws, and all that day in the highest air it abode without moving, insomuch that when the sun was hot and most high there was no difference in shining betwixt them.

But when the day of the nativity was passed the Star ascended up into the firmament, and it had right many long streaks and beams, more burning and brighter than a brand of fire; and, as an eagle flying and beating the air with his wings, right so the streaks and beams of the Star stirred about.

Then all the people, both man and woman, of all that country about when they saw this marvelous Star, were full of wonder thereat; yet they knew well that it was the Star that was prophesied of Balaam, and long time was desired of all the people in that country.

Now, when the three worshipful kings, who at that time reigned in Ind, Chaldea, and Persia, were informed by the astronomers of this Star, they were right glad that they had grace to see the Star in their days.

Wherefore these three worshipful kings, Melchior, Balthazar, and Jasper (in the same hour the Star appeared to all three), though each of them was far from the other, and none knew of the others' purpose, decided to go and seek and worship the Lord and King of the Jews, that was new born, as the appearance of the Star announced.

So each king prepared great and rich gifts, and

trains of mules, camels, and horses charged with treasure, and together with a great multitude of people they set forth on their journeys.

THE CHILD

Now, when these three worshipful kings were passed forth out of their kingdoms, the Star went before each king and his people. When they stood still and rested, the Star stood still; and when they went forward again, the Star always went before them in virtue and strength and gave light all the way.

And, as it is written, in the time that Christ was born, there was peace in all the world, wherefore in all the cities and towns through which they went there was no gate shut neither by night nor by day; and all the people of those same cities and towns marveled wonderfully as they saw kings and vast multitudes go by in great haste; but they knew not what they were, nor whence they came, nor whither they should go.

Furthermore these three kings rode forth over hills, waters, valleys, plains, and other divers and perilous places without hindrance, for all the way seemed to them plain and even. And they never took shelter by night nor by day, nor ever rested, nor did their horses and other beasts ever eat or drink till they had come to Bethlehem. And all this time it did seem to them as one day.

But when the three blessed kings had come near to Jerusalem, then a great cloud of darkness hid the Star from their sight. And when Melchior and his people were come fast by the city, they abode in fog and darkness. Then came Balthazar, and he abode under the same cloud near unto Melchior. Thereupon appeared Jasper with all his host.

So these three glorious kings, each with his host and burdens and beasts, met together in the highway without the city of Jerusalem. And, notwithstanding that none of them ever before had seen the other, nor knew him, nor had heard of his coming, yet at their meeting each one with great reverence and joy kissed the other. So afterward, when they had spoken together and each had told his purpose and the cause of his journey, they were much more glad and fervent. So they rode forth, and at the uprising of the sun, they came into Jerusalem. And yet the Star appeared not.

So then these three worshipful kings, when they were come into the city, asked of the people concerning the Child that was born; and when Herod heard this he was troubled and all Jerusalem with him, and he privately summoned to him these three kings and learned of them the time when the Star appeared. He then sent them forth, bidding them find the young Child and return to him.

Now when these three kings were passed out of Jerusalem the Star appeared to them again as it did erst, and went before them till they were come to Bethlehem.

Now, the nearer the kings came to the place where Christ was born, the brighter shined the Star, and they entered Bethlehem the sixth hour of the day. And they rode through the streets till they came before a little house. There the Star stood still, and then descended and shone with so great a light that the little house was full of radiance; till anon the Star went upward again into the air, and stood still always above the same place.

And the three kings went into the little house and found the Child with his mother, and they fell down and worshiped him, and offered him gifts.

And you shall understand that these three kings had brought great gifts from their own lands, rich ornaments and divers golden vessels, and many jewels and precious stones, and both gold and silver, — these they had brought to offer to the King of the Jews. But when they found the Lord in a little house, in poor clothes, and when they saw that the Star gave so great and holy a light in all the place that it seemed as though they stood in a furnace of fire, then were they so sore afraid, that of all the rich jewels and ornaments they had brought with them, they chose from their treasures what came first to their hands. For Melchior took a round apple of gold in his hand, and thirty gilt pennies, and these he offered unto our Lord; and Balthazar took out of his treasury incense; and Jasper took out myrrh, and that he offered with weeping and tears.

And now after these three kings had worshiped the Lord, they abode in Bethlehem for a little space, and as they abode, there came a command to them, in their sleep, that they should not return to Herod; and so by another way they went home to their kingdoms. But the Star that had gone before appeared no more.

So these three kings, who had suddenly met together in the highway before Jerusalem, went home together with great joy and honor. And when, after many days' journey over perilous places, they had come to the Hill of Vaws, they made there a fair chapel in worship of the Child they had sought. Also they agreed to meet together at the same place once in the year, and they ordained that the Hill of Vaws should be the place of their burial.

So when the three worshipful kings had done what they would, they took leave of each other, and each one with his people rode to his own land rejoicing.

HOW THEY CAME TO COLOGNE

Now, after many years, a little before the feast of Christmas, there appeared a wonderful Star above the cities where these three kings dwelt, and they knew thereby that their time was come when they should pass from earth. Then with one consent they built, at the Hill of Vaws, a fair and large tomb, and there the three Holy Kings, Melchior, Balthazar, and Jasper died, and were buried in the same tomb by their sorrowing people.

Now after much time had passed away, Queen Helen, the mother of the Emperor Constantine, began to think greatly of the bodies of these three kings, and she arrayed herself, and, accompanied by many attendants, went into the Land of Ind.

And you shall understand that after she had found the bodies of Melchior, Balthazar, and Jasper, Queen Helen put them into one chest and ornamented it with great riches, and she brought them into Constantinople, with joy and reverence, and laid them in a church that is called Saint Sophia; and this church the Emperor Constantine did make, — he alone, with a little child, set up all the marble pillars thereof.

Now, after the death of the Emperor Constantine a persecution against the Christian faith arose, and in this persecution the bodies of the three worshipful kings were set at naught. Then came the Emperor Mauricius of Rome, and, through his counsel, the bodies of these three kings were carried to Italy, and there they were laid in a fair church in the city of Milan.

Then afterward, in the process of time, the city of Milan rebelled against the Emperor Frederick the First, and he, being sore beset, sent to Rainald, Archbishop of Cologne, asking for help.

This Archbishop with his army did take the city of Milan, and delivered it to the Emperor. And for this service did the Emperor grant, at the Archbishop's great entreaty, that he should carry forth to Cologne the bodies of the three blessed kings.

Then the Archbishop, with great solemnity and in procession, did carry forth from the city of Milan the bodies of the three kings, and brought them unto Cologne and there placed them in the fair church of Saint Peter. And all the people of the country roundabout, with all the reverence they might, received these relics, and there in the city of Cologne they are kept and beholden of all manner of nations unto this day.

Thus endeth the legend of these three blessed kings, — Melchior, Balthazar, and Jasper.

ARBOR DAY

THE LITTLE TREE THAT LONGED FOR OTHER LEAVES

BY FRIEDRICH RÜCKERT (TRANSLATED)

THERE was a little tree that stood in the woods through both good and stormy weather, and it was covered from top to bottom with needles instead of leaves. The needles were sharp and prickly, so the little tree said to itself: —

"All my tree comrades have beautiful green leaves, and I have only sharp needles. No one will touch me. If I could have a wish I would ask for leaves of pure gold."

When night came the little tree fell asleep, and, lo! in the morning it woke early and found itself covered with glistening, golden leaves.

"Ah, ah!" said the little tree, "how grand I am! No other tree in the woods is dressed in gold."

But at evening time there came a peddler with a great sack and a long beard. He saw the glitter of the golden leaves. He picked them all and hurried away leaving the little tree cold and bare.

"Alas! alas!" cried the little tree in sorrow; "all my golden leaves are gone! I am ashamed to stand among the other trees that have such beautiful foliage. If I only had another wish I would ask for leaves of glass."

Then the little tree fell asleep, and when it woke early, it found itself covered with bright and shining leaves of glass.

"Now," said the little tree, "I am happy. No tree in the woods glistens like me."

But there came a fierce storm-wind driving through the woods. It struck the glass, and in a moment all the shining leaves lay shattered on the ground.

"My leaves, my glass leaves!" moaned the little tree; "they lie broken in the dust, while all the other trees are still dressed in their beautiful foliage. Oh! if I had another wish I would ask for green leaves."

Then the little tree slept again, and in the morning it was covered with fresh, green foliage. And it laughed merrily, and said: "Now, I need not be ashamed any more. I am like my comrades of the woods."

But along came a mother-goat, looking for grass and herbs for herself and her young ones. She saw the crisp, new leaves; and she nibbled, and nibbled, and nibbled them all away, and she ate up both stems and tender shoots, till the little tree stood bare.

"Alas!" cried the little tree in anguish, "I

want no more leaves, neither gold ones nor glass ones, nor green and red and yellow ones! If I could only have my needles once more, I would never complain again."

And sorrowfully the little tree fell asleep, but when it saw itself in the morning sunshine, it laughed and laughed and laughed. And all the other trees laughed, too, but the little tree did not care. Why did they laugh? Because in the night all its needles had come again! You may see this for yourself. Just go into the woods and look, but do not touch the little tree. Why not? *Because it pricks.*

WHY THE EVERGREEN TREES NEVER LOSE THEIR LEAVES

BY FLORENCE HOLBROOK

WINTER was coming, and the birds had flown far to the south, where the air was warm and they could find berries to eat. One little bird had broken its wing and could not fly with the others. It was alone in the cold world of frost and snow. The forest looked warm, and it made its way to the trees as well as it could, to ask for help.

First it came to a birch tree. "Beautiful birch tree," it said, "my wing is broken, and my friends have flown away. May I live among your branches till they come back to me?"

"No, indeed," answered the birch tree, drawing her fair green leaves away. "We of the great forest have our own birds to help. I can do nothing for you."

"The birch is not very strong," said the little bird to itself, "and it might be that she could not hold me easily. I will ask the oak." So the bird said: "Great oak tree, you are so strong, will you not let me live on your boughs till my friends come back in the springtime?"

"In the springtime!" cried the oak. "That is a long way off. How do I know what you might do in all that time? Birds are always looking for something to eat, and you might even eat up some of my acorns."

"It may be that the willow will be kind to me," thought the bird, and it said: "Gentle willow, my wing is broken, and I could not fly to the south with the other birds. May I live on your branches till the springtime?"

The willow did not look gentle then, for she drew herself up proudly and said: "Indeed, I do not know you, and we willows never talk to people whom we do not know. Very likely there are trees somewhere that will take in strange birds. Leave me at once."

The poor little bird did not know what to do. Its wing was not yet strong, but it began to fly away as well as it could. Before it had gone far a voice was heard. "Little bird," it said, "where are you going?"

"Indeed, I do not know," answered the bird sadly. "I am very cold."

"Come right here, then," said the friendly spruce tree, for it was her voice that had called. "You shall live on my warmest branch all winter if you choose."

"Will you really let me?" asked the little bird eagerly.

"Indeed, I will," answered the kind-hearted spruce tree. "If your friends have flown away, it is time for the trees to help you. Here is the branch where my leaves are thickest and softest."

"My branches are not very thick," said the friendly pine tree, "but I am big and strong, and I can keep the North Wind from you and the spruce."

"I can help, too," said a little juniper tree. "I can give you berries all winter long, and every bird knows that juniper berries are good."

So the spruce gave the lonely little bird a home; the pine kept the cold North Wind away from it; and the juniper gave it berries to eat. The other trees looked on and talked together wisely.

"I would not have strange birds on my boughs," said the birch.

"I shall not give my acorns away for any one," said the oak.

"I never have anything to do with strangers," said the willow, and the three trees drew their leaves closely about them.

In the morning all those shining, green leaves lay on the ground, for a cold North Wind had come in the night, and every leaf that it touched fell from the tree.

"May I touch every leaf in the forest?" asked the wind in its frolic.

"No," said the Frost King. "The trees that have been kind to the little bird with the broken wing may keep their leaves."

This is why the leaves of the spruce, the pine, and the juniper are always green.

WHY THE ASPEN QUIVERS

OLD LEGEND

LONG, long ago, so the legend says, when Joseph and Mary and the Holy Babe fled out of Bethlehem into Egypt, they passed through the green wildwood. And flowers and trees and plants bent their heads in reverence.

But the proud aspen held its head high and refused even to look at the Holy Babe. In vain the birds sang in the aspen's branches, entreating it to gaze for one moment at the wonderful One; the proud tree still held its head erect in scorn.

Then outspake Mary, his mother. "O aspen

tree," she said, "why do you not gaze on the Holy Child? Why do you not bow your head? A star arose at his birth, angels sang his first lullaby, kings and shepherds came to the brightness of his rising; why, then, O aspen, do you refuse to honor your Lord and mine?"

But the aspen could not answer. A strange shivering passed through its stem and along its boughs, which set its leaves a-quivering. It trembled before the Holy Babe.

And so from age to age, even unto this day, the proud aspen shakes and shivers.

THE WONDER TREE

BY FRIEDRICH ADOLPH KRUMMACHER (ADAPTED)

ONE day in the springtime, Prince Solomon was sitting under the palm trees in the royal gardens, when he saw the Prophet Nathan walking near.

"Nathan," said the Prince, "I would see a wonder."

The Prophet smiled. "I had the same desire in the days of my youth," he replied.

"And was it fulfilled?" asked Solomon.

"A Man of God came to me," said Nathan, "having a pomegranate seed in his hand. 'Behold,' he said, 'what will become of this.' Then he made a hole in the ground, and planted the seed, and covered it over. When he withdrew his hand the clods of earth opened, and I saw two small leaves coming forth. But scarcely had I beheld them, when they joined together and became a small stem wrapped in bark; and the stem grew before my eyes, — and it grew thicker and higher and became covered with branches.

"I marveled, but the Man of God motioned me to be silent. 'Behold,' said he, 'new creations begin.'

"Then he took water in the palm of his hand, and sprinkled the branches three times, and, lo! the branches were covered with green leaves, so that a cool shade spread above us, and the air was filled with perfume.

"'From whence come this perfume and this shade?' cried I.

"'Dost thou not see,' he answered, 'these crimson flowers bursting from among the leaves, and hanging in clusters?'

"I was about to speak, but a gentle breeze moved the leaves, scattering the petals of the flowers around us. Scarcely had the falling flowers reached the ground when I saw ruddy pomegranates hanging beneath the leaves of the tree, like almonds on Aaron's rod. Then the Man of God left me, and I was lost in amazement."

"Where is he, this Man of God?" asked Prince Solomon eagerly. "What is his name? Is he still alive?"

"Son of David," answered Nathan, "I have spoken to thee of a vision."

When the Prince heard this he was grieved to the heart. "How couldst thou deceive me thus?" he asked.

But the Prophet replied: "Behold in thy father's gardens thou mayest daily see the unfolding of wonder trees. Doth not this same miracle happen to the fig, the date, and the pomegranate? They spring from the earth, they put out branches and leaves, they flower, they fruit, — not in a moment, perhaps, but in months and years, — but canst thou tell the difference betwixt a minute, a month, or a year in the eyes of Him with whom one day is as a thousand years, and a thousand years as one day?"

THE PROUD OAK TREE

OLD FABLE [1]

(TRANSLATED)

THE oak said to the reed that grew by the river: "It is no wonder that you make such a sorrowful moaning, for you are so weak that the little wren is a burden for you, and the lightest breeze must seem like a storm-wind. Now look at me! No

[1] From *Deutsches Drittes Lesebuch,* by W. H. Weick and C. Grebner. Copyright, 1886, by Van Antwerp, Bragg & Co. American Book Company, publishers.

storm has ever been able to bow my head. You will be much safer if you grow close to my side so that I may shelter you from the wind that is now playing with my leaves."

"Do not worry about me," said the reed; "I have less reason to fear the wind than you have. I bow myself, but I never break. He who laughs last, laughs best!"

That night there came a fearful hurricane. The oak stood erect. The reed bowed itself before the blast. The wind grew more furious, and, uprooting the proud oak, flung it on the ground.

When the morning came there stood the slender reed, glittering with dewdrops, and softly swaying in the breeze.

BAUCIS AND PHILEMON

ADAPTED FROM H. P. MASKELL'S RENDERING OF THE GREEK MYTH

On the slopes of the Phrygian hills, there once dwelt a pious old couple named Baucis and Philemon. They had lived all their lives in a tiny cottage of wattles, thatched with straw, cheerful and content in spite of their poverty.

As this worthy couple sat dozing by the fireside one evening in the late autumn, two strangers came and begged a shelter for the night. They had to stoop to enter the humble doorway, where the old man welcomed them heartily and bade them rest their weary limbs on the settle before the fire.

Meanwhile Baucis stirred the embers, blowing them into a flame with dry leaves, and heaped on the fagots to boil the stew-pot. Hanging from the blackened beams was a rusty side of bacon. Philemon cut off a rasher to roast, and, while his guests refreshed themselves with a wash at the rustic trough, he gathered pot-herbs from his patch of garden. Then the old woman, her hands trembling with age, laid the cloth and spread the table.

It was a frugal meal, but one that hungry wayfarers could well relish. The first course was an omelette of curdled milk and eggs, garnished with radishes and served on rude oaken platters. The cups of turned beechwood were filled with home-made wine from an earthen jug. The second course consisted of dried figs and dates, plums, sweet-smelling apples, and grapes, with a piece of clear, white honeycomb. What made the meal more grateful to the guests was the hearty spirit in which it was offered. Their hosts gave all they had without stint or grudging.

But all at once something happened which startled and amazed Baucis and Philemon. They poured out wine for their guests, and, lo! each time the pitcher filled itself again to the brim.

The old couple then knew that their guests were not mere mortals; indeed, they were no other than Jupiter and Mercury come down to earth in the disguise of poor travelers. Being ashamed of their humble entertainment, Philemon hurried out and gave chase to his only goose, intending to kill and roast it. But his guests forbade him, saying: —

"In mortal shape we have come down, and at a hundred houses asked for lodging and rest. For answer a hundred doors were shut and locked against us. You alone, the poorest of all, have received us gladly and given us of your best. Now it is for us to punish these impious people who treat strangers so churlishly, but you two shall be spared. Only leave your cottage and follow us to yonder mountain-top."

So saying, Jupiter and Mercury led the way, and the two old folks hobbled after them. Presently they reached the top of the mountain, and Baucis and Philemon saw all the country round, with villages and people, sinking into a marsh; while their own cottage alone was left standing.

And while they gazed, their cottage was changed into a white temple. The doorway became a porch with marble columns. The thatch grew into a roof of golden tiles. The little garden about their home became a park.

Then Jupiter, regarding Baucis and Philemon

with kindly eyes, said: "Tell me, O good old man and you good wife, what may we do in return for your hospitality?"

Philemon whispered for a moment with Baucis, and she nodded her approval. "We desire," he replied, "to be your servants, and to have the care of this temple. One other favor we would ask. From boyhood I have loved only Baucis, and she has lived only for me. Let the selfsame hour take us both away together. Let me never see the tomb of my wife, nor let her suffer the misery of mourning my death."

Jupiter and Mercury, pleased with these requests, willingly granted both, and endowed Baucis and Philemon with youth and strength as well. The gods then vanished from their sight, but as long as their lives lasted Baucis and Philemon were the guardians of the white temple that once had been their home.

And when again old age overtook them, they were standing one day in front of the sacred porch, and Baucis, turning her gaze upon her husband, saw him slowly changing into a gnarled oak tree. And Philemon, as he felt himself rooted to the ground, saw Baucis at the same time turning into a leafy linden.

And as their faces disappeared behind the green foliage, each cried unto the other, "Farewell, dearest love!" and again, "Dearest love, farewell!" And their human forms were changed to trees and branches.

And still, if you visit the spot, you may see an oak and a linden tree with branches intertwined.

THE UNFRUITFUL TREE

BY FRIEDRICH ADOLPH KRUMMACHER

A FARMER had a brother in town who was a gardener, and who possessed a magnificent orchard full of the finest fruit trees, so that his skill and his beautiful trees were famous everywhere.

One day the farmer went into town to visit his brother, and was astonished at the rows of trees that grew slender and smooth as wax tapers.

"Look, my brother," said the gardener; "I will give you an apple tree, the best from my garden, and you, and your children, and your children's children shall enjoy it."

Then the gardener called his workmen and ordered them to take up the tree and carry it to his brother's farm. They did so, and the next morning the farmer began to wonder where he should plant it.

"If I plant it on the hill," said he to himself, "the wind might catch it and shake down the delicious fruit before it is ripe; if I plant it close to the road, passers-by will see it and rob me of its luscious apples; but if I plant it too near the door of my house, my servants or the children may pick the fruit."

So, after he had thought the matter over, he planted the tree behind his barn, saying to himself: "Prying thieves will not think to look for it here."

But behold, the tree bore neither fruit nor blossoms the first year nor the second; then the farmer sent for his brother the gardener, and reproached him angrily, saying: —

"You have deceived me, and given me a barren tree instead of a fruitful one. For, behold, this is the third year and still it brings forth nothing but leaves!"

The gardener, when he saw where the tree was planted, laughed and said: —

"You have planted the tree where it is exposed to cold winds, and has neither sun nor warmth. How, then, could you expect flowers and fruit? You have planted the tree with a greedy and suspicious heart; how, then, could you expect to reap a rich and generous harvest?"

THE DRYAD OF THE OLD OAK

BY JAMES RUSSELL LOWELL (ADAPTED)

IN olden times there was a youth named Rhœcus. One day as he wandered through the wood he saw an ancient oak tree, trembling and about to fall.

Full of pity for so fair a tree, Rhœcus carefully propped up its trunk, and as he did so he heard a soft voice murmur: —

"Rhœcus!"

It sounded like the gentle sighing of the wind through the leaves; and while Rhœcus paused bewildered to listen, again he heard the murmur like a soft breeze: —

"Rhœcus!"

And there stood before him, in the green glooms of the shadowy oak, a wonderful maiden.

"Rhœcus," said she, in low-toned words, serene and full, and as clear as drops of dew, "I am the Dryad of this tree, and with it I am doomed to live and die. Thou hadst compassion on my oak, and in saving it thou hast saved my life. Now, ask me what thou wilt that I can give, and it shall be thine."

"Beauteous nymph," answered Rhœcus, with a flutter at the heart, "surely nothing will satisfy the craving of my soul save to be with thee forever. Give to me thy love!"

"I give it, Rhœcus," answered she with sadness in her voice, "though it be a perilous gift. An hour before sunset meet me here."

And straightway she vanished, and Rhœcus could see nothing but the green glooms beneath the shadowy oak. Not a sound came to his straining ears but the low, trickling rustle of the leaves, and, from far away on the emerald slope, the sweet sound of an idle shepherd's pipe.

Filled with wonder and joy Rhœcus turned his steps homeward. The earth seemed to spring beneath him as he walked. The clear, broad sky looked bluer than its wont, and so full of joy was he that he could scarce believe that he had not wings.

Impatient for the trysting-time, he sought some companions, and to while away the tedious hours, he played at dice, and soon forgot all else.

The dice were rattling their merriest, and Rhœcus had just laughed in triumph at a happy throw, when through the open window of the room there hummed a yellow bee. It buzzed about his ears, and seemed ready to alight upon his head. At this Rhœcus laughed, and with a rough, impatient hand he brushed it off and cried: —

"The silly insect! does it take me for a rose?"

But still the bee came back. Three times it buzzed about his head, and three times he rudely beat it back. Then straight through the window flew the wounded bee, while Rhœcus watched its flight with angry eyes.

And as he looked — O sorrow! — the red disk of the setting sun descended behind the sharp mountain peak of Thessaly.

Then instantly the blood sank from his heart, as if its very walls had caved in, for he remembered the trysting-hour — now gone by! Without a word he turned and rushed forth madly through the city and the gate, over the fields into the wood.

Spent of breath he reached the tree, and, listening fearfully, he heard once more the low voice murmur: —

"Rhœcus!"

But as he looked he could see nothing but the deepening glooms beneath the oak.

Then the voice sighed: "O Rhœcus, nevermore shalt thou behold me by day or night! Why didst thou fail to come ere sunset? Why didst thou scorn my humble messenger, and send it back to me with bruised wings? We spirits only show ourselves to gentle eyes! And he who scorns the smallest thing alive is forever shut away from all that is beautiful in woods and fields. Farewell! for thou canst see me no more!"

Then Rhœcus beat his breast and groaned aloud.

"Be pitiful," he cried. "Forgive me yet this once!"

"Alas," the voice replied, "I am not unmerciful! I can forgive! But I have no skill to heal thy spirit's eyes, nor can I change the temper of thy heart." And then again she murmured, "Nevermore!"

And after that Rhœcus heard no other sound, save the rustling of the oak's crisp leaves, like surf upon a distant shore.

DAPHNE

BY OVID (ADAPTED)

IN ancient times, when Apollo, the god of the shining sun, roamed the earth, he met Cupid, who with bended bow and drawn string was seeking human beings to wound with the arrows of love.

"Silly boy," said Apollo, "what dost thou with the warlike bow? Such burden best befits my shoulders, for did I not slay the fierce serpent, the Python, whose baleful breath destroyed all that came nigh him? Warlike arms are for the mighty, not for boys like thee! Do thou carry a torch with which to kindle love in human hearts, but no longer lay claim to my weapon, the bow!"

But Cupid replied in anger: "Let thy bow shoot what it will, Apollo, but my bow shall shoot *thee!*" And the god of love rose up, and beating the air with his wings, he drew two magic arrows from his quiver. One was of shining gold and with its barbed point could Cupid inflict wounds of love; the other arrow was of dull silver and its wound had the power to engender hate.

The silver arrow Cupid fixed in the breast of Daphne, the daughter of the river-god Peneus; and forthwith she fled away from the homes of men, and hunted beasts in the forest.

With the golden arrow Cupid grievously

wounded Apollo, who fleeing to the woods saw there the Nymph Daphne pursuing the deer; and straightway the sun-god fell in love with her beauty. Her golden locks hung down upon her neck, her eyes were like stars, her form was slender and graceful and clothed in clinging white. Swifter than the light wind she flew, and Apollo followed after.

"O Nymph! daughter of Peneus," he cried, "stay, I entreat thee! Why dost thou fly as a lamb from the wolf, as a deer from the lion, or as a dove with trembling wings flees from the eagle! I am no common man! I am no shepherd! Thou knowest not, rash maid, from whom thou art flying! The priests of Delphi and Tenedos pay their service to me. Jupiter is my sire. Mine own arrow is unerring, but Cupid's aim is truer, for he has made this wound in my heart! Alas! wretched me! though I am that great one who discovered the art of healing, yet this love may not be healed by my herbs nor my skill!"

But Daphne stopped not at these words, she flew from him with timid step. The winds fluttered her garments, the light breezes spread her flowing locks behind her. Swiftly Apollo drew near even as the keen greyhound draws near to the frightened hare he is pursuing. With trembling limbs Daphne sought the river, the home of her father, Peneus. Close behind her was Apollo, the sun-god. She felt his breath on her hair and his hand on her shoulder. Her strength was spent, she grew pale, and in faint accents she implored the river: —

"O save me, my father, save me from Apollo, the sun-god!"

Scarcely had she thus spoken before a heaviness seized her limbs. Her breast was covered with bark, her hair grew into green leaves, and her arms into branches. Her feet, a moment before so swift, became rooted to the ground. And Daphne was no longer a Nymph, but a green laurel tree.

When Apollo beheld this change he cried out and embraced the tree, and kissed its leaves. "Beautiful Daphne," he said, "since thou cannot be my bride, yet shalt thou be my tree. Henceforth my hair, my lyre, and my quiver shall be adorned with laurel. Thy wreaths shall be given to conquering chiefs, to winners of fame and joy; and as my head has never been shorn of its locks, so shalt thou wear thy green leaves, winter and summer — forever!"

Apollo ceased speaking and the laurel bent its new-made boughs in assent, and its stem seemed to shake and its leaves gently to murmur.

BIRD DAY

THE OLD WOMAN WHO BECAME A WOODPECKER

BY PHŒBE CARY (ADAPTED)

AFAR in the Northland, where the winter days are so short and the nights so long, and where they harness the reindeer to sledges, and where the children look like bear's cubs in their funny, furry clothes, there, long ago, wandered a good Saint on the snowy roads.

He came one day to the door of a cottage, and looking in saw a little old woman making cakes, and baking them on the hearth.

Now, the good Saint was faint with fasting, and he asked if she would give him one small cake wherewith to stay his hunger.

So the little old woman made a *very small* cake and placed it on the hearth; but as it lay baking she looked at it and thought: "That is a big cake, indeed, quite too big for me to give away."

Then she kneaded another cake, much smaller, and laid that on the hearth to cook, but when she turned it over it looked larger than the first.

So she took a tiny scrap of dough, and rolled it out, and rolled it out, and baked it as thin as a wafer; but when it was done it looked so large that she could not bear to part with it; and she said: "My cakes are much too big to give away," — and she put them on the shelf.

Then the good Saint grew angry, for he was hungry and faint. "You are too selfish to have a human form," said he. "You are too greedy to deserve food, shelter, and a warm fire. Instead, henceforth, you shall build as the birds do, and get your scanty living by picking up nuts and berries and by boring, boring all the day long, in the bark of trees."

Hardly had the good Saint said this when the little old woman went straight up the chimney, and came out at the top changed into a red-headed woodpecker with coal-black feathers.

And now every country boy may see her in the woods, where she lives in trees boring, boring, boring for her food.

THE BOY WHO BECAME A ROBIN

AN OJIBBEWAY LEGEND

BY HENRY R. SCHOOLCRAFT (ADAPTED)

ONCE upon a time there was an old Indian who had an only son, whose name was Opeechee. The boy had come to the age when every Indian lad makes a long fast, in order to secure a Spirit to be his guardian for life.

Now, the old man was very proud, and he

wished his son to fast longer than other boys, and to become a greater warrior than all others. So he directed him to prepare with solemn ceremonies for the fast.

After the boy had been in the sweating lodge and bath several times, his father commanded him to lie down upon a clean mat, in a little lodge apart from the rest.

"My son," said he, "endure your hunger like a man, and at the end of *twelve days*, you shall receive food and a blessing from my hands."

The boy carefully did all that his father commanded, and lay quietly with his face covered, awaiting the arrival of his guardian Spirit who was to bring him good or bad dreams.

His father visited him every day, encouraging him to endure with patience the pangs of hunger and thirst. He told him of the honor and renown that would be his if he continued his fast to the end of the twelve days.

To all this the boy replied not, but lay on his mat without a murmur of discontent, until the ninth day; when he said: —

"My father, the dreams tell me of evil. May I break my fast now, and at a better time make a new one?"

"My son," replied the old man, "you know not what you ask. If you get up now, all your glory will depart. Wait patiently a little longer. You have but three days more to fast, then glory and honor will be yours."

The boy said nothing more, but, covering himself closer, he lay until the eleventh day, when he spoke again: —

"My father," said he, "the dreams forebode evil. May I break my fast now, and at a better time make a new one?"

"My son," replied the old man again, "you know not what you ask. Wait patiently a little longer. You have but one more day to fast. To-morrow I will myself prepare a meal and bring it to you."

The boy remained silent, beneath his covering, and motionless except for the gentle heaving of his breast.

Early the next morning his father, overjoyed at having gained his end, prepared some food. He took it and hastened to the lodge intending to set it before his son.

On coming to the door of the lodge what was his surprise to hear the boy talking to some one. He lifted the curtain hanging before the doorway, and looking in saw his son painting his breast with vermilion. And as the lad laid on the bright color as far back on his shoulders as he could reach, he was saying to himself: —

"My father has destroyed my fortune as a man. He would not listen to my requests. I shall be happy forever, because I was obedient to my parent; but he shall suffer. My guardian Spirit has given me a new form, and now I must go!"

At this his father rushed into the lodge, crying: "My son! my son! I pray you leave me not!"

But the boy, with the quickness of a bird, flew to the top of the lodge, and perching upon the highest pole, was instantly changed into a most beautiful robin redbreast.

He looked down on his father with pity in his eyes, and said: —

"Do not sorrow, O my father, I am no longer your boy, but Opeechee the robin. I shall always be a friend to men, and live near their dwellings. I shall ever be happy and content. Every day will I sing you songs of joy. The mountains and fields yield me food. My pathway is in the bright air."

Then Opeechee the robin stretched himself as if delighting in his new wings, and caroling his sweetest song, he flew away to the near-by trees.

THE TONGUE-CUT SPARROW

BY A. B. MITFORD (ADAPTED)

ONCE upon a time there lived a little old man and a little old woman. The little old man had a kind heart, and he kept a young sparrow, which he cared for tenderly. Every morning it used to sing at the door of his house.

Now, the little old woman was a cross old thing,

and one day when she was going to starch her linen, the sparrow pecked at her paste. Then she flew into a great rage and cut the sparrow's tongue and let the bird fly away.

When the little old man came home from the hills, where he had been chopping wood, he found the sparrow gone.

"Where is my little sparrow?" asked he.

"It pecked at my starching-paste," answered the little old woman, "so I cut its evil tongue and let it fly away."

"Alas! Alas!" cried the little old man. "Poor thing! Poor thing! Poor little tongue-cut sparrow! Where is your home now?"

And then he wandered far and wide seeking his pet and crying: —

"Mr. Sparrow, Mr. Sparrow, where are you living?"

And he wandered on and on, over mountain and valley, and dale and river, until one day at the foot of a certain mountain he met the lost bird. The little old man was filled with joy and the sparrow welcomed him with its sweetest song.

It led the little old man to its nest-house, introduced him to its wife and small sparrows, and set before him all sorts of good things to eat and drink.

"Please partake of our humble fare," sang the sparrow; "poor as it is, you are welcome."

"What a polite sparrow," answered the little old man, and he stayed for a long time as the bird's guest. At last one day the little old man said that he must take his leave and return home.

"Wait a bit," said the sparrow.

And it went into the house and brought out two wicker baskets. One was very heavy and the other light.

"Take the one you wish," said the sparrow, "and good fortune go with you."

"I am very feeble," answered the little old man, "so I will take the light one."

He thanked the sparrow, and, shouldering the basket, said good-bye. Then he trudged off leaving the sparrow family sad and lonely.

When he reached home the little old woman was very angry, and began to scold him, saying:—

"Well, and pray where have you been all these days? A pretty thing, indeed, for you to be gadding about like this!"

"Oh," he replied, "I have been on a visit to the tongue-cut sparrow, and when I came away it gave me this wicker basket as a parting gift."

Then they opened the basket to see what was inside, and lo and behold! it was full of gold, silver, and other precious things!

The little old woman was as greedy as she was cross, and when she saw all the riches spread before her, she could not contain herself for joy.

"Ho! Ho!" cried she. "Now I'll go and call on the sparrow, and get a pretty present, too!"

She asked the old man the way to the sparrow's house and set forth on her journey. And she wandered on and on over mountain and valley, and dale and river, until at last she saw the tongue-cut sparrow.

"Well met, well met, Mr. Sparrow," cried she. "I have been looking forward with much pleasure to seeing you." And then she tried to flatter it with soft, sweet words.

So the bird had to invite her to its nest-house, but it did not feast her nor say anything about a parting gift. At last the little old woman had to go, and she asked for something to carry with her to remember the visit by. The sparrow, as before, brought out two wicker baskets. One was very heavy and the other light.

The greedy little old woman, choosing the heavy one, carried it off with her.

She hurried home as fast as she was able, and closing her doors and windows so that no one might see, opened the basket. And, lo and behold! out jumped all sorts of wicked hobgoblins and imps, and they scratched and pinched her to death.

As for the little old man he adopted a son, and his family grew rich and prosperous.

THE QUAILS

A LEGEND OF THE JATAKA

FROM THE RIVERSIDE FOURTH READER

AGES ago a flock of more than a thousand quails lived together in a forest in India. They would have been happy, but that they were in great dread of their enemy, the quail-catcher. He used to imitate the call of the quail; and when they gathered together in answer to it, he would throw a great net over them, stuff them into his basket, and carry them away to be sold.

Now, one of the quails was very wise, and he said: —

"Brothers! I've thought of a good plan. In future, as soon as the fowler throws his net over us, let each one put his head through a mesh in the net and then all lift it up together and fly away with it. When we have flown far enough, we can let the net drop on a thorn bush and escape from under it."

All agreed to the plan; and next day when the fowler threw his net, the birds all lifted it together in the very way that the wise quail had told them, threw it on a thorn bush and escaped. While the fowler tried to free his net from the thorns, it grew dark, and he had to go home.

This happened many days, till at last the

fowler's wife grew angry and asked her husband: —

"Why is it that you never catch any more quail?"

Then the fowler said: "The trouble is that all the birds work together and help one another. If they would only quarrel, I could catch them fast enough."

A few days later, one of the quails accidentally trod on the head of one of his brothers, as they alighted on the feeding-ground.

"Who trod on my head?" angrily inquired the quail who was hurt.

"Don't be angry, I did n't mean to tread on you," said the first quail.

But the brother quail went on quarreling.

"I lifted all the weight of the net; you did n't help at all," he cried.

That made the first quail angry, and before long all were drawn into the dispute. Then the fowler saw his chance. He imitated the cry of the quail and cast his net over those who came together. They were still boasting and quarreling, and they did not help one another lift the net. So the hunter lifted the net himself and crammed them into his basket. But the wise quail gathered his friends together and flew far away, for he knew that quarrels are the root of misfortune.

THE MAGPIE'S NEST

BY JOSEPH JACOBS

ALL the birds of the air came to the magpie and asked her to teach them how to build nests. For the magpie is the cleverest bird of all at building nests. So she put all the birds round her and began to show them how to do it. First of all she took some mud and made a sort of round cake with it.

"Oh, that's how it's done!" said the thrush, and away it flew; and so that's how thrushes build their nests.

Then the magpie took some twigs and arranged them round in the mud.

"Now I know all about it!" said the blackbird, and off it flew; and that's how the blackbirds make their nests to this very day.

Then the magpie put another layer of mud over the twigs.

"Oh, that's quite obvious!" said the wise owl, and away it flew; and owls have never made better nests since.

After this the magpie took some twigs and twined them round the outside.

"The very thing!" said the sparrow, and off he went; so sparrows make rather slovenly nests to this day.

Well, then Madge magpie took some feathers and stuff, and lined the nest very comfortably with it.

"That suits me!" cried the starling, and off it flew; and very comfortable nests have starlings.

So it went on, every bird taking away some knowledge of how to build nests, but none of them waiting to the end.

Meanwhile Madge magpie went on working and working without looking up, till the only bird that remained was the turtle-dove, and that had n't paid any attention all along, but only kept on saying its silly cry: "Take two, Taffy, take two-o-o-o!"

At last the magpie heard this just as she was putting a twig across, so she said: "One's enough."

But the turtle-dove kept on saying: "Take two, Taffy, take two-o-o-o!"

Then the magpie got angry and said: "One's enough, I tell you!"

Still the turtle-dove cried: "Take two, Taffy, take two-o-o-o!"

At last, and at last, the magpie looked up and saw nobody near her but the silly turtle-dove, and then she got rarely angry and flew away and refused to tell the birds how to build nests again.

And that is why different birds build their nests differently.

THE GREEDY GEESE

FROM IL LIBRO D'ORO (ADAPTED)

MANY years ago there was near the sea a convent famed for the rich crops of grain that grew on its farm. On a certain year a large flock of wild geese descended on its fields and devoured first the corn, and then the green blades.

The superintendent of the farm hastened to the convent and called the lady abbess.

"Holy mother," said he, "this year the nuns will have to fast continually, for there will be no food."

"Why is that?" asked the abbess.

"Because," answered the superintendent, "a flood of wild geese has rained upon the land, and they have eaten up the corn, nor have they left a single green blade."

"Is it possible," said the abbess, "that these wicked birds have no respect for the property of the convent! They shall do penance for their misdeeds. Return at once to the fields, and order the geese from me to come without delay to the convent door, so that they may receive just punishment for their greediness."

"But, mother," said the superintendent, "this is not a time for jesting! These are not sheep to be guided into the fold, but birds with long, strong wings, to fly away with."

"Do you understand me!" answered the abbess. "Go at once, and bid them come to me without delay, and render an account of their misdeeds."

The superintendent ran back to the farm, and found the flock of evildoers still there. He raised his voice and clapping his hands, cried: —

"Come, come, ye greedy geese! The lady abbess commands you to hasten to the convent door!"

Wonderful sight! Hardly had he uttered these words than the geese raised their necks as if to listen, then, without spreading their wings, they placed themselves in single file, and in regular order began to march toward the convent. As they proceeded they bowed their heads as if confessing their fault and as though about to receive punishment.

Arriving at the convent, they entered the courtyard in exact order, one behind the other, and there awaited the coming of the abbess. All night they stood thus without making a sound, as if struck dumb by their guilty consciences. But when morning came, they uttered the most pitiful cries as though asking pardon and permission to depart.

Then the lady abbess, taking compassion on the repentant birds, appeared with some nuns upon a balcony. Long she talked to the geese, asking them why they had stolen the convent grain. She threatened them with a long fast, and then, softening, began to offer them pardon if they would never again attack her lands, nor eat her corn. To which the geese bowed their heads low in assent. Then the abbess gave them her blessing and permission to depart.

Hardly had she done so when the geese, spreading their wings, made a joyous circle above the convent towers, and flew away. Alighting at some distance they counted their number and found one missing. For, alas! in the night, when they had been shut in the courtyard, the convent cook, seeing how fat they were, had stolen one bird and had killed, roasted, and eaten it.

When the birds discovered that one of their number was missing, they again took wing and, hovering over the convent, they uttered mournful cries, complaining of the loss of their comrade, and imploring the abbess to return him to the flock.

Now, when the lady abbess heard these melancholy pleas, she assembled her household, and inquired of each member where the bird might be. The cook, fearing that it might be already known to her, confessed the theft, and begged for pardon.

"You have been very audacious," said the abbess, "but at least collect the bones and bring them to me."

The cook did as directed, and the abbess at a word caused the bones to come together and to assume flesh, and afterwards feathers, and, lo! the original bird rose up.

The geese, having received their lost companion, rejoiced loudly, and, beating their wings gratefully, made many circles over the sacred cloister, before they flew away. Neither did they in future ever dare to place a foot on the lands of the convent, nor to touch one blade of grass.

THE KING OF THE BIRDS

BY THE BROTHERS GRIMM (TRANSLATED)

ONE day the birds took it into their heads that they would like a master, and that one of their number must be chosen king. A meeting of all the birds was called, and on a beautiful May morning they assembled from woods and fields and meadows. The eagle, the robin, the bluebird, the owl, the lark, the sparrow were all there. The cuckoo came, and the lapwing, and so did all the other birds, too numerous to mention. There also came a very little bird that had no name at all.

There was great confusion and noise. There was piping, hissing, chattering and clacking, and finally it was decided that the bird that could fly the highest should be king.

The signal was given and all the birds flew in a

great flock into the air. There was a loud rustling and whirring and beating of wings. The air was full of dust, and it seemed as if a black cloud were floating over the field.

The little birds soon grew tired and fell back quickly to earth. The larger ones held out longer, and flew higher and higher, but the eagle flew highest of any. He rose, and rose, until he seemed to be flying straight into the sun.

The other birds gave out and one by one they fell back to earth; and when the eagle saw this he thought, "What is the use of flying any higher? It is settled: I am king!"

Then the birds below called in one voice: "Come back, come back! You must be our king! No one can fly as high as you."

"Except me!" cried a shrill, shrill voice, and the little bird without a name rose from the eagle's back, where he had lain hidden in the feathers, and he flew into the air. Higher and higher he mounted till he was lost to sight, then, folding his wings together, he sank to earth crying shrilly: "I am king! I am king!"

"You, our king!" the birds cried in anger; "you have done this by trickery and cunning. We will not have you to reign over us."

Then the birds gathered together again and made another condition, that he should be king who could go the deepest into the earth.

How the goose wallowed in the sand, and the duck strove to dig a hole! All the other birds, too, tried to hide themselves in the ground. The little bird without a name found a mouse's hole, and creeping in cried: —

"I am king! I am king!"

"You, our king!" all the birds cried again, more angrily than before. "Do you think that we would reward your cunning in this way? No, no! You shall stay in the earth till you die of hunger!"

So they shut up the little bird in the mouse's hole, and bade the owl watch him carefully night and day. Then all the birds went home to bed, for they were very tired; but the owl found it lonely and wearisome sitting alone staring at the mouse's hole.

"I can close one eye and watch with the other," he thought. So he closed one eye and stared steadfastly with the other; but before he knew it he forgot to keep that one open, and both eyes were fast asleep.

Then the little bird without a name peeped out, and when he saw Master Owl's two eyes tight shut, he slipped from the hole and flew away.

From this time on the owl has not dared to show himself by day lest the birds should pull him to pieces. He flies about only at night-time, hating and pursuing the mouse for having made the hole into which the little bird crept.

And the little bird also keeps out of sight, for he fears lest the other birds should punish him for his cunning. He hides in the hedges, and when he thinks himself quite safe, he sings out: "I am king! I am king!"

And the other birds in mockery call out: "Yes, yes, the hedge-king! the hedge-king!"

THE DOVE WHO SPOKE TRUTH

BY ABBIE FARWELL BROWN

THE dove and the wrinkled little bat once went on a journey together. When it came toward night a storm arose, and the two companions sought everywhere for a shelter. But all the birds were sound asleep in their nests and the animals in their holes and dens. They could find no welcome anywhere until they came to the hollow tree where old Master Owl lived, wide awake in the dark.

"Let us knock here," said the shrewd bat; "I know the old fellow is not asleep. This is his prowling hour, and but that it is a stormy night he would be abroad hunting. — What ho, Master Owl!" he squeaked, "will you let in two storm-tossed travelers for a night's lodging?"

Gruffly the selfish old owl bade them enter, and grudgingly invited them to share his supper. The poor dove was so tired that she could scarcely eat, but the greedy bat's spirits rose as soon as he saw the viands spread before him. He was a sly fellow, and immediately began to flatter his host into good humor. He praised the owl's wisdom and his courage, his gallantry and his generosity; though every one knew that however wise old Master Owl might be, he was neither brave nor gallant. As for his generosity — both the dove and the bat well remembered his selfishness toward the poor wren, when the owl alone of all the birds refused to give the little fire-bringer a feather to help cover his scorched and shivering body.

All this flattery pleased the owl. He puffed and ruffled himself, trying to look as wise, gallant, and brave as possible. He pressed the bat to help himself more generously to the viands, which invitation the sly fellow was not slow to accept.

During this time the dove had not uttered a word. She sat quite still staring at the bat, and wondering to hear such insincere speeches of flattery. Suddenly the owl turned to her.

"As for you, Miss Pink-Eyes," he said gruffly, "you keep careful silence. You are a dull table-companion. Pray, have you nothing to say for yourself?"

"Yes," exclaimed the mischievous bat; "have you no words of praise for our kind host? Methinks he deserves some return for this wonderfully generous, agreeable, tasteful, well-appointed, luxurious, elegant, and altogether acceptable banquet. What have you to say, O little dove?"

But the dove hung her head, ashamed of her companion, and said very simply: "O Master Owl, I can only thank you with all my heart for the hospitality and shelter which you have given me this night. I was beaten by the storm, and you took me in. I was hungry, and you gave me your best to eat. I cannot flatter nor make pretty speeches like the bat. I never learned such manners. But I thank you."

"What!" cried the bat, pretending to be shocked, "is that all you have to say to our obliging host? Is he not the wisest, bravest, most gallant and generous of gentlemen? Have you no praise for his noble character as well as for his goodness to us? I am ashamed of you! You do not deserve such hospitality. You do not deserve this shelter."

The dove remained silent. Like Cordelia in the play she could not speak untruths even for her own happiness.

"Truly, you are an unamiable guest," snarled the owl, his yellow eyes growing keen and fierce with anger and mortified pride. "You are an ungrateful bird, Miss, and the bat is right. You do not deserve this generous hospitality which I have offered, this goodly shelter which you asked. Away with you! Leave my dwelling! Pack off into the storm and see whether or not your silence will soothe the rain and the wind. Be off, I say!"

"Yes, away with her!" echoed the bat, flapping his leathery wings.

And the two heartless creatures fell upon the poor little dove and drove her out into the dark and stormy night.

Poor little dove! All night she was tossed and beaten about shelterless in the storm, because she had been too truthful to flatter the vain old owl. But when the bright morning dawned, draggled and weary as she was, she flew to the court of King Eagle and told him all her trouble. Great was the indignation of that noble bird.

"For his flattery and his cruelty let the bat never presume to fly abroad until the sun goes down," he cried. "As for the owl, I have already doomed him to this punishment for his treatment of the wren. But henceforth let no bird have anything to do with either of them, the bat or the owl. Let them be outcasts and night-prowlers, enemies to be attacked and punished if they appear among us, to be avoided by all in their loneliness. Flattery and inhospitality, deceit and cruelty, — what are more hideous than these? Let them cover themselves in darkness and shun the happy light of day.

"As for you, little dove, let this be a lesson to you to shun the company of flatterers, who are sure to get you into trouble. But you shall always be loved for your simplicity and truth. And as a token of our affection your name shall be used by poets as long as the world shall last to rhyme with *love*."

THE BUSY BLUE JAY

BY OLIVE THORNE MILLER (ADAPTED)

I

ONE of the most interesting birds who ever lived in my Bird Room was a blue jay named Jakie. He was full of business from morning till night, scarcely ever a moment still.

Poor little fellow! He had been stolen from the nest before he could fly, and reared in a house, long before he was given to me. Of course he could not be set free, for he did not know how to take care of himself.

Jays are very active birds, and being shut up in a room, my blue jay had to find things to do, to keep himself busy. If he had been allowed to grow up out of doors, he would have found plenty to do, planting acorns and nuts, nesting, and bringing up families.

Sometimes the things he did in the house were what we call mischief because they annoy us, such as hammering the woodwork to pieces, tearing bits out of the leaves of books, working holes in chair seats, or pounding a cardboard box to pieces. But how is a poor little bird to know what is mischief?

Many things which Jakie did were very funny. For instance, he made it his business to clear up the room. When he had more food than he could eat at the moment, he did not leave it around, but put it away carefully, — not in the garbage pail, for that was not in the room, but in some safe nook where it did not offend the eye. Sometimes it was behind the tray in his cage, or among the books on the shelf. The places he liked best were about me, — in the fold of a ruffle or the loop of a bow on my dress, and sometimes in the side of my slipper. The very choicest place of all was in my loosely bound hair. That, of course, I could not allow, and I had to keep very close watch of him, for fear I might have a bit of bread or meat thrust among my locks.

In his clearing up he always went carefully over the floor, picking up pins, or any little thing he could find, and I often dropped burnt matches, buttons, and other small things to give him something to do. These he would pick up and put nicely away.

Pins Jakie took lengthwise in his beak, and at first I thought he had swallowed them, till I saw him hunt up a proper place to hide them. The place he chose was between the leaves of a book.

He would push a pin far in out of sight, and then go after another. A match he always tried to put in a crack, under the baseboard, between the breadths of matting, or under my rockers. He first placed it, and then tried to hammer it in out of sight. He could seldom get it in far enough to suit him, and this worried him. Then he would take it out and try another place.

Once the blue jay found a good match, of the parlor match variety. He put it between the breadths of matting, and then began to pound on it as usual. Pretty soon he hit the unburnt end and it went off with a loud crack, as parlor matches do. Poor Jakie jumped two feet into the air, nearly frightened out of his wits; and I was frightened, too, for I feared he might set the house on fire.

Often when I got up from my chair a shower of the bird's playthings would fall from his various hiding-places about my dress, — nails, matches, shoe-buttons, bread-crumbs, and other things. Then he had to begin his work all over again.

Jakie liked a small ball or a marble. His game was to give it a hard peck and see it roll. If it rolled away from him, he ran after it and pecked again; but sometimes it rolled toward him, and then he bounded into the air as if he thought it would bite. And what was funny, he was always offended at this conduct of the ball, and went off sulky for a while.

He was a timid little fellow. Wind or storm outside the windows made him wild. He would fly around the room, squawking at the top of his voice; and the horrible tin horns the boys liked to blow at Thanksgiving and Christmas drove him frantic.

Once I brought a Christmas tree into the room to please the birds, and all were delighted with it except my poor little blue jay, who was much afraid of it. Think of the sadness of a bird being afraid of a tree!

II

Jakie had decided opinions about people who came into the room to see me, or to see the birds. At some persons he would squawk every moment. Others he saluted with a queer cry like "Ob-ble! ob-ble! ob-ble!" Once when a lady came in with a baby, he fixed his eyes on that infant with a savage look as if he would like to peck it, and jumped back and forth in his cage, panting but perfectly silent.

Jakie was very devoted to me. He always greeted me with a low, sweet chatter, with wings quivering, and, if he were out of the cage, he would come on the back of my chair and touch my cheek or lips very gently with his beak, or offer me a bit of food if he had any; and to me alone when no one else was near, he sang a low, exquisite song. I afterwards heard a similar song sung by a wild blue jay to his mate while she was sitting, and so I knew that my dear little captive had given me his sweetest — his love-song.

One of Jakie's amusements was dancing across the back of a tall chair, taking funny little steps, coming down hard, "jouncing" his body, and whistling as loud as he could. He would keep up this funny performance as long as anybody would stand before him and pretend to dance too.

My jay was fond of a sensation. One of his dearest bits of fun was to drive the birds into a panic. This he did by flying furiously around the room, feathers rustling, and squawking as loud as he could. He usually managed to fly just over the head of each bird, and as he came like a catapult, every one flew before him, so that in a minute the room was full of birds flying madly about, trying to get out of his way. This gave him great pleasure.

Once a grasshopper got into the Bird Room, probably brought in clinging to some one's dress in the way grasshoppers do. Jakie was in his cage, but he noticed the stranger instantly, and I opened the door for him. He went at once to look at the grasshopper, and when it hopped he was so startled that he hopped too. Then he picked the insect up, but he did not know what to do with it, so he dropped it again. Again the grasshopper jumped directly up, and again the jay did the same. This they did over and over, till every one was tired laughing at them. It looked as if they were trying to see who could jump the highest.

There was another bird in the room, however, who knew what grasshoppers were good for. He was an orchard oriole, and after looking on awhile, he came down and carried off the hopper to eat. The jay did not like to lose his plaything; he ran after the thief, and stood on the floor giving low cries and looking on while the oriole on a chair was eating the dead grasshopper. When the oriole happened to drop it, Jakie, — who had got a new idea what to do with grasshoppers, — snatched it up and carried it under a chair and finished it.

I could tell many more stories about my bird, but I have told them before in one of my "grown-up" books, so I will not repeat them here.

BABES IN THE WOODS

BY JOHN BURROUGHS

ONE day in early May, Ted and I made an expedition to the Shattega, a still, dark, deep stream that loiters silently through the woods not far from my cabin. As we paddled along, we were on the alert for any bit of wild life of bird or beast that might turn up.

There were so many abandoned woodpecker

chambers in the small dead trees as we went along that I determined to secure the section of a tree containing a good one to take home and put up for the bluebirds. "Why don't the bluebirds occupy them here?" inquired Ted. "Oh," I replied, "blue birds do not come so far into the woods as this. They prefer nesting-places in the open, and near human habitations." After carefully scrutinizing several of the trees, we at last saw one that seemed to fill the bill. It was a small dead tree-trunk seven or eight inches in diameter, that leaned out over the water, and from which the top had been broken. The hole, round and firm, was ten or twelve feet above us. After considerable effort I succeeded in breaking the stub off near the ground, and brought it down into the boat. "Just the thing," I said; "surely the bluebirds will prefer this to an artificial box." But, lo and behold, it already had bluebirds in it! We had not heard a sound or seen a feather till the trunk was in our hands, when, on peering into the cavity, we discovered two young bluebirds about half grown. This was a predicament indeed!

Well, the only thing we could do was to stand the tree-trunk up again as well as we could, and as near as we could to where it had stood before. This was no easy thing. But after a time we had it fairly well replaced, one end standing in the mud of the shallow water and the other resting against a tree. This left the hole to the nest about ten feet below and to one side of its former position. Just then we heard the voice of one of the parent birds, and we quickly paddled to the other side of the stream, fifty feet away, to watch her proceedings, saying to each other, "Too bad! too bad!" The mother bird had a large beetle in her beak. She alighted upon a limb a few feet above the former site of her nest, looked down upon us, uttered a note or two, and then dropped down confidently to the point in the vacant air where the entrance to her nest had been but a few moments before. Here she hovered on the wing a second or two, looking for something that was not there, and then returned to the perch she had just left, apparently not a little disturbed. She hammered the beetle rather excitedly upon the limb a few times, as if it were in some way at fault, then dropped down to try for her nest again. Only vacant air there! She hovers and hovers, her blue wings flickering in the checkered light; surely that precious hole *must* be there; but no, again she is baffled, and again she returns to her perch, and mauls the poor beetle till it must be reduced to a pulp. Then she makes a third attempt, then a fourth, and a fifth, and a sixth, till she becomes very much excited. "What could have happened? Am I dreaming? Has that beetle hoodooed me?" she seems to say, and in her dismay she lets the bug drop, and looks bewilderedly about her. Then she flies away through the woods, calling. "Going for her mate," I said to Ted. "She is in deep trouble, and she wants sympathy and help."

In a few minutes we heard her mate answer, and presently the two birds came hurrying to the spot, both with loaded beaks. They perched upon the familiar limb above the site of the nest, and the mate seemed to say, "My dear, what has happened to you? I can find that nest." And he dived down, and brought up in the empty air just as the mother had done. How he winnowed it with his eager wings! How he seemed to bear on to that blank space! His mate sat regarding him intently, confident, I think, that he would find the clue. But he did not. Baffled and excited, he returned to the perch beside her. Then she tried again, then he rushed down once more, then they both assaulted the place, but it would not give up its secret. They talked, they encouraged each other, and they kept up the search, now one, now the other, now both together. Sometimes they dropped down to within a few feet of the entrance to the nest, and we thought they would surely find it. No, their minds and eyes were intent only upon that square foot of space where the nest had been. Soon they withdrew to a large limb many feet higher up, and seemed to say to themselves,

"Well, it is not there, but it must be here somewhere; let us look about." A few minutes elapsed, when we saw the mother bird spring from her perch and go straight as an arrow to the nest. Her maternal eye had proved the quicker. She had found her young. Something like reason and common sense had come to her rescue; she had taken time to look about, and behold! there was that precious doorway. She thrust her head into it, then sent back a call to her mate, then went farther in, then withdrew. "Yes, it is true, they are here, they are here!" Then she went in again, gave them the food in her beak, and then gave place to her mate, who, after similar demonstrations of joy, also gave them his morsel.

Ted and I breathed freer. A burden had been taken from our minds and hearts, and we went cheerfully on our way. We had learned something, too; we had learned that when in the deep woods you think of bluebirds, bluebirds may be nearer you than you think.

THE PRIDE OF THE REGIMENT

BY HARRY M. KIEFFER (ADAPTED)

"OLD ABE" was the war-eagle of the Eighth Wisconsin Volunteers. Whoever it may have been that first conceived the idea, it was certainly a happy thought to make a pet of an eagle. For the eagle is our national bird, and to carry an eagle along with the colors of a regiment on the march, and in battle, and all through the whole war, was surely very appropriate, indeed.

"Old Abe's" perch was on a shield, which was carried by a soldier, to whom, and to whom alone, he looked as to a master. He would not allow any one to carry or even to handle him, except this soldier, nor would he ever receive his food from any other person's hands. He seemed to have sense enough to know that he was sometimes a burden to his master on the march, however, and, as if to relieve him, would occasionally spread his wings and soar aloft to a great height, the men of all regiments along the line of march cheering him as he went up.

He regularly received his rations from the commissary, like any enlisted man. Whenever fresh meat was scarce, and none could be found for him by foraging parties, he would take things into his own claws, as it were, and go out on a foraging expedition himself. On some such occasions he would be gone two or three days at a time, during which nothing whatever was seen of him; but he would invariably return, and seldom would come back without a young lamb or a chicken in his talons. His long absences occasioned his regiment not the slightest concern, for the men knew that, though he might fly many miles away in quest of food, he would be quite sure to find them again.

In what way he distinguished the two hostile armies so accurately that he was never once known to mistake the gray for the blue, no one can tell. But so it was, that he was never known to alight save in his own camp, and amongst his own men.

At Jackson, Mississippi, during the hottest part of the battle before that city, "Old Abe" soared up into the air, and remained there from early morning until the fight closed at night, no doubt greatly enjoying his bird's-eye view of the battle. He did the same at Mission Ridge. He was, I believe, struck by Confederate bullets two or three times, but his feathers were so thick that his body was not much hurt. The shield on which he was carried, however, showed so many marks of Confederate balls that it looked on top as if a groove plane had been run over it.

At the Centenial celebration held in Philadelphia, in 1876, "Old Abe" occupied a prominent place on his perch on the west side of the nave in the Agricultural Building. He was evidently growing old, and was the observed of all observers. Thousands of visitors, from all sections of the country, paid their respects to the grand old bird, who, apparently conscious of the honors conferred upon him, overlooked the sale of his biography and photographs going on beneath his perch with entire satisfaction.

As was but just and right, the soldier who had carried him during the war continued to have charge of him after the war was over, until the day of his death, which occurred at the capital of Wisconsin, in 1881.

THE MOTHER MURRE

BY DALLAS LORE SHARP

ONE of the most striking cases of mother-love which has ever come under my observation, I saw in the summer of 1912 on the bird rookeries of the Three-Arch Rocks Reservation off the coast of Oregon.

We were making our slow way toward the top of the outer rock. Through rookery after rookery of birds, we climbed until we reached the edge of the summit. Scrambling over this edge, we found ourselves in the midst of a great colony of nesting murres — hundreds of them — covering this steep rocky part of the top.

As our heads appeared above the rim, many of the colony took wing and whirred over us out to sea, but most of them sat close, each bird upon its egg or over its chick, loath to leave, and so expose to us the hidden treasure.

The top of the rock was somewhat cone-shaped.

and in order to reach the peak and the colonies on the west side we had to make our way through this rookery of the murres. The first step among them, and the whole colony was gone, with a rush of wings and feet that sent several of the top-shaped eggs rolling, and several of the young birds toppling over the cliff to the pounding waves and ledges far below.

We stopped, but the colony, almost to a bird, had bolted, leaving scores of eggs, and scores of downy young squealing and running together for shelter, like so many beetles under a lifted board.

But the birds had not every one bolted, for here sat two of the colony among the broken rocks. These two had not been frightened off. That both of them were greatly alarmed, any one could see from their open beaks, their rolling eyes, their tense bodies on tiptoe for flight. Yet here they sat, their wings out like props, or more like gripping hands, as if they were trying to hold themselves down to the rocks against their wild desire to fly.

And so they were, in truth, for under their extended wings I saw little black feet moving. Those two mother murres were not going to forsake their babies! No, not even for these approaching monsters, such as they had never before seen, clambering over their rocks.

What was different about these two? They had

their young ones to protect. Yes, but so had every bird in the great colony its young one, or its egg, to protect, yet all the others had gone. Did these two have more mother-love than the others? And hence, more courage, more intelligence?

We took another step toward them, and one of the two birds sprang into the air, knocking her baby over and over with the stroke of her wing, and coming within an inch of hurling it across the rim to be battered on the ledges below. The other bird raised her wings to follow, then clapped them back over her baby. Fear is the most contagious thing in the world; and that flap of fear by the other bird thrilled her, too, but as she had withstood the stampede of the colony, so she caught herself again and held on.

She was now alone on the bare top of the rock, with ten thousand circling birds screaming to her in the air above, and with two men creeping up to her with a big black camera that clicked ominously. She let the multitude scream, and with threatening beak watched the two men come on. A motherless baby, spying her, ran down the rock squealing for his life. She spread a wing, put her bill behind him and shoved him quickly in out of sight with her own baby. The man with the camera saw the act, for I heard his machine click, and I heard him say something under his breath that you would hardly expect a mere man and a game-warden to say. But most men have a good deal of the mother in them; and the old bird had acted with such decision, such courage, such swift, compelling instinct, that any man, short of the wildest savage, would have felt his heart quicken at the sight.

"Just how compelling might that mother-instinct be?" I wondered. "Just how much would that mother-love stand?" I had dropped to my knees, and on all fours had crept up within about three feet of the bird. She still had chance for flight. Would she allow me to crawl any nearer? Slowly, very slowly, I stretched forward on my hands, like a measuring-worm, until my body lay flat on the rocks, and my fingers were within three *inches* of her. But her wings were twitching, a wild light danced in her eyes, and her head turned toward the sea.

For a whole minute I did not stir. I was watching — and the wings again began to tighten about the babies, the wild light in the eyes died down, the long, sharp beak turned once more toward me.

Then slowly, very slowly, I raised my hand, touched her feathers with the tip of one finger — with two fingers — with my whole hand, while the loud camera click-clacked, click-clacked hardly four feet away!

It was a thrilling moment. I was not killing

anything. I had no long-range rifle in my hands, coming up against the wind toward an unsuspecting creature hundreds of yards away. This was no wounded leopard charging me; no mother-bear defending with her giant might a captured cub. It was only a mother-bird, the size of a wild duck, with swift wings at her command, hiding under those wings her own and another's young, and her own boundless fear!

For the second time in my life I had taken captive with my bare hands a free wild bird. No, I had not taken her captive. She had made herself a captive; she had taken herself in the strong net of her mother-love.

And now her terror seemed quite gone. At the first touch of my hand I think she felt the love restraining it, and without fear or fret she let me reach under her and pull out the babies. But she reached after them with her bill to tuck them back out of sight, and when I did not let them go, she sidled toward me, quacking softly, a language that I perfectly understood, and was quick to respond to. I gave them back, fuzzy and black and white. She got them under her, stood up over them, pushed her wings down hard around them, her stout tail down hard behind them, and together with them pushed in an abandoned egg that was close at hand. Her own baby, some one else's baby, and some one else's forsaken egg! She could cover no more; she had not feathers enough. But she had heart enough; and into her mother's heart she had already tucked every motherless egg and nestling of the thousands of frightened birds, screaming and wheeling in the air high over her head.

THE END

REFERENCE LISTS
FOR STORY-TELLING AND COLLATERAL READING

REFERENCE LISTS

FOR STORY-TELLING AND COLLATERAL READING

(The grades assigned are merely suggestive, as some of the stories may be used in higher or lower grades than here indicated.)

NEW YEAR'S DAY

For grades 1–4.

An All-the-Year-Round Story, in Poulsson, *In the Child's World;* Peter the Stone-Cutter, in Macdonell, *Italian Fairy Book;* The Forest Full of Friends, in Alden, *Why the Chimes Rang.*

For grades 5–8.

A Chinese New Year's in California, in *Our Holidays Retold from St. Nicholas;* A New Year's Talk, in Stevenson, *Days and Deeds* (prose); Story of the Year, in Andersen, *Stories and Tales;* The Animals' New Year's Eve, in Lagerlöf, *Further Adventures of Nils.*

LINCOLN'S BIRTHDAY

For grades 1–4.

A Westfield Incident, in Moores, *Abraham Lincoln,* page 87; Lincoln and the Little Horse, in *Werner's Readings,* no. 45; Lincoln and the Pig, in Gross, *Lincoln's Own Stories;* Lincoln and the Small Dog, in Moores, *Abraham Lincoln,* page 25.

For grades 5–6.

A Backwoods Boyhood, in Moores, *Abraham Lincoln;* Choosing Abe Lincoln Captain, in Schauffler, *Lincoln's Birthday;* Following the Surveyor's Chain, in Baldwin, *Abraham Lincoln;* His Good Memory of Names, in Gallaher, *Best Lincoln Stories;* Lincoln and the Doorkeeper, in Gross,

Lincoln's Own Stories, page 78; Lincoln and the Unjust Client, in Moores, *Abraham Lincoln,* page 46; Lincoln's Kindness to a Disabled Soldier, in Gallaher, *Best Lincoln Stories;* The Clary's Grove Boys, in Noah Brooks, *Abraham Lincoln,* page 51; The Snow Boys, in Noah Brooks, *Abraham Lincoln,* page 122.

For grades 7–8.

Counsel Assigned, Andrews; *He Knew Lincoln,* Tarbell; *Lincoln and the Sleeping Sentinel,* Chittenden; Lincoln Remembered Him, in Gallaher, *Best Lincoln Stories;* Lincoln's Springfield Farewell, in Moores, *Abraham Lincoln,* page 82; *Perfect Tribute,* Andrews.

SAINT VALENTINE'S DAY

For grades 1–4.

A Sunday Valentine, in White, *When Molly was Six;* Beauty and the Beast, in Lang, *Blue Fairy Book;* East of the Sun and West of the Moon, in Lang, *Blue Fairy Book;* The Fair One With Golden Locks, in Scudder, *Children's Book;* The Sleeping Beauty in the Wood, in Scudder, *Children's Book;* The Valentine (poem), in Brown, *Fresh Posies.*

For grades 5–6.

Gracieuse and Percinet, in D'Aulnoy, *Fairy Tales;* Jorinda and Joringel, in Grimm, *German Household Tales;* The Day-Dream, Tennyson (poem), in *Story-Telling Poems;* The Singing, Soaring Lark, in Grimm, *German Household Tales;* William and the Werewolf, in Darton, *Wonder Book of Old Romance.*

For grades 7–8.

As You Like It, Shakespeare; Brunhild, in Baldwin, *Story of Siegfried;* Floris and Blanchefleur, in Darton, *Wonder Book of Old Romance;* Palamon and Arcita, in Darton, *Tales of the Canterbury Pilgrims; The Fair Maid of Perth,* Scott, chapters 2–6; *The Singing Leaves,* Lowell (poem); *The Tempest,* Shakespeare.

WASHINGTON'S BIRTHDAY

For grades 1–4.

Little George Washington, and Great George Washington, in Wiggin and Smith, *Story Hour;* The Virginia Boy, in Wilson, *Nature Study,* Second Reader.

For grades 5–6.

A Christmas Surprise, in Tappan, *American Hero Stories,* Dolly Madison, in Tappan, *American Hero Stories;* Going to Sea, in Scudder, *George Washington,* page 33; How George Washington was Made Commander-in-Chief, in Tomlinson, *War for Independence;* The Home of Washington, and The Appearance of the Enemy, in Madison, *Peggy Owen at Yorktown;* Young Washington in the Woods, in Eggleston, *Strange Stories from History.*

For grades 7–8.

Anecdotes and Stories, in Schauffler, *Washington's Birthday;* He Resigns his Commission, in Lodge, *George Washington,* vol. I, page 338; The British at Mount Vernon, in Lodge, *George Washington,* vol. I, page 295; The Young Surveyor, in Scudder, *George Washington;* Washington Offered the Supreme Power, in Lodge, *George Washington,* vol. I, page 328; Washington's Farewell to His Officers, in Lodge, *George Washington,* vol. I, page 337.

RESURRECTION DAY (EASTER)

For grades 1–4.

Easter Eggs, von Schmid; The Boy Who Discovered the Spring, in Alden, *Why the Chimes Rang;* Herr Oster Hase, in Bailey and Lewis, *For the Children's Hour;* The Legend of Easter Eggs, O'Brien (poem), in *Story-Telling Poems; The Rabbit's Ransom,* Vawter; The White Hare, in Stevenson, *Days and Deeds* (prose).

For grades 5–8.

Easter, Gilder (poem); The General's Easter Box, in *Our Holidays Retold from St. Nicholas; The Trinity Flower,* Ewing; What Easter is, in Stevenson, *Days and Deeds* (prose).

MAY DAY

For grades 1–4.

A Story of the Springtime, in Kupfer, *Legends of Greece and Rome;* How the Water Lily Came, in Judd, *Wigwam Stories;* The Brook in the King's Garden, in Alden, *Why the Chimes Rang;* The Legend of the Dandelion, in Bailey and Lewis, *For the Children's Hour;* The Lilac Bush, in *Riverside Fourth Reader;* The Maple Leaf and the Violet, in Wiggin and Smith, *Story Hour;* The Story of the Anemone, in Coe, *First Book of Stories for the Story-Teller;* The Story of the First Butterflies, inHolbrook, *Book of Nature Myths;* The Story of the First Snowdrops, in Holbrook, *Book of Nature Myths;* The Story of the Rainbow, in Coe, *First Book of Stories for the Story-Teller;* Two Little Seeds, in MacDonald, *David Elginbrod*, chapter, "The Cave in the Straw"; Why the Morning-Glory Climbs, in Bryant, *How to Tell Stories to Children.*

For grades 5–6.

Ladders to Heaven, Ewing; The Daisy, in Andersen, *Wonder Stories;* Five out of One Shell, in Andersen, *Stories and Tales;* The Pomegranate Seeds, in Hawthorne, *Tanglewood Tales.*

For grades 7–8.

The May-Pole at Merry Mount, in Hawthorne, *Twice-Told Tales;* The Opening of the Eyes of Jasper, in Dyer, *The Richer Life;* The Prisoner and the Flower, in Stevenson, *Days and Deeds* (prose).

MOTHERS' DAY

For grades 1–4.

Hans and the Wonderful Flower, in Bailey and Lewis, *For the Children's Hour;* The Closing Door, in Lindsay, *Mother Stories;* The Daughter of a Samurai, in Nixon-Roulet, *Japanese Folk-Stories;* The Fairy Who Came to our House, in Bailey and Lewis, *For the Children's Hour;* The Little Traveler, in Lindsay, *Mother Stories;* Thorwald and the Star-Children, in Boyesen, *Modern Vikings.*

For grades 5–6.

Lincoln's Letter to a Mother, in Moores, *Abraham Lincoln*, page 105; My Angel Mother, in Baldwin, *Abraham Lincoln;* Napoleon and the English Sailor Boy, Campbell (poem), in *Story-Telling Poems;* The Song of the Old Mother, Yeats (poem), in *Riverside Eighth Reader;* Valentine and Ursine (poem), in Lanier, *Boy's Percy.*

For grades 7–8.

A Patriot Mother, in Tomlinson, *War for Independence;* Lincoln's Letter, in Gross, *Lincoln's Own Stories;* President for One Hour, in *St. Nicholas Christmas Book; The Conqueror's Grave*, Bryant (poem); The Gracchi, in Morris, *Historical Tales* (Roman); The Knight's Toast attributed to Scott (poem), in *Story-Telling Poems;* Young Manhood, in Noah Brooks, *Abraham Lincoln.*

MEMORIAL AND FLAG DAYS

For grades 3–6.

A Boy Who Won the Cross, in Hart and Stevens, *Romance of the Civil War;* A Story of the Flag, in *Our Holidays Retold from St. Nicholas;* Betsy's Battle Flag, Irving (poem), in Stevenson, *Poems of American History;* Noteworthy Flag Incidents, in Smith, *Our Nation's Flag;* The Legs of Duncan Ketcham, in Price, *Lads and Lassies of Other Days;* The Origin of Memorial Day, in Stevenson, *Days and Deeds* (prose); The Planting of the Colors, in Thomas, *Captain Phil*, page 227.

For grades 7–8.

Kearny at Seven Pines, Stedman (poem); Quivíra, Guiterman (poem), in *Story-Telling Poems;* Reading the List, in Schauffler, *Memorial Day;* Remember the Alamo, in Lodge and Roosevelt, *Hero Tales;* Reuben James, Roche, (poem), in *Story-Telling Poems;* The Defense of the Alamo, Miller (poem), in Stevenson, *Poems of American History;* The Fire Rekindled, in Schauffler, *Memorial Day;* The Flag-Bearer, in Lodge and Roosevelt, *Hero Tales;* The March of the First Brigade, in *Riverside Eighth Reader.*

INDEPENDENCE DAY

For grades 3–6.

A Winter at Valley Forge, in Tappan, *American Hero Stories;* Cornwallis's Buckles, in *Revolutionary Stories Retold from St. Nicholas;* Ethan Allen, in Johonnot, *Stories of Heroic Deeds;* Fourth of July Among the Indians, in *Indian Stories Retold from St. Nicholas;* How "Mad Anthony" Took Stony Point, in Tappan, *American Hero Stories;* How the "Swamp Fox" Made the British Miserable, in Tappan, *American Hero Stories;* John Paul Jones, in Tappan, *American Hero Stories;* Lætitia and the Redcoats, in *Revolutionary Stories Retold from St. Nicholas;* Molly Pitcher, in *Revolutionary Stories Retold from St. Nicholas;* Paul Revere's Ride, Longfellow (poem), in *Story-Telling Poems;* Prescott and the Yankee Boy, in Johonnot, *Stories of Heroic Deeds;* Rodney's Ride, Brooks (poem), in *Story-Telling Poems;* The Boston Massacre, in Hawthorne, *Grandfather's Chair;* The Bulb of the Crimson Tulip, in *Revolutionary Stories Retold from St. Nicholas;* The First Day of the Revolution, in Tappan, *American Hero Stories.*

For grades 7–8.

A Woman's Heroism, in Tomlinson, *War for Independence; Grandmother's Story of Bunker-Hill Battle,* Holmes (poem); How the Major Joined Marion's Men, in Tomlinson, *War for Independence;* Molly Pitcher, Sherwood (poem), in Stevenson, *Poems of American History;* Patrick Henry, in Morris, *Historical Tales, American,* Second Series; *Song of Marion's Men,* Bryant (poem); That Bunker Hill Powder, in *Revolutionary Stories Retold from St. Nicholas; The Mantle of St. John de Matha,* Whittier (poem); The Tory's Farewell, in Hawthorne, *Grandfather's Chair.*

LABOR DAY

For grades 1–4.

Dust Under the Rug, in Lindsay, *Mother Stories;* Giant Energy and Fairy Skill, in Lindsay, *Mother Stories;* How Flax was Given to Men, in Holbrook, *Book of Nature Myths;* My Friend the Housekeeper, in *Riverside Fourth Reader;*

Peasant Truth, in *Riverside Third Reader;* Prometheus, the Giver of Fire, in Coe, *First Book of Stories for the Story-Teller;* Six Soldiers of Fortune, in Grimm, *German Household Tales;* The Country Maid and her Milk-Pail, in Scudder, *Book of Fables and Folk-Stories;* The Flax, in Andersen, *Wonder Stories;* The Hammer and the Anvil, in Ramaswami Raju, *Indian Fables;* The Honest Woodman, in Poulsson, *In the Child's World;* The Little Gray Pony, in Lindsay, *Mother Stories;* The Little House in the Wood, in Grimm, *German Household Tales;* The Old Man Who Lived in a Wood (poem), in *Story-Telling Poems;* The Pixy Flower, in Rhys, *Fairy-Gold;* The Spandies, in Gilchrist, *Helen and the Uninvited Guests,* page 15; The Three Trades, in Grimm, *German Household Tales;* The Toy of the Giant's Child, von Chamisso (poem), in *Story-Telling Poems;* Vegetable Lambs, in Curtis, *Story of Cotton;* Vulcan the Mighty Smith, in Poulsson, *In the Child's World.*

For grades 5–6.

A Handful of Clay, in *Riverside Sixth Reader;* How they Built the Ship Argo in Iolcos, in Kingsley, *Greek Heroes;* Icarus and Dædalus, in Peabody, *Old Greek Folk-Stories;* Master of All Masters, in Jacobs, *English Fairy Tales;* The Dwarf's Gifts, in Brown, *In the Days of Giants;* The Forging of Balmung, in Baldwin, *Hero Tales;* The Giant Builder, in Brown, *In the Days of Giants;* The God of Fire, in Francillon, *Gods and Heroes;* The Wicked Hornet, in Baldwin, *The Sampo;* The Wish-Ring, in *Fairy Stories Retold from St. Nicholas;* The Wounds of Labor, in d'Amicis, *Heart* (*Cuore*); Weland's Sword, in Kipling, *Puck of Pook's Hill.*

For grades 7–8.

Careers of Danger and Daring, Moffett; David Maydole, Hammer-Maker, in *Riverside Seventh Reader;* Jack Farley's Flying Switch, in Warman, *Short Rails;* Histories of Two Boys, in *Riverside Seventh Reader;* History of Labor Day, in Stevenson, *Days and Deeds* (prose); The Arms of Æneas, in Church, *Stories from Virgil;* The Blacksmith Boy and the Battle, in Marden, *Winning Out;* The Duke's Armorer, in

Stories of Chivalry Retold from St. Nicholas; The Scullion Boy's Opportunity, in Marden, *Winning Out;* The Vision of Anton the Clockmaker, in Dyer, *The Richer Life;* Tubal Cain, Mackay (poem), in *Story-Telling Poems.*

COLUMBUS DAY

For grades 4–8.

Columbus, Miller (poem), in *Riverside Seventh Reader;* Columbus at the Convent, Trowbridge (poem), in Stevenson, *Poems of American History;* Guanahani, in Moores, *Christopher Columbus;* How Diego Mendez Got Food for Columbus, in Higginson, *American Explorers;* How Diego Mendez Saved Columbus, in Higginson, *American Explorers;* In Search of the Grand Khan, in Moores, *Christopher Columbus;* The Garden of Eden, in Moores, *Christopher Columbus.*

HALLOWEEN

For grades 1–4.

The Smith and the Fairies, in Grierson, *Children's Book of Celtic Stories;* The Witch, in Lang, *Yellow Fairy Book;* The Witch That was a Hare, in Rhys, *English Fairy Book;* Tom-Tit Tot (Rumpelstiltskin), in Jacobs, *English Fairy Tales.*

For grades 5–6.

Mr. Fox, in Jacobs, *English Fairy Tales;* The Godfather, in Grimm, *German Household Tales;* The Golden Arm, in Jacobs, *English Fairy Tales;* The Robber Bridegroom, in Grimm, *German Household Tales; The Story of a Cat,* Bedolière; The Youth Who Could not Shiver or Shake, in Grimm, *German Household Tales.*

For grades 7–8.

Alice Brand, in Scott, *Lady of the Lake* (poem); All-Hallow-Eve Myths, in *Our Holidays Retold from St. Nicholas;* Black Andie's Tale of Tod Lapraik, in Stevenson, *David Balfour;* History of Hallowe'en, in Stevenson, *Days and Deeds* (prose); *Legend of Sleepy Hollow,* and *Rip Van Winkle,* Irving; *Macbeth,* Shakespeare; The Bottle Imp, in Stevenson, *Island Nights' Entertainments; The Devil and Tom*

Walker, Irving; *The Fire-King*, Scott (poem); The Speaking Rat, in Dickens, *Uncommercial Traveller*, chapter 15.

THANKSGIVING DAY

For grades 1–4.

A Thanksgiving Dinner, in White, *When Molly was Six;* The Chestnut Boys, in Poulsson, *In the Child's World;* The First Thanksgiving Day, in Wiggin and Smith, *Story Hour;* The Marriage of Mondahmin, in Judd, *Wigwam Stories;* The Turkey's Nest, in Lindsay, *More Mother Stories;* The Visit, in Lindsay, *More Mother Stories;* Turkeys Turning the Tables, in Howells, *Christmas Every Day.*

For grades 5–6.

A Dinner That Ran Away, in Miller, *Kristy's Surprise Party;* A Mystery in the Kitchen, in Miller, *Kristy's Surprise Party;* Ann Mary, Her Two Thanksgivings, in Wilkins, *Young Lucretia;* An Old-Time Thanksgiving, in *Indian Stories Retold from St. Nicholas;* The Coming of Thanksgiving, and The Season of Pumpkin Pies, in Warner, *Being a Boy;* The Magic Apples, in Brown, *In the Days of Giants;* St. Francis's Sermon to the Birds, Longfellow (poem), in *Story-Telling Poems.*

For grades 7–8.

An Old-Fashioned Thanksgiving, Alcott; The First Thanksgiving Day, Preston (poem), in *Story-Telling Poems;* The Night Before Thanksgiving, in Jewett, *The Queen's Twin;* The Peace Message (poem), in Stevenson, *Poems of American History;* The Turkey Drive, in Sharp, *Winter.*

CHRISTMAS DAY

For grades 1–4.

A Christmas Tree Reversed, in Brown, *Little Miss Phœbe Gay;* Babouscka, Thomas (poem), in *Story-Telling Poems; Christmas Every Day*, Howells; Fulfilled, in Bryant, *How to Tell Stories to Children;* His Christmas Turkey, in Vawter, *The Rabbit's Ransom;* In the Great Walled Country, in Alden,

Why the Chimes Rang; Little Girl's Christmas, in Dickinson and Skinner, *Children's Book of Christmas Stories;* Santa Claus and the Mouse, Poulsson (poem), in *St. Nicholas Christmas Book;* The Christmas Cake, in Lindsay, *More Mother Stories;* The Christmas Tree, in Austin, *Basket Woman;* The First New England Christmas, in Stone and Fickett, *Every-Day Life in the Colonies;* The Golden Cobwebs, in Bryant, *How to Tell Stories to Children;* The Moon of Yule, in Davis, *The Moons of Balbanca;* The Rileys' Christmas, in White, *When Molly was Six;* The Story of Gretchen, in Lindsay, *Mother Stories;* The Three Kings of Cologne, Field (poem), in *Story-Telling Poems; The Turkey Doll,* Gates; The Voyage of the Wee Red Cap, in Dickinson and Skinner, *Children's Book of Christmas Stories;* Toinette and the Elves, in Dickinson and Skinner, *Children's Book of Christmas Stories; 'T was the Night Before Christmas,* Moore (poem); *Why the Chimes Rang,* Alden.

For grades 5–6.

Christmas Before Last, in Stockton, *Bee-Man of Orn;* Christmas in the Alley, in Miller, *Kristy's Queer Christmas; Dog of Flanders,* Ramée; Felix, in Stein, *Troubadour Tales;* Good King Wenceslas (poem), in *Story-Telling Poems;* Hope's Christmas Tree, in Miller, *Kristy's Surprise Party;* How a Bear Brought Christmas, in Miller, *Kristy's Queer Christmas;* How Santa Claus Came to Simpson's Bar, in Harte, *Luck of Roaring Camp;* How Uncle Sam Observes Christmas, in *Our Holidays Retold from St. Nicholas;* Lottie's Christmas Tree, in Miller, *Kristy's Rainy Day Picnic;* St. Nicholas and the Innkeeper, in Walsh, *Story of Santa Klaus;* St. Nicholas and the Robbers, in Walsh, *Story of Santa Klaus;* St. Nicholas and the Slave Boy, in Walsh, *Story of Santa Klaus; Santa Claus on a Lark,* Gladden; *Solomon Crow's Christmas Pockets,* Stuart; *The Birds' Christmas Carol,* Wiggin; The Coming of the Prince, in Field, *Christmas Tales and Christmas Verse;* The Festival of St. Nicholas, in Dodge, *Hans Brinker; The Peace Egg,* Ewing; The Symbol and the Saint, in Field, *Christmas Tales and Christmas Verse.*

For grades 7–8.

A Christmas Carol, Dickens; A Still Christmas, Repplier, in Morris, *In the Yule-Log Glow; The First Christmas Tree,* Van Dyke; *The Lost Word,* Van Dyke; *The Mansion,* Van Dyke; *The Other Wise Man,* Van Dyke; Cosette, in Hugo, *Les Misérables,* book 3; *Where Love is, There God is Also,* Tolstoy.

ARBOR DAY

For grades 1–4.

Flower of the Almond and Fruit of the Fig, in Foote, *Little Fig-Tree Stories;* Karl and the Dryad, in Brown, *Star Jewels;* The Girl Who Became a Pine Tree, in Judd, *Wigwam Stories;* The Kind Old Oak, in Poulsson, *In the Child's World;* The Oak Tree, in Vawter, *The Rabbit's Ransom;* The Workman and the Trees, in Ramaswami Raju, *Indian Fables.*

For grades 5–6.

Apple-Seed John, Child (poem), in *Story-Telling Poems;* How the Children Saved Hamburg, in Marden, *Winning Out;* How the Indians Learned to Make Maple Sugar, in University of the State of New York, *Legends and Poetry of the Forests;* Old Pipes and the Dryad, in Stockton, *Bee-Man of Orn;* Tale of Old Man and the Birch Tree, in University of the State of New York, *Legends and Poetry of the Forests;* The Elm and the Vine, Rosas (poem), in *Story-Telling Poems;* The Gourd and the Palm (poem), in *Story-Telling Poems;* The Planting of the Apple Tree, Bryant (poem), in *Riverside Fifth Reader.*

For grades 7–8.

Brier-Rose, Boyesen (poem), in *Story-Telling Poems;* How the Charter was Saved, in Morris, *Historical Tales, American;* O-So-Ah, the Tall Pine Speaks, in University of the State of New York, *Legends and Poetry of the Forests;* The Eliot Oak, in Drake, *New England Legends;* The First of the Trees, in University of the State of New York, *Legends and Poetry of the Forests;* The Liberty Tree, in Hawthorne, *Grandfather's Chair,* part 3, chapter 2; The Plucky Prince, May Bryant (poem), in *Story-Telling Poems; The Story of a Thousand-Year Pine,* Mills; The Washington Elm, in Drake, *New England Legends.*

BIRD DAY

For grades 1–4.

Out of the Nest, in Lindsay, *More Mother Stories;* The Fox and the Crow, in Jacobs, *Æsop's Fables;* The Jackdaw and the Doves, in Scudder, *Book of Fables and Folk-Stories;* The Jay and the Peacock, in Jacobs, *Æsop's Fables;* The King, the Falcon, and the Drinking Cup, in Dutton, *The Tortoise and the Geese;* The Lark and her Young Ones, in Scudder, *Book of Fables and Folk-Stories;* The Monk and the Bird, in Scudder, *Book of Legends;* The Owl and his School, in Ramaswami Raju, *Indian Fables;* The Owl and the Pussy-Cat, Lear (poem), in *Story-Telling Poems;* The Partridge and the Crow, in Dutton, *The Tortoise and the Geese;* The Pious Robin, in Brown, *Curious Book of Birds;* The Rustic and the Nightingale, in Dutton, *The Tortoise and the Geese;* The Sparrows, Thaxter (poem), in *Story-Telling Poems;* The Sparrows and the Snake, in Dutton, *The Tortoise and the Geese;* The Spendthrift and the Swallow, in Scudder, *Book of Fables and Folk-Stories;* The Story of the First Mocking-Bird, in Holbrook, *Book of Nature Myths;* The Story of the Oriole, in Holbrook, *Book of Nature Myths;* The Wren Who Brought Fire, in Brown, *Curious Book of Birds;* Why the Peacock's Tail has a Hundred Eyes, in Holbrook, *Book of Nature Myths;* Why the Peetweet Cries for Rain, in Holbrook, *Book of Nature Myths.*

For grades 5–6.

A Madcap Thrush, in Miller, *True Bird Stories;* Antics in the Bird Room, in Miller, *True Bird Stories;* Fate of the Children of Lir, in Grierson, *Children's Book of Celtic Stories;* Halcyone, in Brown, *Curious Book of Birds;* St. Francis's Sermon to the Birds, Longfellow (poem), in *Story-Telling Poems;* Saint Kentigern and the Robin, in Brown, *Book of Saints and Friendly Beasts;* The Donkey and the Mocking-Bird, Rosas (poem), in *Story-Telling Poems;* The Early Girl, in Brown, *Curious Book of Birds;* The Nightingale, in Andersen,

Wonder Stories; The Parrot, Campbell (poem), in *Story-Telling Poems;* The Phœnix, in Brown, *Curious Book of Birds; The Robin,* Whittier (poem); The Saucy Oriole, in Miller, *True Bird Stories;* The Wild Swans, in Andersen, *Wonder Stories; Walter von der Vogelweid,* Longfellow (poem).

For grades 7–8.

Arnaux, the Chronicle of a Homing Pigeon, in Thompson-Seton, *Animal Heroes;* King Edwin's Feast, Chadwick (poem), in *Story-Telling Poems;* Our New Neighbors at Ponkapog, in *Riverside Seventh Reader;* The Abbot of Inisfalen, Allingham (poem), in *Story-Telling Poems; The Birds of Killingworth,* Longfellow (poem); The Downy Woodpecker, in *Bird Stories from Burroughs; The Eagle,* Tennyson (poem); The Emperor's Bird's-Nest, Longfellow (poem), in *Story-Telling Poems; The Falcon of Ser Federigo,* Longfellow (poem); The Gulls, in Breck, *Wilderness Pets,* pages 103, 161; The House Wren, in *Bird Stories from Burroughs;* The Keeper of the Nest, in Roberts, *The Feet of the Furtive;* The Screech Owl, in *Bird Stories from Burroughs;* The Song Sparrow, in *Bird Stories from Burroughs.*

INDEXES

SUBJECT INDEX

INDEX OF TITLES

INDEX OF AUTHORS